The L[illegible]s
U[illegible]

Northern Ireland through the eyes of its exiles

Barry Gibson

The Conrad Press

The Land That Makes Us Refugees

Published by The Conrad Press in the United Kingdom 2025
Tel: +44(0)1227 472 874
www.theconradpress.com
info@theconradpress.com
ISBN 978-1-917673-15-0

Typesetting and Cover Design by: Levellers
The Conrad Press logo was designed by Maria Priestley.
Printed and bound in Great Britain by Clays Ltd, Elcograf S.p.A.

For Ciara and Fergal

Contents

INTRODUCTION

It's over in a second.

One moment I'm rowing along the river, the next moment I'm in it.

A one-man scull is the easiest rowing boat to flip, all it needs is for that one man – or teenaged boy in my case – to make a single mistake and over he goes.

I snagged one of my oars on something in the river Lagan and half a second later my boat was upside down and I was waist-deep in the water.

Gareth, my instructor that Sunday afternoon back in 1993, rowed over and patiently talked me through the process of dragging my boat over to the riverbed and stepping back into it.

I was pleasantly surprised that I managed to get back in my scull at the second attempt.

Then we made our way back along the river to Belfast Rowing Club, where my dad was waiting to take me home in his about-to-get-damp Fiat.

I know that I will go into the Lagan for a second time, though I've no idea when.

I'm middle-aged now, so my days of rowing – and indeed of drunkenly staggering over bridges late at night – are a distant memory.

When it comes, my second immersion in my native city's lifeblood will not be the result of a blink-of-the-eye accident, but rather the culmination of a decades-old decision.

More than ten years ago, as my partner Jenny and I were about to become parents, we decided to make our wills.

We drove a few miles to a solicitors' office in Huddersfield to draw up our plans.

I knew, going into that brief meeting on a humdrum Tuesday morning, that I was about to have the opportunity to put on legal record what I wished to happen to whatever money and possessions I have to my name when I die.

But I hadn't anticipated that the solicitor would also offer me the chance to record, in my last will and testament, what I wanted to happen to my body when the clock stops.

I was in my mid-thirties back then, a relatively young man who'd never considered his funeral arrangements.

But, while I was totally unprepared for the solicitor's question, I found I needed no time to consider a response.

My home – not the place where I lived, but the place where I'm from – came into view in my mind's eye with immediate clarity:

"Please could you put down that, when I die, I want to be cremated and my ashes sprinkled in the river Lagan?

"There's a place opposite Belfast Rowing Club called Annadale. That's where I want to go in."

It was an almost out-of-body experience to be suddenly yanked back to the place where I was born and bred.

I had left Northern Ireland a decade earlier, determined never to return.

Since that day at the solicitors' office more than a decade ago, I've learnt more fully than I would ever wish that none of us knows how long we have left.

I hope it's a very long time until I make my return to the Lagan. But I just don't know.

I have no belief in an after-life – a childhood spent in Northern Ireland can be a very effective inoculation against religious belief – but I do like to think that after I die, I'll return to my roots.

Back with my ancestors.

Northern Ireland's emotional pull is enduring, but not strong enough to drag me back this side of the deathbed.

I left in 2002, first for Taiwan, then South Korea and I'm now long since settled in England.

There were two reasons for getting on that plane to Taipei just before Chinese New Year more than twenty years ago – next-to-no job opportunities for recent graduates and a political system that had replaced tit-for-tat murder with tit-for-tat grudge-settling.

As Northern Ireland settled in to a couple of decades of dysfunction, I waved goodbye with rather less regret than I would have expected.

Ten years later I had settled in Yorkshire and Jenny and I had become parents – Ciara was born in 2012 and Fergal the following year.

Jenny and I agreed that we should give our children Irish names partly because I knew they would be children of Yorkshire, not Ulster.

I love hearing their little Pennine voices enunciate phrases like "you can't say owt," but I know they'll never yell the likes of "go on ye, boy, ye" with the same native energy.

I'm delighted that their voices come from their mother and their names from their father.

I love the way they enjoy visiting Northern Ireland and have taken on their dad's homeland as part of their identity.

But they're too young to understand the true nature of Northern Irish society, the reason why their father lives on the British side of the Irish Sea.

Becoming a parent made me more determined than ever to stay away from Northern Ireland, to make sure my children grew up without developing the skill of determining a stranger's religion without ever asking them.

I'm happy that my son wears a Northern Ireland kit with his own name on the back.

But at some point I'll have to explain to him that, if he walks down the street in Belfast wearing that green and white shirt, some of the people he passes will hate him because he supports Northern Ireland.

And others will hate him because he's called Fergal.

This book is about the many people like me who left Northern Ireland and why most of us have no urge to return.

Every year a whole university-worth of eighteen-year-olds drain out of Northern Ireland.

They fill the campuses of Dublin, Durham and Dundee with their GAA tops and their vowel sounds that have stumped Hollywood's finest.

We should remember that this isn't a privilege that isn't open to everyone.

As English-speakers with European passports, we have options that are closed off to people from other much more dysfunctional societies.

And, on a human level, the high level of emigration is in some ways a good thing.

Why should a young person who grew up in Belfast, Banbridge, or Bellaghy go to university close enough to home to be able to nip back at the weekend to get their ma to do their washing?

It's good that thousands of young people from Northern Ireland get to broaden their minds and cut themselves loose from the apron-strings of home.

The problem is not how many 18-year-olds head to Larne Port or Belfast City Airport every year.

It's how few of them walk back through those terminals for anything other than fleeting visits to a homeland from which they've grown apart.

John Fitzgerald, one of Ireland's leading economists, has studied the impact of Northern Ireland's high emigration rate.

He noted in 2022 that the North's excellent education system coexists with an economy that can't retain its graduates:

When students (from Northern Ireland) studying in GB complete their first qualification at third level, only a third return to a job in Northern Ireland, and ten per cent of those who studied in Northern Ireland take their first job outside Northern Ireland.

Thus, while the progression to third level of young people is high by UK standards, Northern Ireland loses many of them once they graduate.[1]

I was one of those who resisted the urge to go to uni across the water, spending my undergraduate years at Queen's University, Belfast, studying politics four miles from my childhood front door.

But when I look back on that time now, I realise how frayed the connection with home has become.

By far the most worthwhile thing I did during my university years was spending the summers of 1999 and 2000 in Washington, DC working as an intern on the Young Leaders Program, now called the Washington Ireland Program.

It gives university students from Ireland the chance to work in offices in the US capital – including for two lucky interns, the White House – in order to gain the experience and confidence to become the leaders of tomorrow.

Today the programme, quite rightly, has an all-Ireland focus.

But back then it was very Northern-centric, an attempt in the early years of the peace process to bring young members of the two communities together in a neutral atmosphere.

---

[1] p37, One Island, Two Labour Markets; John Fitzgerald, Irish Studies in International Affairs, 2022.

I was encouraged to apply in 1999 because they were short of Protestants.

I got the gig, despite being the wrong type of Prod[2].

We were perhaps three-quarters Northern back then, though our smattering of Southerners did provide the programme's best-known alumnus – an ambitious but slightly awkward medical student from Dublin called Leo.

But as I look back now at the class of 2000, I see that the programme hasn't worked in its central aim of building Northern Ireland's leaders of tomorrow.

Most of us are making whatever mark we're making on life outside our native land.

Going through our Facebook Messenger group (long since dormant) I check my Northern classmates' locations: London, Belfast, Dublin, Bangor (County Down), Newry, Slaithwaite, Liverpool, Devon, Sydney, London, Liverpool, Manchester, Washington.

Of the thirteen of us Nordies on the group, only three remain in Northern Ireland now. As many live in the north west of England.

Going back a little further into my past and the strings holding my friends to the old country are just as thin.

In 2022 I was invited to the twenty-fifth reunion of my high school class. The idea of it being a quarter of a century since I last darkened the door of a school classroom was too depressing to think about, let alone celebrate, so I declined the invitation.

And looking at my Facebook friends who were also invited, most of them would have had a schlep to get back to Holywood, County Down: Bangor, Lisburn, Birmingham, Manchester, Nottingham, Belfast, Nottingham, Belfast, Dublin, London, Derry, London, Guildford (Western Australia), Cork, Anchorage.

---

[2] Unlike most Northern Protestants, I believe our people would be happier in a united Ireland than we are in the United Kingdom.

Of fifteen old classmates, only five of them still lived in Northern Ireland.

I accepted this all my life – the idea that many of us would leave Northern Ireland and most of us would never go back.

Then one February day, stuck on the M62 making my way home from another early shift, Spotify decided I should listen to the track Homesick[3] by the US folk singer Noah Kahan.

In it, he sings with despair about his native Vermont – a place that he knows defines him but that he desperately wants to leave:

...this place is such great motivation. For anyone tryna move the fuck away from hibernation.

With no actual moving traffic to concentrate on, my mind was free to concentrate on his lyrics:

Time moves so damn slow
I swear I feel my organs failing
I stopped caring 'bout a month ago
Since then, it's been smooth sailing

And that's when I realised he was singing about me, about my feelings towards a homeland that defines me and infuriates me in equal measure.

Then, like the sleep-deprived journalist I was, a word came into my weary mind and wouldn't leave: "Why?"

Why do so many of us leave Northern Ireland?

Why do so few of us go back?

Why does nobody in power in Northern Ireland seem to care?

Despite being a full-time shift worker with two children, I realised that I had to carve out the time to try to answer these questions.

When I started writing this book, I envisaged it as an angry examination of why Northern Ireland repels so many

[3] From his excellent 2023 album Stick Season (We'll All Be Here Forever).

of its young people and what the Northern Ireland Executive should do to start to reverse this.

But looking back now at my first notes, I see how much the book you're holding has moved on from the original vision.

A few months after my Damascene moment a couple of miles east of Junction 23, I went on an outside broadcast to the Open.

I'm no golf fan, but the demands of working for a breaking news and sports station such as BBC Radio 5 Live, often means turning your hand to a topic about which you have little knowledge or interest.

Journalists aren't supposed to have comfort zones.

So I found myself leading a team of four to bring our listeners the excitement of the first day of the Open from Royal Liverpool Golf Club in the town of Hoylake on the Wirral – the kind of place that gives the lie to the stereotype that all Scousers are poor and left-wing.

Golf is not a sport that worries about the price of bread so, on arrival at the course's press centre, each visiting journalist was handed a goodie bag of branded Open items.

I'm not sure when I'll have call to wear my Open tie, but my son's friend, Rhys – who is a massive golf fan – happily took the branded baseball cap and water bottle off my hands.

That just left a grand-looking Open notebook complete with attached bookmark ribbon.

I used it to plan this book, filling it with contact details of camogie clubs in New Zealand, Orange lodges in Toronto and even a table recording the sex and religion of each interviewee, in the interests of achieving a rough balance across the piece.

Right at the beginning, I also used the Open notebook to outline what I thought would be the book's structure, how each chapter would flow into the next one.

When I look back at the start of this endeavour from the vantage point of the end, I'm struck by how much it has changed.

The book I had planned to write, before I'd asked anyone for an interview, or scanned any Facebook group for contacts, was very different from the one which you're about to read.

In my first outline there were no fewer than three chapters based around how the Good Friday Agreement had failed (the past, the present, the future) and how this drives emigration.

The very first thing I wrote in my notebook was that the aim of the Introduction would be to "explain why high emigration is a problem for Northern Ireland."

The tone of my first scribblings is much more preachy, more judgmental than the final version of the book: High emigration is a bad thing, the Executive should try to reduce it, a Northern Ireland less repellent to its young people would be a happier, wealthier place.

I believe all these things today just as much as I did when I first wrote them in my Open notebook.

But, in the course of speaking to so many other people who've left Northern Ireland, I realised that this was not the most interesting thing to say about those of us who've abandoned the place.

About halfway through talking to people for this book, I came to understand that it shouldn't be a cry for a change, but rather a reflection of reality.

By speaking to fellow emigrants about why they left, I had the chance to tell the story of Northern Ireland's atrocious past, its infuriating present and its unsure future in a unique way.

Northern Ireland's sorrows are well documented, but never before in this way, by dozens of people who left the place for good.

With one exception[4], the emigrants I spoke to expressed affection towards Northern Ireland, the place where they grew up, the unique society that formed them.

But, with no exceptions, my interviewees were frustrated with Northern Ireland.

When they return home, they see their birthplace through the eyes of an informed outsider.

Their perspectives on the place's problems are unique and valuable for this reason – they know what Northern Ireland is and they know what it could be.

But before we get to that I feel that I need to explain why Northern Irish people are scattered to the winds.

The first part of the book covers the final destination of most of my conversations for this book, regardless of the age or the religion of the person I happened to be interviewing: The Troubles.

There is more than a little truth in the old jibe that Irish people exaggerate their suffering – our wars are happy, but our songs are sad.

If you were to present our death toll to a Ukrainian or a Palestinian, they would urge you to thank whatever God you believe in that things weren't much worse.

But by the standards of stable Western democracies, the Troubles stands out for the scale and, above all, the length of the suffering it inflicted.

From the deployment of British troops to the streets of Belfast and Derry in 1969 to the year the Good Friday Agreement was signed in 1998, 3,500 people were killed in Northern Ireland – more than half of them civilians.

At first glance, this figure might not seem too high – yes, 3,500 tragedies, but spread out over three decades can they really resonate so much another thirty years on?

---

[4] Ryan Cosgrave – not his real name – who features in the chapter The Most Likely To Go

But that ignores the fact of how intimately small Northern Ireland is.

Its population now is pushing towards two million, but during the Troubles there were only a million and a half of us.

Great Britian's population today is around thirty times greater than Northern Ireland's. America's is roughly 160 times larger.

Now look back at those 3,500 deaths and imagine more than 100,000 funerals in Britain over thirty years, or think about 560,000 grieving American families after three decades of hurt.

How would either society sit with this suffering? How would their political systems manage all that trauma? How would their cultures reflect all that pain?

And that's before we think about the 47,000 people injured during the Troubles.

Some of the wounded were patched up there and then, back at work in a day or two.

But many others sat up in their hospital bed to look at their wheelchair for the first time, knowing that it would be with them for every moment of the rest of their life.

I won't do the comparative British and American figures as I hope you've got the message about the scale of the suffering.

We often refer to the pain of the Troubles as the empty chair round the dinner table, the seat that will never be filled by a loved one taken away.

But the Troubles itself is like an empty chair in every discussion about Northern Irish politics – the third person who is always present, even when they're not explicitly acknowledged.

A book about why people leave Northern Ireland has to start there, in those bitter days, those unresolved times whose secrets still torment.

Before interviewing some of the emigrants I spoke to, I was already aware of some of the details of their suffering during the Troubles.

But many others brought up their experiences during the conflict unprompted.

The Good Friday Agreement ended the Troubles but did not resolve them.

In some ways it ended them because it didn't resolve them.

There's something fundamental to the agreement itself that makes it at once one of the most effective peace deals of modern times and one of the least successful governing models.

The cemeteries are no longer being filled with people whose only crime was to go out for a drink at the wrong time or drive their taxi into the wrong area.

This is the agreement's great success and it should never be downplayed.

But that enormous gain sits alongside its government structure, which by any standards, has been a failure.

Since the agreement was reached in 1998, Northern Ireland has had a functioning executive for just over fifty per cent of the time.

The problem is that the agreement – or more precisely its bastard offspring the St Andrew's Agreement of 2003 – allows the largest unionist party and the largest nationalist party to collapse the executive and prevent any return until their demands are met.

This is what is known in Northern Ireland as ransom politics.

The DUP – the largest unionist party for the last twenty years – condemns Sinn Fein when they collapse the institutions.

And Sinn Fein, which has been the dominant party on the nationalist side for the last two decades, castigates the

DUP when they give Stormont a bit of the old Samson treatment.

But these condemnations ring hollow when neither party – despite repeated invitations from politicians of other groups or from journalists – will promise not to use their veto in the future.

Back in 2017, Sinn Fein collapsed the Executive in protest at the DUP's handling of a flawed heating programme.[5]

They then kept Northern Ireland without any government for three years while haggling with the DUP over an Irish Language Act.

A deal was reached in 2020, through the New Decade, New Approach agreement, a title which instantly struck the cynical Ulster mind as hopelessly optimistic.

Sure enough, the DUP decided soon after the agreement was reached to take their ball home, bringing Northern Ireland's executive down in protest at the UK government's attempt to manage the hard Brexit on which the DUP had played a key part in introducing in the first place.

Neither the DUP nor Sinn Fein had more than thirty per cent of the vote when they condemned Northern Ireland to years without a government.

No other governing system anywhere in the world gives a minority party the right to block the formation of any government. No other society emerging from conflict today would follow this example.

And these long periods of stasis have real impacts for people in Northern Ireland, including many of those who voted for the two parties responsible for the breakdowns.

---

[5] Brilliantly explained in Sam McBride's book *Burned: The Inside Story of the 'Cash-for-Ash' Scandal and Northern Ireland's Secretive New Elite*

With Northern Ireland's politicians unable to agree on forming a new executive its civil servants – never the most dynamic group of bureaucrats at the best of times – were left without the democratic accountability to take anything more than the most basic house-keeping decisions.

Over in Westminster the ministers who were at least theoretically responsible for governance mixed their traditional cocktail of bewilderment and indifference, adding a stiff dash of condescension to the mix.

Meanwhile in Northern Ireland, ailing patients' wait for surgery stretched into years, rather than months and Lough Neagh – the largest inland waterway in Britain and Ireland – filled up with algae.

When I started to write this book, Northern Ireland had no government. As I write these lines, it does.

By the time you read them, who knows?

But either way, the weaknesses of the Good Friday Agreement are all too apparent.

And they form the basis of the second chapter of the book, Our Imperfect Peace, looking at those of us who left Northern Ireland after the bullets stopped flying.

A sense of hope unfulfilled permeates the pages of the second chapter.

The third chapter – Generation Betrayed – tells the story of ceasefire babies, those too young to have any memory of the Troubles, but who nevertheless concluded that even a peaceful Northern Ireland was unfulfilling.

Chapter Four: The Most Likely To Go explores how growing up gay in the most homophobic part of Britain and Ireland fuels the very high migration rate for same-sex attracted people.

We hear their stories of judgmental families, limited opportunities and even conversion therapy.

And in the final chapter, A Line On A Map, all of the emigrants turn their minds to the future – how they, now living abroad, would react to a border poll.

Northern Ireland's days within the United Kingdom may be numbered, but whether they are or not, the emigrants bring the insight of outsiders to judge the challenges that unity may bring.

Each interviewee said something that surprised me, every single one recounted an experience that I realised could illuminate Northern Irish society's peculiarities to those who weren't brought up there.

I felt that when Fidelma McCorry told me how her ex-boyfriend was murdered or when Mark Aiken mentioned that his uncle had been shot dead.

Both men had been going about their normal working days – one as a builder, the other driving a taxi – when they were shot dead for no other reason than their religion.

I also felt that sense of illumination when Gareth Patterson told me about the conversion therapy he had endured or when Rory Hughes wondered aloud if transgenerational trauma from the Troubles was the reason he suffers from ulcerative colitis.

All of them mentioned these painful experience in passing, while making a wider point.

In typical Ulster fashion, none of them wallowed in their pain.

And, despite the painful experiences that Northern Ireland inflicted on them, all of them celebrated the land that makes us refugees.

For all its flaws, they acknowledged how our homeland gave them the strength to endure the challenges of living as an outsider in someone else's country.

During my adult life I've endured three episodes of months-long pain.

One was health related, the other two were the outworking of the fractious end of a relationship.

But in all three cases, I either returned to the office as soon as a doctor would allow me, or carried on working even when those around me were advising me to take some time off.

In all three instances, my English colleagues remarked admiringly about my ability to keep going through adversity.

Northern Ireland made me that way.

The Troubles made me that way.

Which is not to say I had an awful, conflicted childhood. I grew up in one of the more peaceful parts of Belfast.

Yes, my family had some difficult moments, but unlike some of the people you'll read about in the following pages, we don't have a gravestone to go and visit of a loved one who was murdered during the conflict.

But even for those of us who avoided the pain of burying a family member, the Troubles were always there in the background.

Not just the noise of bombs and helicopters, not just the sobbing relatives on the news, but all those curtailed plans, all those guarded conversations, all that constant vigilance.

The Troubles made us stoic. Perhaps it's better to say they made us more stoic.

They made us resilient.

Northern Ireland is now – and has always been – a sick society.

From the next page onwards, you will see how it has failed to provide its citizens with a stable and prosperous foundation around which to build their lives.

But it is a sick society which builds healthy people, whether they choose to leave or remain.

This book is about them.

This book is by them.

This book is for them.

TIT FOR TAT

"If you usually go home through the main gate, you'll have to go out the back gate this afternoon."

Our deputy headmaster Mr Long is his typical matter-of-fact self as he pokes his head round the classroom door to explain the change of plan for the end of the school day.

The thirty of us in that drafty room are only aged ten, but all of us in Miss Ireland's P6 class know why the route home has had to change today.

We heard why half an hour earlier.

The windows of our classroom rattled as a bomb went off. Not a big one, but certainly a close one.

About 200 yards from our classroom – and a twenty-second walk from the school pitch where some of us were playing football thirty minutes earlier – a man's life has just ended.

We learn on the news that night that he was a retired police officer. Blown to bits by a bomb placed under his car by an IRA member, identity to this day unknown.

The victim's family[6], his friends and his former colleagues must have been devastated when they found out. However, I imagine that at the moment each of them were told the news they were shocked, but not surprised.

A terrible thing had happened to them – but not an unexpected thing.

For the rest of us, normal life resumed almost immediately.

I remember seeing our school on the local news that evening. And I recall our teacher, the redoubtable Miss

[6] Shamefully, I had to search the internet for the victim's name as I didn't know it. He was Gabriel Mullaly, a fifty-four-year-old retired police inspector. He had six children. May they live to see their dad's killers brought to justice.

Ireland, commenting a few days later that whoever planted that bomb had no job calling themselves a Christian.

But other than that, life went on. There was no special reassuring talk from our headmistress at assembly the following day.

There was no discussion of counselling, as I hope there would be now if someone was murdered right outside my children's school.

But, even if we had been offered psychological help, it would've seemed strange to accept it. We all just moved on. The car bomb wasn't the talk of the playground the following day, it wasn't something I had any desire to talk to my mum and dad about.

It was a terrible thing, but a terrible thing that had happened to someone I didn't know.

It is this, the everyday nature of the Troubles, which is hard to describe to those who didn't live through it and difficult to explain without seeming insensitive to those who suffered.

For most of us, most of the time, the conflict was background noise – helicopters whirring overhead, soldiers patrolling the streets, paramilitary graffiti on walls. It was the constant inconvenience of bomb scares and checkpoints.

Michael Campbell is older than me[7] and from a much more conflicted part of Belfast – west to my east – so his Troubles were much worse than mine.

He ducked out of the St Patrick's Day celebrations at Christchurch Irish Society to talk to me on Zoom from his car, proudly wearing his Ireland rugby shirt.

---

[7] The Troubles were far more intense in their early years – over half of all deaths occurred between 1969 and 1976. Thus, in general terms, my parents' generation of Baby Boomers suffered far more than their Gen X kids.

As Michael tells me his life story, the Troubles is the uninvited guest in our conversation, constantly elbowing its way into his narrative:

"My best man, his father was shot a few years after I got married. A Protestant had been killed the night before, so it was 'let's shoot a Catholic'. He never did a bad thing to anyone in his life...I remember once I was driving to pick up my wife and there had been rioting, I drove past 105 burnt-out cars and buses between the Falls Road and the Andersonstown Road...I started working for Guinness in 1988, I remember one day – the 30th of January 1991 – we had an all-day meeting at the Lansdowne Court Hotel on the Antrim Road. The next day the IRA blew it up and three other pubs – Robinsons, the Chimney Corner...I forget the fourth one. But, yeah, all of them Guinness pubs. It was punishment for not paying protection money. But fair play to Guinness, they never paid them."

Two things strike me as I speak to Michael. The first is his impressive memory. He recalls the exact date of a work meeting more than thirty years ago and tells me that, after a period of rioting, he drove past 105 burnt-out cars, rather than just a hundred.

The other thing I note is that, when Michael mentions the Troubles, he does so without even a trace of self-pity. Why me? Why us? These are not questions that sit well with the traditional Northern Irish value of stoicism.

But despite his lack of self-pity, Michael is clear that the Troubles are the key reason he's speaking to me from Christchurch rather than Belfast:

"I was born in the Lagan Valley Hospital in Lisburn in 1964 and adopted at birth. I spent the first ten years of my life living in Stockmans Gardens off the Andersonstown Road.

"The Troubles started when I was five and we moved to Ballymena five years later. My dad thought it would be quieter there. There were only three Catholic families living on the road, but we were round the corner from Liam Neeson.

"I went to boarding school, which insulated me a bit from the Troubles. When I was fifteen, we moved back to Belfast, to Fortwilliam, which was a bit quieter than west Belfast. I started working for Winemark and then in 1987 I met Mary, who was from Turf Lodge[8].

"We got married two years later. But even before we got married, we were talking about leaving. We went to New Zealand in 1992 and loved it, so we moved here a year later – the 24th of June 1993."

Michael and his wife welcomed sons to the world in 1994, 1996 and 1998 and have built a happy Irish emigrant life in New Zealand:

"About twenty-two per cent of people in New Zealand claim some Irish ancestry. We've got Gaelic football and hurling here in Christchurch, we send a competitor to the Rose of Tralee.[9]

"There's loads of Irish pubs, you could go to an Irish music session every night of the week if you wanted. Some people hear my accent and ask if I'm Canadian, some people guess Scottish – I tell them I'm from Northern Ireland, so in a way I'm half-Scottish.

"Sometimes people ask me if I'm Protestant or Catholic and I always just say 'well, if I wasn't from Northern Ireland, you wouldn't ask me that.'"

Compared with Michael's fulfilling life in New Zealand, a peaceful but still economically deprived Northern Ireland has little to offer:

"On one hand, the Troubles have ended, but the place is still a basket case.

---

[8] An area of west Belfast.

[9] The Irish beauty competition only slightly parodied as the Lovely Girl Contest in an episode of Father Ted.

"I was over a few years ago, I had a coffee in Castle Court[10] and then I went out on to Royal Avenue[11] and the shops and offices were all empty. And across the border you've got a country with double the GDP.

"We're doing well here, we've got three sons born and brought up here. Look, we could sell up in New Zealand and we'd have half a million to buy a house in Belfast...a nice house on the Malone Road[12]? No, we wouldn't be interested."

Michael is far from the only exile I spoke to who chafed at paramilitaries' desire to police the communities they claimed to protect.

Shortly after the Troubles started the various loyalist and republican armed groups which emerged turned their attentions inwards, enforcing discipline on the very people in whose name they were taking lives.

In the absence of an impartial, trustworthy police force, the men in balaclavas stepped in, dishing out their version of justice to political opponents, petty criminals, business owners who refused to help their cause and residents who dared to show a romantic interest in someone from the other side of the sectarian divide.

Thousands of people were subjected to punishment attacks during the Troubles – in more than 100 cases the attacks were fatal. The violence and intimidation continues – especially in loyalist areas – decades after the end of the conflict[13].

---

[10] Belfast's first major shopping centre which heralded a new era of confidence when it was built in the early 90s, despite repeated attempts by the IRA to blow it up.

[11] The main shopping street in Belfast city centre.

[12] Belfast's poshest road, whose inhabitants accept they will always be the butt of 'the haves and the have yachts' jokes from their more deprived neighbours.

[13] The role of paramilitary punishment attacks and intimidation in death by suicide in Northern Ireland, Sharon Mallon, Open University, 2017

Sometimes, as with Michael's example of the Belfast pubs whose owners refused to bend the knee to the IRA, the violence was, as it were, just business.

But on other occasions, like for Yvonne O'Hagan's family, it was much more personal. She speaks to me in her blue and white checked shirt from the attic of her home in Wellington.

Unusually for someone from a Catholic background, Yvonne always refers to the place the two of us left as "Northern Ireland" rather than "the North".

As our conversation goes on, I realise that her use of the term "Northern Ireland" is pointed, an indication that she rejects the stifling conformity of her background:

"I grew up in a very nationalist area, Galbally which is between Dungannon and Ballygawley in County Tyrone. I'm one of six, working class, grew up in a housing estate.

"I was one of the shyest in my family. I'm not quite sure how my parents managed it, but somehow they brought us all up to think that everyone was equal and no-one had the right to take someone else's life. It's only now that I can look back and reflect on that.

"A lot of the boys I knew at school went on to join the IRA, the boys who were killed at Loughgall.[14]

"I remember when I was seven, we were standing by this hedge waiting for the bus to school and then I saw soldiers with their faces blacked up hiding in the hedge. I said 'hi' to them and one of my friends said, 'why are you talking to those British bastards?'

"But my parents were different, if it came on the news that a British soldier had been killed, they would say 'that was somebody's son.'

---

[14] On May 8, 1987, eight members of the IRA were killed in an SAS ambush as they prepared to attack a police station in the County Armagh village. It was the IRA's biggest loss of life in a single incident during the Troubles.

"When I was eight, I remember walking up the lane to school and there were five IRA men walking towards us with their guns and their balaclavas. They had the look like they'd just done something, whatever it was, like they were finished.

"As I walked past one of them, he said 'Hi, Yvonne'. I knew his voice, I knew who he was. No, Barry, never worry, I won't say his name. He's dead now.

"But I remember at the time thinking that these are our neighbours. I can see how those young lads thought they were fighting for their country.

"Those lads at Loughgall, they were only twenty-one, what a waste of life. What was it all for? Did it achieve anything?"

By 1981 Yvonne and her family found that there was nowhere left to hide their opposition to the IRA. In that tumultuous year, ten republican prisoners starved themselves to death in an attempt to force the British government to recognise that they were political prisoners rather than criminals.

The hunger strikes led to a surge of support for the IRA and Sinn Fein on both sides of the border. Those who lived in areas already dominated by the republican movement were expected to show their support for the hunger strikers, regardless of any reservations they might have had:

"I was 16 during the hunger strike and I was studying at college in Dungannon. When news came through that one of the hunger strikers had died, all the Catholic students would walk out of class and all the Protestants would stay.

"I remember walking out, but asking myself why I was doing it. I was very conflicted, thinking 'does that mean that I support the cause?'

"When a hunger striker died, everyone else in our estate would put up a black flag on their house but my dad wouldn't. That was really brave of him – and really stupid. He was targeted because of that.

"The IRA came in one night, they smashed the kitchen window and kicked in the back door. It was snowing that night and my mum took my brother – who was the only one of us there at the time – out into the snow.

"They said to my dad: 'This is how we do things here.' They beat him up in the kitchen. They told him: 'If you don't do it our way, this is what's going to happen.' I remember coming back and seeing him with black eyes.

"He stood up for what he believed in – that it's wrong to take someone else's life. He was bloody harmless. I don't think he was ever the same after that."[15]

Like Michael Campbell, Yvonne felt the hand of the Troubles on her shoulder, pushing her out the door:

"When I was a teenager I didn't do normal things, like going out, because you couldn't, it wasn't safe. There was a lot of missed years. It's different for my girls, they just go out, they jump on a train and it's no bother.

"I remember odd things from the Troubles, like every now and again they'd blow up the petrol station in the village and we'd all be in the field next day trying to find any packets of cigarettes that had been blown away.

"I remember telling my family that I wanted to move to London. They tried to talk me out of it but I went over there, I lived in London for seven years."

Yvonne eventually decided to move much further away from her conflicted Tyrone upbringing:

"When I was about twenty-five or twenty-six this woman from New Zealand moved into our flat, it had been

---

[15] As she tells me the story, I can't help but think of a friend of mine from a different, but equally republican, town in the North. He spoke out against the IRA and was beaten over the head with a baseball bat one night. Just like Yvonne's father, my friend was never the same after that.

all Irish girls before that. I met some more Kiwis and they were such good fun, it sparked my interest in the country.

"Me and my friend Jenny went to New Zealand for six months, then we went to Australia for six months. But my visa ran out both times so I ended up back in Northern Ireland."

But her enforced return home only strengthened Yvonne's resolve to leave again. Like many emigrants I spoke to who had to come home, she found that all the frustrations that had driven her from Northern Ireland still held:

"I came home to the same estate where my parents lived. It was just after the ceasefires in 1994. I went out with a friend to the Dunowen Inn in Dungannon. We were talking to a couple of guys, who said they were RUC.

"When we were getting in a taxi outside, the driver saw us talking to them. He told my brother. He told me: 'You guys were talking to police officers, that's not how we do things here.' My brother wouldn't be involved or anything like that, it's just that he's lived there his whole life."

In common with other emigrants, Yvonne couldn't fight the thought that she was an outsider in Northern Ireland:

"I just thought to myself: 'I'm not living somewhere where people tell me who I can and can't talk to.' That was when I had my lightbulb moment. I didn't fit in.

"I got a job at a school in New Zealand and later I met my partner Marty and we had three girls. They're sixteen, eighteen and twenty now. We lived in Malahide in Dublin from 2000 to 2008, up until the crash.

"Our daughters were all born in Dublin. I had this idea with our first girl that I'd like to give birth to her in Tyrone but it didn't work out in the end.

"I was working as a teacher and we bought a house near the airport, easy enough for heading North. People in Dublin would talk about 'youse Northerners with your problems' it was banter but underneath it, they really do think that we're different from them.

"I remember the first time I brought Marty to meet my family. He was driving from the airport, on the road up to the estate there's tricolours flying from every lamppost.

"Then the army stopped us at a checkpoint. The soldier's holding his GPMG[16] – God, even that I know what a GPMG is – and asking for ID. As soon as Marty shows him his New Zealand driving license the fella relaxes and just waves us through.

"So, I thought it was no bother. Marty's usually a cool character, but he pulled the car over. I just said, 'don't worry, that's normal' and he said 'Yvonne, there's nothing normal about that.'"

On her most recent visit home Yvonne was reminded of the cruel intimacy of Northern Ireland:

"I went home last year with my three daughters. It was the first time I'd been over from New Zealand in six years. We were in a pub with my mum and I saw this guy sitting in the alcove, he kept looking over at us.

"I asked my mum who he was and she said: 'That's one of the boys who beat up your dad.' I wasn't angry with him, I just thought: 'You poor thing, you were only young and you got dragged into doing that to my dad because you thought it was for the cause.'

"The look on his face, it was a look of guilt."

Like many of the people I speak to, Yvonne's feelings about Northern Ireland are conflicted. On the one hand her determination never to move back is strengthened with each brief visit:

"I went back when my dad died six years ago. I wanted to carry his coffin but I was told that wasn't how we do

---

[16] General Purpose Machine Gun, the rifle routinely carried by British soldiers during the Troubles.

things. Afterwards I told my mother that I'm carrying her coffin no matter what."

But she appreciates the resilience she imbibed as part of her Northern Irish childhood:

"I'm sixty next year but it's only in the last few years I've started to think about what we all went through.

"When Marty left me, I had this huge resilience because of the place I grew up in. I was able to keep going."

Yvonne has a powerful affection for the old country and a desire to help other emigrants:

"I work in a law firm in Wellington. I have a friend from Belfast and she helped me get the job. When I hear an Irish accent it causes a reaction in my bones, like when I heard your accent tonight.

"I'm not over here just to hang out with other Irish people but you do gravitate towards your own because they feel like your family. I live in a lovely wee village and you wouldn't believe how many Irish people are here.

"I was down at the coffee cart and I saw this fella with a Northern accent, I could see his Union Jack tattoos. I got talking to him, turns out he was in the RUC.

"I invited him to the Irish Society but he said he felt like he wouldn't be welcome there. He never came along.

"I think of Ireland as home, not necessarily Northern Ireland. When I hear Irish music, I can hear it in my heart. I would never go back...what made me leave is still there...it's still there.

"Some of the people may be long gone but it's still in the psyche. When I went home to visit a while ago, they'd be going round the houses, round the pubs selling that paper – what's it called? An Phoblacht.[17]

"God, if I'd stayed there, I'd have been kneecapped and feathered by now. I'd have been speaking out about what I believed in, I'd have ended up like my dad."

---

[17] A republican newspaper.

Like Michael and Yvonne, Jim McAuley grew up at the start of the Troubles in a working-class area which quickly came under the control of the hard men who lived there.

But, unlike the two adopted Kiwis, Jim regularly visits Northern Ireland. In part this is because a journey home for him is no more complicated than a drive from Huddersfield to Manchester Airport followed by a fifty-minute flight back to the City Airport in his native east Belfast.

But Jim's frequent returns home are also a result of his career in academia, which he has dedicated to the study of Northern Ireland.

Indeed, of all the emigrants I spoke to, Jim seems to have left Northern Ireland the least, both physically and emotionally. Not only did he end up marrying a Belfast woman who he met in a pub in Huddersfield, he also took a job that entailed regular, prolonged trips back home.

Jim is one of the few people I speak to who is old enough to have clear memories of Northern Ireland before the Troubles.

It's sometimes difficult to explain to people who aren't from Northern Ireland what a watershed moment 1969 was. People of my parents' generation will sometimes speak of the pre-Troubles time in the same way that older British people used to talk of the years before 1939.

Which is not to say that the Troubles were on anything like the scale of the Second World War of course. But more to note that, for those like Jim who are old enough to remember the years before communal violence subsumed Northern Ireland, their lives are divided – sometimes subconsciously – into the years before and the years after:

"I was born in 1956, there was me and my twin sister and we lived in Willowfield in east Belfast. It was a typical working-class Protestant upbringing, my da was a welder in the shipyard, all my uncles worked in the shipyard.

"I was very ill with asthma as a child so I used to spend most of my time at my granny's because she lived on the same street as the doctor. But you know I have only good memories of my childhood, I can't point to any drama.

"It was a very sharing community and people did look after each other. I know it's a cliché but we didn't lock our door during the day, I don't think anybody on our street did. At least not until 1969."

Jim goes on to explain his memories of that pivotal time, as the society he had grown up in slipped away forever:

"I was 13 when the Troubles started. I remember the bombs going off on the Woodstock Road and seeing the burnt-out buildings.

"One time there was shooting on our street and a man literally grabbed me and threw me into a house to get me out of harm's way.

"But because I lived in east Belfast, there wasn't so much rioting. There's only one interface, at the Short Strand, and that wasn't particularly close to us. If you wanted to go rioting, you'd have to go out of your way.

"But the paramilitaries were very active around us. There was a sense that our community was under attack and that the whole of Northern Ireland was in danger."

Like Yvonne, Jim had to deal with the strange feeling of realising that some of his friends and neighbours had joined paramilitary groups, while retaining the identities they had before the violence began:

"I remember the fella who ran the shop at the end of our street, he'd be selling you a pound of cheese in the afternoon and then in the evening, he'd be out on the street with a balaclava on.

"Loyalists in the area set up a no-go area in protest at the republican no-go area in Derry. So there was all this barricade round my granny's street. But it was strange because I knew who all these paramilitaries were.

"My best friend was arrested for UVF membership."

Given Jim's imposing frame, he would have been a welcome recruit to the loyalist groups operating in the streets where he grew up.

But music, football and family stopped him from turning the corner into the cul-de-sac of life in the paramilitaries:

"I joined Castlereagh Glentoran[18] Supporters Club when I was sixteen and, looking back, that was why I didn't join the paramilitaries. At the weekend I was focussed on going to the football and then going into town to buy records.

"But also, I was respectable working class. My granny never touched alcohol or cigarettes, neither did my mum.

"We had a full set of Encyclopaedia Britannica at home. My uncles were involved in the Northern Ireland Labour Party, I remember them all talking about politics.

"It had an effect on me, I was never going to go to uni to study engineering after that."

But, though his family's politics and respectability helped keep him of jail, Jim was less keen to follow in his father's footsteps at work:

"I went to Cregagh Technical College because my father wanted me to have a trade like him. After two weeks it became clear that I could barely hammer a nail into a piece of wood, so I left and did some O Levels instead.

"I left school at sixteen and started working for BT as a support engineer. I was just thinking about the Ulster Workers Strike[19] because it was the fiftieth anniversary the other day. I worked every day through that strike.

"BT sponsored me to go through university so I studied sociology and social anthropology at the University of

[18] The best of Belfast's four football teams.

[19] The general strike by loyalists, accompanied by much violence and intimidation, which brought down the power sharing government formed by the Sunningdale Agreement.

Ulster and then I was offered the chance to do a PhD in Leeds in 1983. It wasn't really that I wanted to leave Northern Ireland at the time, it was just a good opportunity to do a PhD.

"In 1984 I was playing for my rugby team in a match in Huddersfield. We were meant to go home after the match but we all decided to stay for a few drinks instead.

"Halfway through the night, I tripped over this woman and heard her Belfast accent. We got talking and it turned out she grew up 500 yards from where I grew up, my parents knew her parents and all that."

But Jim and his wife-to-be decided against returning to Belfast to build their family:

"Steph's more against moving back to Northern Ireland than me. She lost people in the Troubles and I didn't.

"We settled in Huddersfield and we both had academic jobs where we could live in the same place, which is hard to do in England and much harder in Northern Ireland, so it got to the point were going back was inconceivable."

By the time Jim and Steph were welcoming their son and daughter into the world, the Troubles were well into their second decade. The British people around them had become accustomed to the occasional IRA bomb on their streets and the much more regular return of their young soldiers in coffins.

This was the IRA's long war strategy, the group's attempt to wear down the British state until the point where Her Majesty's Government agreed to sit down and negotiate the terms of its withdrawal.

It was a late Twentieth Century attempt to recreate the conditions in the early 1920s, when the previous iteration of the IRA led by Michael Collins had effectively forced Britain to give up control of 26 of Ireland's counties.

But the Tan War of 1919 to 1921 was of much greater intensity than the Troubles – more than two thousand people were killed in those two years. The IRA's active membership at the time was in five figures and Sinn Fein had majority support across the island.

Conditions in the North two generations later were nowhere near as fertile for revolution, a point the republican movement inadvertently demonstrated when it adopted the 'Armalite and ballot box' strategy in the 1980s, buoyed by initial electoral success in the wake of the hunger strike.

When they started to contest elections, Sinn Fein settled in to a bulletproof vote a little over 10% - well behind their rival for Catholic votes, the SDLP, whose support tended to be in the high teens or early 20s.

Sinn Fein contested local authority elections for the first time in 1985, emerging as the single largest party in just one of Northern Ireland's 26 council areas.

For a more conventional political party, this would be considered a promising first outing. But for an organisation claiming to act on behalf of the people of Ireland, it exposed the futility of the republican movement's long war strategy.

In effect, a minority of the minority in the North was trying to force Western Europe's largest army to turn and run. It was always a doomed prospect.

But Jim recalls that the IRA's campaign was markedly successful in increasing the level of anti-Irish animosity in Britain:

"There was lots of hostility at the time to people from Northern Ireland. Outside of the uni, there was very little knowledge of the situation, people would just say: 'Why do we have to keep sending our boys over there to get killed?'

"And there was a general anti-Irish, far-right feeling in Leeds at the time. I remember going to see Leeds United and there were National Front guys at the turnstiles selling their paper. That was the last time I went to Elland Road.

"I remember one time I was in a pub in North Yorkshire and these lads overheard my accent. They left the pub and they came back a few minutes later with face coverings on and fired a starting pistol at me. They thought it was hilarious, they were laughing saying 'we just wanted you to feel at home'. It was bizarre.

"But to be honest, I'm six foot four and seventeen stone so maybe I didn't get the same level of hostility as other people got."

Jim has spent large periods of his professional life in Northern Ireland, seeing how the place has changed – and how it hasn't – in the years since the IRA abandoned its 'one more bomb, bro' strategy of the 1980s:

"I still feel very close to Northern Ireland because I've been doing research there for forty years. I'd spend Christmas there, Easter there. I'd be over twelve to fifteen times a year, maybe for two to three months cumulatively so I've seen how the place has changed.

"The Good Friday Agreement...look, no-one in their right mind wasn't pleased when the agreement was reached, given that it brought peace. It's not the agreement itself that's the problem, it's the idea that it's written in stone.

"The assembly's been operational for four and a half of the last seven years, it clearly isn't working. We can't go on with this situation where one party is able to bring everything down and say: 'Give us so many billions and then we'll go back.'"

Jim's children have differing approaches to the identity that their parents bequeathed to them:

"It's funny, they have different attitudes to their heritage. I don't think Roan would ever say he's English, but he wouldn't say he's Irish either. He has a British passport, but Charlotte has an Irish passport.

"She goes to watch the Northern Ireland football team and the Irish rugby team with me. She's living in Dubai now and she's in a Gaelic football team, I think she feels more at home with the Irish ex-pats than the English ex-pats."

Jim is not quite committed to moving back home permanently. The problems of Northern Ireland – problems he knows only too well – still discourage his head from making the move that his heart appears to have already made:

"Steph and I have been living in Groomsport[20] for the past few months. The development used to be a caravan park, Steph's family had a caravan here when she was a kid.

"But then you look at what's happened to the NHS here. My niece's wee girl had a very high temperature the other day and the best they could do for her was a phone call from a GP.

"Will we stay? I don't know. We're going back to England in a few weeks. The state of the NHS in Northern Ireland is a big factor, but also we've lived most of our adult lives in Yorkshire.

"I think the high emigration rate is a reflection of a failed society that's largely based on sectarianism. I don't necessarily mean violence, it's the benign apartheid where we have to have two of everything.

"This whole idea that British and Irish are polar opposites...this is still a very conflicted society."

Jim's frustrations with the Good Friday Agreement are backed up by research carried out by the Belfast thinktank Pivotal.

In 2021, it asked young people why they had chosen to leave Northern Ireland:

Students consistently reported that the religious/political divides in Northern Ireland are a 'push' factor for studying elsewhere.

Students described being "sick" of ongoing community tension and disengaged from the historical context of the conflict in Northern Ireland.

[20] A small coastal village about 10 miles outside Belfast

Notably, many students felt that the heavily segregated nature of education created limited contact with young people from different religious/political backgrounds and contributed to a desire to study elsewhere to gain a more varied experience of society...Students consistently described concern and dissatisfaction with government functioning in Northern Ireland.

A perceived lack of progress by the Northern Ireland Executive, a focus on identity politics and neglect of wider social and economic issues were cited as 'push' factors for the majority of the participants.

There was a clear perception of incompetence amongst politicians and a failure to represent issues of priority to young people.[21]

Meanwhile, Jim's experience of anti-Irish prejudice in West Yorkshire is backed up by a less rigorous academic source, er, me.

When he told me his memories of animosity in Leeds in the 1980s, I couldn't help feeling like it was a fuller-fat version of what I experienced twenty years later, twenty miles down the road in Huddersfield.

In one workplace, a colleague routinely referred to me as 'Irishman', not as a description of my nationality, but as though it were my name, as in: 'Come over here, Irishman.'

I had first encountered this particular form of linguistic prejudice a few months earlier, when watching The Damned United, the excellent adaptation of David Peace's book about Brian Clough's disastrous brief spell as Leeds manager in 1974.

The film includes a much YouTubed scene where Michael Sheen's Clough addresses his new charges ahead of their first training session.

---

[21] p5-6, Should I Stay Or Should I Go? Reasons for leaving Northern Ireland for work and study; Pivotal, Public Policy Forum Northern Ireland, 2021

He tells the league champions standing in front of him that their many successes under his hated predecessor Don Revie mean nothing to him:

"The first thing you can do for me is to chuck all your medals, and all your caps and all your pots and all your pans into the biggest fucking dustbin you can find because you've never won any of them fairly – you've done it all by cheating."

Having made his general discontent with the team's lack of sportsmanship crystal clear, Sheen's Clough then singles out the two midfielders he considers to have manned the engine room of thuggery under Revie.

First he upbraids the Scottish maestro Billy Bremner, demanding "good, clean attractive football from my captain."

Then he turns to his midfield partner, Johnny Giles: "And you, Irishman. God gave you skill, intelligence and the best passing ability in the game. What God did not give you is six studs to wrap around another player's knee."

A perhaps fictionalised version of Clough's robust language in 1974 is one thing. But the same term used for real more than thirty years later really rankles.

However, my colleague doesn't see it that way, so he carries on referring to me as though my nationality were my name when the fancy takes him.

I suppose I'm lucky compared with the "dagos" and "jungle bunnies" he mentions in conversation. Most of the rest of my colleagues are embarrassed by his behaviour, but nothing ever gets done about it. I suppose that was the Noughties for you.

Many other colleagues engage in milder anti-Irish "banter" around me for their own amusement. Ironically, in an office featuring several functioning alcoholics, there are digs about me drinking too much because I'm Irish.

I still recall the day there was a bomb scare in town. In the end it's nothing but a hoax, but several colleagues take the opportunity to dust off some old favourites they haven't had much chance to use since the first IRA ceasefire fifteen years before.

"I see you've been up to your old tricks again, Barry." I stop counting at half a dozen. I'm not angry, so much as bored.

While I don't feel like making excuses for my overtly racist colleague, over the years I've come to realise that the other prejudices I encountered – the jibes about bombs and booze – probably came from a less hateful place than I first assumed.

English people consider Irish people – all of us, whatever side of the border we're from and whichever foot we kick with – as family. Yes, we're different, but not different like a Dane or an Italian.

As such, we're targets for banter like everyone else in these islands. People from Belfast drink too much and blow things up, just like Scousers nick things, Scots refuse to get their round in and people from the West Country have a unhealthy romantic interest in their cousins.

So, it would be wrong to portray my experience of life outside Northern Ireland as a tidal wave of hostility. Far more common is the feeling of the gently lapping waves of indifference.

Back in the Noughties, those who did want to talk to me about Northern Ireland tended to be ex-soldiers. None of the former squaddies I've passed the time of day with gave the impression of having any trauma at what they experienced in Northern Ireland.

Rather they expressed a general sense of bafflement at the pointlessness of it all and a feeling of detachment from the people whom they used to look at down the barrel of a gun.

On a press trip to Brussels in 2009, I had a few drinks with Nigel Farage and his Yorkshire UKIP representative

Godfrey Bloom in an Irish pub right outside the European Parliament.

Having picked up on my accent, Godfrey took a sip of beer before summing up his Troubles experience in typically blunt fashion: "Two tours in the 70s, Barry – only damage I did was to my fucking liver."

But for those who moved from Northern Ireland to England during the Troubles, the hostility was often more marked than the fleeting animosity I experienced.

Liam Devlin grew up in one of the most deprived parts of Belfast at the height of the Troubles. So when he got on the ferry in 1989 to move to one of the poshest universities in England, he quickly felt out of place:

"For most of them I was some sort of exotic animal. I remember one girl called Tamzin, she had blonde hair and I quite fancied her. I was talking to her and she said: 'Oh my god, you're actually really nice.'

"I asked her why she was surprised. I hadn't realised that most of students in our halls were afraid of me because I was from Belfast.

"When I was in Manchester people referred to me as 'Paddy'. I was happy I wasn't there for the bomb in 1996 because I know I would have been lifted[22]. I was always stopped for questioning on the ferry because I'm called Liam Devlin."

Liam and I meet in a pub in Slawit, the West Yorkshire village we both now call home. At the time Liam was working with my wife Jenny at Huddersfield University and, as it turns out, he was very keen to discuss the old country.

After we talk for a while, I realise who he reminds me of – my uncle Bill.[23] Like Liam, Bill left Northern Ireland to study. Both men have the same abiding affection for their

[22] Belfast slang for "arrested".

[23] Perhaps appropriately, as "Liam" is the Irish form of "William".

birthplace, alongside a frustration at Northern Ireland's sectarianism.

They each seem to gravitate towards people from the other community – Catholics in Bill's case, Protestants for Liam – not out of any animosity to their own side, but perhaps as a subconscious attempt to escape the sectarianism that defined their upbringing.

It's certainly a frustration that seems to weigh heavily on Liam:

"The moment you're born, you're given this huge baggage of history and you're not allowed to say: 'I don't want it' you're just not allowed.

"I was born in 1971 in Twinbrook. It's an estate on the edge of west Belfast that was built because of the overcrowding in the centre of Belfast. I remember it as a place of incredible freedom. There were lots of young families.

"We were this big group of kids and we could just run around in this close-knit community. We ran out the door in the morning and then we weren't expected back until the evening. Because it was on the edge of town, I could run across the street and be out in the fields. It was a place of freedom and imagination.

"But it was also a place of vicious violence. When the police and army came in, they would come in force, to raid someone's home. There was a very real sense that they hated us.

"There was never any chance that I was going to get involved. But for some of the kids I grew up with, it didn't go well for them.

"I had one friend who stole cars. He was kneecapped by the IRA but that didn't stop him. He kept nicking cars and then one day he drove through an army checkpoint and they shot him dead."

When he was 15, Liam and his family left their entirely Catholic housing estate in Belfast to move to the much more religiously mixed – and much more peaceful – town of Newcastle in County Down.

For Liam it was his first chance to get to know the other side:

"I got five crappy O Levels and then went to the tech in Downpatrick. All my best friends there were Protestants.

"I went to Manchester University to study astrophysics. I had this mad idea that Manchester would be just like Coronation Street. I hated having a background you couldn't get rid of in Belfast. But in Manchester I had no bearings.

"Most of the other students were from very wealthy backgrounds. There was one fella from Eton and another who had a chequebook from Coutts. They didn't really have any consequences for their actions, they could do what they want."

Liam returned to Ireland in the Nineties. A brief period studying archaeology at Queen's was brought to an end by the rather fundamental issue that he "wasn't really interested in archaeology."

In 1996, Liam moved to the Dublin Institute of Technology to study photography. As he went on to build a career as a photographer, it seems fair to say that he eventually chose the right subject – but not the right city.

In our hourlong conversation, Liam comes across as a man who is generally at ease with the world. The only time he becomes agitated is when discussing his disappointment that the Republic he experienced as a young man fell far short of his childhood memories of the state:

"Before I went to live in Dublin, I had fond memories of the Republic. When we were kids, we would go on holiday to Donegal.

"We always got stopped at the border, pulled over and searched. When we got across the border, we would cheer. So I had this rose-tinted view of the Republic, but Dublin got rid of that very quickly.

"Dublin was a Victorian city with a rigid class structure. Behind the Guinness factory, there'd be all these street kids running around, it was like Dickens.

"The city was so corrupt. There were whole swathes of the population who were just abandoned. The state was run by friends of friends, it was incredibly nepotistic.

"I know people from the North who got hassled in Dublin. I know a young woman from Belfast who got on a bus in Dublin. Someone heard her accent and told her to go back to her own country.

"My best friend is from Lambeg[24] and he moved to Cork. He always felt he was being judged. People had these preconceptions about him because he's a Protestant. He feels like an outsider.

"In 2008 I moved to Bristol to do a PhD. I was glad to leave Dublin. It's a difficult place, very, very expensive. It's quite a mean place."

Now happily ensconced in West Yorkshire, Liam remains attached to the old country:

"I go home regularly, but mostly to Newcastle. I don't really know many people in Belfast now. I love the place and I feel tied to it umbilically. In the 2000s young people in Belfast were starting to feel invested in the place. But Brexit killed the energy in Belfast.

"I would move back for my family. There's a certain camaraderie in Northern Ireland, a way of talking to each other.

"You could have an amazing quality of life there. But still...I remember going out with my Protestant friends in Dundonald, or this one time in a UDA bar in Holywood.[25] I would pretend my name was Peter.

---

[24] A small village in County Antrim that gives its name to the enormous drums played during Orange Order parades in rural areas.

[25] The small town in County Down which is one 'l' of a long way from the Hollywood in Los Angeles

"Maybe I'm still overly cautious about these things. I find the politics of the place depressing. John Hume was incredible and, looking back now, so was David Trimble[26]. He was a man of his culture."

But life as an emigrant seems to suit Liam better. None of the other customers enjoying the surprisingly reasonably priced craft ale in the Hideaway in Slawit knows or cares about his religious background:

"I wanted out at eighteen. I didn't want to be a Catholic and everything that that entails. When you meet someone new, you get into this little conversational dance with them where you're trying to find out their religion.

"I remember telling myself that I would stop doing this when I met someone new. But I couldn't manage to do it. I feel a connection to people from Northern Ireland, without a doubt. You have to get the Protestant-Catholic thing out of the way but then there's this lovely balance between being very warm but not suffering fools. The quality of conversation is great."

As someone who grew up in one of the most violent parts of Belfast at the height of the Troubles, Liam knows he carries more than most:

"I think I have an acute sense of trouble, when I think something's not right I'm very sensitive to that.

"I remember in Dublin, I would tense up if I was driving and someone in an SUV came up behind me because it sounds like an army jeep.

---

[26] When Liam mentions Trimble being a man of his culture I tell him an anecdote I heard about him years ago. In the early 70s, Trimble was a young law lecturer in Belfast with hardline unionist views. But when one of his students was interned for suspected republican paramilitary involvement, Trimble went to Long Kesh several times to teach him. Not out of any sympathy with the student's politics, but because of his Protestant sense of duty. Liam is genuinely delighted to hear this little story.

"I was at the DART[27] station behind Trinity once. There was car parked underneath the line with no-one in it. I couldn't relax until the train left the station. My rational brain told me that it was just someone parking there and going in the Spar. But my fear wouldn't let me relax."

When I ask Liam if he considers Northern Ireland home, he takes a short sip of beer and a long think:

"For all its problems and frustrations, it's still home. I didn't feel at home in the South, I'll always be a Nordie.

"But I never really felt like I belonged anywhere. One of my earliest memories is standing in Twinbrook and thinking 'this isn't me.'

"But I want to be buried in Northern Ireland."

Julie McDonald grew up just a few miles from Liam. But socially, and religiously, hers was a different world to his:

"I was born in July 1959 into a middle-class Protestant family in east Belfast.

"I remember going to Donegal on holiday and visiting my father's family in Bangor every Sunday, things like that. But I also remember in 1968 hearing a bomb go off for the first time.

"But still, I don't remember the early Seventies as being terrible. My parents were very sociable and they would go out and we would invite our friends round and listen to records."

It was only when Julie visited England that she realised how strange her native city had become in the course of her childhood:

"Looking back now you realise it wasn't normal. There were bombs going off in town all the time.

"I remember we went to England and, when we went into Boots, I instinctively opened my bag for the woman working there to check – she just looked at me as if to say,

[27] Dublin Area Rapid Transport, the Irish capital's rail system.

'what are you doing?' It was our normal and it took a while after I left to realise that it wasn't normal for other people."

Julie's choice of career meant she felt she had to leave Northern Ireland:

"I went to a grammar school – Strathearn – and I always had the idea that I would leave and go to GB to study, I suppose like a lot of middle-class Protestants do.

"It wasn't so much the violence, it was that I was bored. Northern Ireland seemed very provincial. We went on holiday to London in 1973 and I just thought to myself that this is where I wanted to be.

"I was always in school plays and in the end I moved to London and tried to become an actress. I was always skint. I did one scene with Ciaran Hinds in a film called December Bride and I was in another film called Hushaby Baby, that was exciting because I got to meet Sinead O'Connor.

"But in the end I failed. It's strange, but in my twenties I dreamed of becoming an actress, of getting a part in a film about Northern Ireland and going back there for a month. It's strange to have this attachment to a place that you don't actually want to live in.

"I felt like I'd made such a Horlicks of my acting career – and of my relationship – that I left London for Paris and I've lived here ever since."

Julie's affinity to Northern Ireland seems to have grown stronger over her three decades in Paris:

"It's thirty years in France now, twenty-seven of them in this apartment. I've always been a Francophile. My son is twenty-six and he lives in Barcelona and my daughter's twenty-three and she works for France 24 here in Paris.

"But they've always had an affinity to Northern Ireland. We used to spend every July there – for rainbows and riots. And we'd go back in the school holidays in May and October.

"We'd go to Northern Ireland at least four times a year. They'd spend a lot of time with their cousins. They speak

Belfast. Do you know how I mean, Barry, they can speak in code?

"So they'd say 'down' in an Ulster accent to an Ulster person, but when they're speaking to an English person, they'd anglicise the vowel sound."

In common with many other emigrants I speak to, Julie mentions that leaving Northern Ireland has given her the chance to mix with people from the other community in a relaxed way that wouldn't be possible if they had both stayed at home:

"I've gravitated towards other Irish people in Paris, but there aren't very many Northerners among us. My best friend over here, Declan, is the same age as me but he grew up in Andersonstown.

"But we're still a small bunch compared with 'the Irish Irish' – which they have been known to call themselves. I go to the Irish cultural centre, I'm a member of Mná na hÉireann,[28] I've never felt as Irish as I do in Paris."

When I ask Julie if she would ever return to live in Northern Ireland, a country which she clearly still holds in much affection, she mentions two problems which will become common themes as my interviews go on – the health service and the segregated school system:

"No, I wouldn't go back to live there. One of the reasons is the NHS being in such a mess. I'm getting older now and the health system in France is much better. But there are other things.

"The separate education systems they have, I still find that vile, I just think it's terrible. I love that France is a secular country, with the separation of church and state. Nearly all the funerals that I go to now are atheist funerals."

Charlotte Forbes also found her way to Paris from Northern Ireland. But, unlike Julie, her story starts in one of the poorest parts of the North – the border town of

---

[28] Women of Ireland, a Paris-based group of female emigrants

Strabane which is notorious for its high unemployment rate:

"I was born in 1982 and I grew up with my two sisters, we're all close in age. Dad was a teacher and mum worked for the Citizens Advice Bureau.

"I'd say our upbringing wasn't impoverished but we weren't well-off either. We didn't have holidays abroad or anything like that. Strabane wasn't exactly a thriving metropolis, there was one Indian family in the town when I was growing up.

"Successive Tory governments haven't given a fuck about Strabane, or the North West in general. And even now if fees like there isn't a local representative who really champions the area.

"There's a kind of inferiority complex, like I remember our teacher warning us before we did our French A Level that we'd have to work hard at it because we'd be up against kids from schools like Methody[29] in Belfast, even though our school was a really high-achieving school."

Charlotte's parents tried to shield her from the reality of the conflicted society she called home:

"My parents tried to protect us from the Troubles, they'd never put the Six O'clock News on because of what you'd see.

"But I had nightmares in my teenage years about bombs. I know one girl who wouldn't come out of her room all summer because she was having nightmares about the Troubles.

"I remember Greysteel,[30] that was shocking for me because it was near Derry, where we would go to do our shopping. I can still remember hearing about the shooting on a tinny wireless we used to have. And I remember

---

[29] Methodist College Belfast, the city's third most self-important school.

[30] On October 30, 1993, gunmen from the UDA murdered eight Catholics who were drinking in the Rising Sun Bar in the County Derry village of Greysteel.

thinking we could be next. My parents tried to reassure me but you had this feeling of insecurity, like the rug could be pulled out from under you at any minute."

Despite her affection for her hometown, Charlotte left as soon as she could:

"I've never met people as nice as people from Strabane. It's the kind of place where everyone knows everyone, but there can be a downside to that too.

"When I went to visit Belfast, it was the big smoke. I went to Queen's in 2000 to do European Studies with French. I was living in Alanbrooke Hall, it's been demolished now. I was away from my parents and my sisters and I felt homesick and depressed.

"I didn't go out much at first because I was shy but eventually I made some friends among the international students. In my final year at Queen's I went to the British Council on Fountain Street to sign up to teach English – I jumped at the chance.

"I moved to Paris in 2004 and I've lived here ever since. At first you try not to gravitate to other Irish people because you want to integrate into French life as much as possible. But over the years I've made a lot of Irish friends – mainly from the Republic – and I go to an Irish church on Sundays.

"I'm still teaching after all these years and my French is really good now. A lot of French people have been to Ireland and they have fond memories of the place. When people ask where I'm from, I say that I'm from a place near Derry because lots of people have heard of Derry. No-one's heard of Strabane."

Charlotte is a frequent visitor to her hometown, but each journey back only strengthens her determination not to return permanently:

"I go back to Strabane five times a year and I spent the first lockdown there because the Covid rate was much lower than it was in Paris.

"I find spending time in Strabane gives me energy. But I could never go back there, I could never go back to a place where everyone knows you.

"When I go back to Northern Ireland, some of the changes are for the worse. In the poorer towns like Strabane there's Poundlands, nail bars and pubs, that's it.

"And politically, there's no middle ground anymore – but I suppose you could say the same in France. I was glad to see Alliance make some gains but the UUP and the SDLP have gone way down and I think that's a shame."

No-one is more aware of the decline of the SDLP than Emer Currie.

We were friends at Queen's more than two decades ago. When we speak on Zoom, we begin by showing off our pandemic pups, turned post-Covid dogs, Teddy and Honey.

Then I ask Emer to reflect on her childhood in 1980s Tyrone, growing up as the youngest child of one of the best-known political figures in Northern Ireland:[31]

"When I was ten I already felt like my destiny was plotted out. I would try to pass my eleven plus and get into the convent at Donaghmore, I'd carry on Irish dancing and when I was older I'd go off to the Gaeltacht[32] and try to become a fluent Irish speaker by the age of sixteen like my sisters.

"I would go to uni somewhere and Mum and Dad would carry on living in Donaghmore. Daddy was the oldest of eleven and they all lived within a three-mile radius of Donaghmore Market.

---

[31] Austin Currie, whose occupation of a house in Caledon, County Tyrone to protest against the sectarian housing policy of the Stormont government is widely seen as the key moment in the civil rights movement of the 1960s. He went on to become one of the founders of the SDLP in 1970 and is the only person to have held executive office in both jurisdictions in Ireland.

[32] The areas of Ireland, mainly in the rural West, where Irish is the first language.

"There was nothing to suggest that we would be moving to Dublin. But then one day the phone rang and it was Garrett Fitzgerald[33] on the line.

"They had a good relationship going back to Sunningdale. He asked Daddy to come down to Dublin and get involved with Fine Gael.

"Daddy was forty-nine, there was no sign of Stormont coming back, no prospect of getting into Westminster. Within twenty-four hours they'd decided to give it a go, to take the risk."

For Emer, Dublin was a huge change – a move to a much calmer society from an on-edge upbringing in Tyrone:

"I would get some grief from other kids in the North because of who my dad was but other kids in the class would get grief about other things.

"But, yes, it was an unusual upbringing. I can see now why we didn't have sleepovers. Who would let their kid sleepover at our house when there could be sledgehammers at the door at 4 in the morning?

"There was more of a loyalist threat against my father in the Seventies, before I was born. In the Eighties the threat was coming from the IRA. I felt that within my own community, there would be other children at school whose families were IRA supporters so there was tension there.

"But we had exceptional neighbours who looked out for us, we had Daddy's family, we had party supporters.

"We had bulletproof windows and we used to hit a tennis ball against them, kick a football at them. Home was a sanctuary, there was a lot of love in that house.

"And it all felt normal to me but, now that I have kids of my own, I wonder how my parents coped. How did my mother cope with the RUC always coming round, with not

---

[33] Leader of Fine Gael (traditionally Ireland's second largest party) from 1977 to 1987 and Taoiseach from 1982 to 1987.

knowing if her husband would come home in the evening? I just wasn't aware how high the stakes were.

"I did the first year of grammar school in the North and then I moved down to Dublin with the rest of the family. For a politically sensitive twelve-year-old who'd lived in the circumstances I'd lived in, my life was nothing like the lives of twelve-year-olds in the South.

"There was little understanding of what was happening in the North. Most people had never been to the North, they just knew about the bombs.

"It was a very lonely place for a good few years because I just didn't fit in. Really nobody understood what I was talking about.

"It's only now that I'm older I can understand the whole situation better – I was different from everyone else."

Unlike the vast majority of her Dublin classmates, Emer chose to move back to the North for university:

"I wanted to go somewhere different but still similar, but there was only one other person in my school year who went to the North.

"The moment I really let it go was when I went back up to Queen's and met students who had lived in the North their whole lives and they were sceptical of me because I'd lived in the South.

"That's when I went from being a Nordie to being a Mexican. There's a perception from Northerners that Southerners don't understand the situation so that was the attitude from some people – that I didn't understand what was going on."

Emer doesn't disagree with me that our time at Queen's, straddling the Good Friday Agreement, comprise Northern Ireland's least shit years:[34]

"Yes, the North was completely different to the place I'd left. We were living in an era where we all felt so

---

[34] My phrase, not hers.

confident and optimistic about the future. We were able to have difficult conversations about identity because there wasn't so much at stake as there had been during the Troubles. I think we were all more secure in our own identities than we are today."

But those first halting steps towards reconciliation now seem like a distant memory:

"There hasn't been the integration that we would have hoped for. People are so attached to their identities in the North, there's so much segregation. There is the emergence of a Northern Irish identity, but some people still seemed obsessed with identity. When you live somewhere else, you don't have to think about your identity all the time.

"Before you speak to someone in the South, you don't have to think about not offending them. You don't have to worry so much about not upsetting people. There's an energy that you use when talking to someone else from the North, but you don't realise you're making the effort.

"When you scratch the surface, the Troubles are there. But not to a huge extent, I was one of the lucky ones. But it's in me, it's in my friends from the North. It's part of who you are.

"I used to close all the curtains at night so no-one could see in the house...when the Ballymurphy[35] victims were vindicated a few years ago, I was in tears."

In the 20 years since we last spoke, I'd forgotten just how perceptive Emer is. During our conversation I mention in passing someone I know who positively enjoys the ancient Ulster art of taking offence.

Emer suggests that they behave in this way because of the pain they went through. I know this person and Emer doesn't. But I realise that she's right about their motives.

---

[35] Between August 9 and August 11, 1971, British troops shot dead eleven civilians in the west Belfast housing estate of Ballymurphy. No-one has ever been charged in relation to the massacre, but in 2021 a coroner concluded that all those killed were innocent and that their killings were unjustified.

Later in our conversation, Emer asks me if I decided to write this book because of a feeling of guilt. I hadn't thought about it in those terms. But when I pause for a few moments to ponder Emer's suggestion, I realise she's hit the nail on the head.

When we spoke, Emer was a member of the Irish upper house – the Seanad – for Fine Gael. Later in the year she won a seat in the Dail in the general election which saw her party retain its place in government.

Emer is one of the most high-profile Northerners in the South and thus in a unique position to judge how people from one part of Ireland are viewed in the other:

"I know Northern commentators who come to the South today and they feel there's very little awareness of the North. I used to resent that as a teenager and I can feel they resent it now.

"But I eventually felt accepted in the South and that's when I let the resentment go. It's not personal, it's just that people in the South have a different upbringing, a different life experience.

"And not everywhere in the Republic is like Dublin, if you grew up on the border your knowledge of the situation in the North would be much better.

"A lot of time people in the South are afraid to talk to about the North in case they offend someone."

Emer makes sure her children know their Northern heritage:

"I married a Protestant, and we agreed that our first child would be brought up a Catholic and our second a Protestant. We wanted to be an interfaith family and reflect both our traditions. I'm a Northern Catholic and I want my children to understand that identity and to understand where they come from.

"It's me making sure that my backstory is inculcated in their lives forever and they never forget that part of their identity is Northern Catholic.

"But when we go to Belfast, the thing they're most interested in is Walkers crisps!

"No, Barry, they don't support Tyrone – they support Dublin. They're wee Dubs!"

As my conversation with Emer comes to an end, I think about Liam Devlin's harsh words about life in Dublin and the hostility that Northerners sometimes face in the Republic.

So I ask Emer to reflect on the experience of Garda Commissioner Drew Harris, one of the few Northerners in the South who's more prominent than her.

In 2023 he faced a huge vote of no confidence from his own officers. They were upset, among other things, by his attempt to move their shifts from the pandemic pattern of four days on, four days off back to the more demanding pre-Covid system of six days on, four days off.

Ninety-eight per cent of the Garda Representative Association voted against their boss – the kind of unpopularity that evaded even Liz Truss. Harris, like the leading police officer in any country, is not immune from criticism from the public who pay his wages, or the politicians who put him in position.

And of course, those whom he sends out into harm's way every day have the right to express their reservations about him.

But the lingering sense remains that some of the heat he takes is down to the fact that he's a Nordie (and even worse, a Prod).

The Sunday Times columnist Alison O'Connor told the radio show Newstalk:[36]

I think we don't even realise it a lot of the time, that we have this sort of bias, which is an inherent form of racism, I believe.

---

[36] https://www.newstalk.com/news/northerners-in-the-republic-they-tell-you-theyre-more-irish-than-you-1507320

The amount of people who've never even bothered crossing the border, who have no friends in the North...it all kind of joins up. A lot of us down here see a Northern Irish identity as being somehow inauthentic or threatening. I think it comes from the Troubles, from a place of fear.

When I put Alison O'Connor's point to Emer, she disagrees:

"He might be a bit different and, when you boil down why he's different, that's because he's from the North.

"But I don't think it's prejudice against Northerners. In some ways, as a Northerner in the South, you're a bit of a novelty.

"There are three views – people who like the North, people who don't like the North and people who are totally indifferent.

"Some people just do not want to talk about the North, don't want to hear about the Troubles, don't want anything to do with it."

Tracey Taggart also has experience of being a Nordie in the South.

Before we get started, Tracey and I try to decide what relation we are.

In the end we settle for second cousins. Tracey's late father, Charlie, was my great-uncle, one of my granny's brothers.

But despite being a generation above me, Tracey is only three years my senior – Charlie was the baby of six brothers and sisters and he married relatively late in life.

Halfway through our conversation, our closeness in age is brought home to me when Tracey mentions the effect that massacres from the late Eighties and Nineties – the phase of the Troubles she recalls the most vividly – had on her.

She remembers where she was when she heard of the killings at Milltown, Loughinisland et al. I remember where I was too.

But it's not our closeness in age or shared blood that makes me keen to talk to Tracey. It's her religious background.

Tracey's parents entered into a mixed marriage, something which was controversial in the 1970s but which is thankfully becoming more accepted now:

"Daddy was a Presbyterian and Mummy was a Catholic. When they got married, they found it really hard to get a house because Mummy was Catholic. These were in the days before the Housing Executive.[37]

"After they got married, Daddy was living in Killyleagh with Aunt Iris and Mummy was living in Ardglass.

"It was hard for them. It wasn't until Uncle Bobby was fixing Faulkner's[38] boat one day. He mentioned the problem his brother and his wife were having getting a house and, a week later, they had a house in Kilmore, which is a wee place just outside Crossgar.

"I was born in 1976 and we lived in Kilmore until I was six. There was no issue about religion from either family, but my mum and dad did try to shield me from any of the hostility when I was young. I knew we were different because Mummy went to Mass and Daddy didn't.

---

[37] Northern Ireland's social housing provider. It was set up in 1971 to take responsibility from the unionist-dominated councils of the era, which had allocated housing unfairly. Discrimination against Catholics in housing was one of the key reasons for the emergence of the Civil Rights Movement in the 1960s.

[38] Brian Faulkner, the final Prime Minister of Northern Ireland from 1971 to 1972, and chief executive of the power-sharing executive of 1974 which was brought down by the Ulster Workers Strike. Faulkner loved Strangford Lough, though perhaps not as much as my great uncle Bobby, who spent almost his entire life either on or next to the lough.

"Kilmore was a very Protestant place. Coming up to the Twelfth, the flags would go up and they'd put an Orange arch up as well.

"My mum didn't like the atmosphere in the village in the run-up to the Twelfth. I think they both felt vulnerable. They would make sure the curtains were shut at night and Daddy would check under the car every morning.

"Daddy worked in the shipyard in Belfast, again it was a very Protestant place. Later on he told me how some people at work stopped talking to him when they found out that he'd married a Catholic."

When Tracey was six she and her parents moved twenty minutes' away to the small fishing village of Ardglass. Her mum and dad felt more at ease in a mainly Catholic area than they had in Protestant Kilmore. But Tracey still felt like she didn't fit in:

"Ardglass was a nationalist town, but my parents both felt more comfortable there. My Daddy was a very personable guy, he'd get along with anyone so I guess being one of the few Protestants in the town didn't bother him.

"My parents brought me up to be tolerant but they also brought me up to be careful. When I was around someone I didn't know, I wouldn't talk about my background. My parents gave me a neutral name but my surname – Scott – is very Protestant.

"Sometimes other kids would say things to me like: 'Your da's a Protestant – is he an Orangeman?' you know, things like that."

Like all children who grew up during the Troubles, Tracey's parents couldn't protect her from the conflict forever:

"I think the first time I became aware of the Troubles was my fifth birthday. Bobby Sands died the day before and we were trying to get through Downpatrick but you couldn't because you have to go through a republican estate called the Flying Horse and there was rioting going on.

"I was aware something important had happened but I didn't know what, I just knew it had disrupted my birthday.

"Then later on I remember going up to Belfast to go shopping and before you could get into Royal Avenue, you had to go through a checkpoint – do you remember that checkpoint, Barry?

"Aye, there was one gate for women and children and one gate for men. The Troubles was like a low hum that you don't realise is there until you're not in it anymore."

Like many children of mixed marriages, Tracey didn't feel fully at home in either tradition:

"My Daddy's side were Presbyterian and Church of Ireland going all the way back into history. I was brought up as a Catholic, but Catholicism was always an itchy garment for me that didn't fit right.

"I went to the Catholic primary school in Ardglass and then I went to Assumption Grammar in Ballynahinch, I was taught by nuns.

"I remember one day we were doing comparative religion. My daughters, when they do comparative religion in school on the Isle of Man, they study Islam – you know, an actual other religion. But when we did comparative religion, we studied Presbyterianism, which isn't another religion, it's part of Christianity.

"I ended up having an argument with my teacher because she was saying things about Presbyterians that I knew weren't true. She was talking about Presbyterians as if they were all the same, as if they were all Calvinists.[39]

---

[39] At this point, I find myself remembering a conversation with my great uncle Martin, Tracey's uncle by marriage. A lifelong Presbyterian, on one occasion Martin described to me at great length, and with wry bemusement, the origin of the deep hostility between Killyleagh's two Presbyterian churches – First Killyleagh and Second Killyleagh. And that's before he moved on to the other Presbyterian sect who had their own church just outside the village. Ulster Protestants are a disputatious people. It is arguably our greatest strength – and our greatest weakness.

"She was just reading it from a textbook, but I had more experience of it than she had. I wouldn't apologise and eventually my parents had to come down to school to smooth things over. So yeah, I found convent school quite stultifying."

Tracey recalled a moment of horror in the later part of the Troubles which convinced her to leave:

"In 1994 I was applying to go to uni. I had no idea that there was going to be a ceasefire later in the year. And then Loughinisland[40] happened.

"I knew someone whose great uncle was killed and I remember thinking: 'This is horrible, I don't think I want to live here anymore.' They were just watching the football and those people just went in there and killed them.

"I remember my daddy saying: 'That's not who we are as a people.' Loughinisland was a pivot point for me. I had an offer from Queen's, but I decided to go to Trinity[41] instead to study Irish history."

Like Emer Currie, Tracey felt out of place in the Republic:

"I felt like a bit of an oddity in Dublin. The Troubles might as well have been taking place in another universe. It was remote to them, something they didn't understand.

"I don't know, maybe if you lived in England the Troubles were more real for you, because the IRA would plant bombs there sometimes.

---

[40] On June 18, 1994, UVF gunmen entered the Heights Bar in Loughinisland, near Downpatrick. The small pub was packed with people watching the Republic of Ireland take on Italy in the World Cup. The gunmen shot six people dead and wounded five others in a purely sectarian attack on Catholics. Among the dead was eighty-seven-year-old Barney Green, the oldest victim of the Troubles.

[41] Trinity College Dublin, Ireland's oldest university, which was established in 1592.

"Some people I got to know had never met a Northerner before. There were so many people in Dublin who'd never been to the North.

"It was the days of the Celtic Tiger so everything was on the up in Dublin. It was very different from the North, they had almost an innocence about them that we didn't have.

"I liked that freedom, you didn't have to be quite as careful about who you were with and what you were saying. Dublin didn't have that undertone of political violence."

The final mass murder of the Troubles convinced Tracey to leave Northern Ireland for good:

"I finished at Trinity in 1998 and one of my friends had a job in the Isle of Man so I came over here, I thought it would only be for a year or two.

"Then there was the Omagh bomb and I thought I didn't want to go back to living with all that again. But even then I wouldn't say I'd decided to leave permanently, maybe only for a year or two.

"But then I got married, then we had kids. And then I realised I didn't want to bring up my children in Northern Ireland, I didn't want all the segregation, I didn't want them to worry about all the things that I used to worry about when I was growing up."

Like most of the emigrants I speak to, Tracey's determination not to return to Northern Ireland, to spare her children from its sectarianism, sits alongside an enduring affection for the place and a recognition of how much it has shaped her.

Northern Ireland is the errant parent – damaging but still indisputably hers:

"I still think I'm very Northern Irish, it's still a big part of my identity. I teach about Northern Ireland and I think about it a lot. But yeah, it still stays with you even all these years later.

"I'm sitting here and the blinds are up and I'm not comfortable with that. I know the neighbours aren't going to come in and shoot me but still I'm not comfortable.

"And then when you meet someone else from Northern Ireland you do that wee dance with them, you know the subtle questioning to find out their religion.

"There are things about me that people sometimes find confusing. But also I think, coming from Northern Ireland, you're not shocked by people being violent to each other. You know how bad people can be, but I suppose you know how forgiving people can be too.

"I got a really big bout of homesickness last year because my mum was dying. I was back maybe 10 times in six months.

"Being back was part of the grieving process because once my mum dies that breaks another link with the village I grew up in. Some of the limitations of Ardglass get on your nerves though.

"It's a bit insular, it's small village life where everyone knows who you are. And when you see people you grew up with, they want you to be that old version of yourself.

"I love visiting cities, I love the energy. I love the craic in Belfast now. It's not the old Belfast with that ring of steel, it's great to see tourists there, I love taking my girls there. We've been on a mural tour."

Like Jim McAuley in Huddersfield, Tracey finds that her two children take differing attitudes to their Northern Irish heritage:

"Aine is very political and very interested in Northern Ireland. Eilis isn't as interested. Aine would watch documentaries on TikTok and she's watched Once Upon A Time In Northern Ireland. I showed it to my students too.

"There was a woman explaining why she planted a bomb when she was seventeen. My students they were horrified, but to that woman, it was her normal.

"There's a loyalist paramilitary describing how he went into a sweet shop and shot two people dead, they were horrified.

"And then there's the things we remember – Sean Graham's[42] and what do you call him from Milltown? Michael Stone[43], that's it. Aine was horrified by it all."

When I ask Tracey if she's decided where she'll be buried, her answer is far more confident than Liam Devlin's considered pondering of his options:

"After my mum died, my aunt Joan said to me 'Tommy Edgar wants to know if you're going in the grave with her, he needs to know how much cement to put in there.'

"I told her that I am probably going in there because I know people will come to visit me. Mum and Dad got married in that church – the priest told my dad he had to convert before he'd let them get married in the church, but he relented when they started planning to get married at his church in Killyleagh instead.

"I got married there, I had my first communion there, I had the girls baptised there for mum. I know a lot of people in the graveyard. On a good day you can see the Isle of Man from the graveyard."

Jenny Ryan[44] is also the child of a mixed marriage. And, just like Tracey, she was relieved when her family

---

[42] On February 5, 1992, UDA gunmen entered Sean Graham's bookies on the Ormeau Road in south Belfast and opened fire, killing five people and wounding nine others. The UDA, which incredibly was still a legal organisation at the time, claimed that the sectarian murder of Catholic civilians was in retaliation for the IRA's sectarian murder of eight Protestant workmen at Teebane in County Tyrone a few days earlier. Readers will perhaps not be surprised at this point to learn that the massacre at Sean Graham's did not persuade the IRA to desist from murdering Protestant civilians.

[43] In one of the most infamous attacks of the Troubles, loyalist Michael Stone launched a gun and grenade attack on an IRA funeral at Milltown cemetery in west Belfast, killing three people in front of TV cameras.

[44] Not her real name.

moved from the heavily Protestant village where she spent the early years of her life to a more religiously mixed town:

"Both my parents are from Fermanagh and there were some tensions there between the families, because my mum wasn't Catholic. Dad was a Catholic RUC officer, so it wasn't possible for him to stay in Fermanagh. My parents moved to Carrick and then to Ballycarry when I was three.

"It was a very small village with a very small primary school. I remember my dad working a lot of shifts and my mum saying 'be careful' each time he went out to work. And I knew where the gun was in the house, not that I could reach it, of course.

"My parents didn't talk about my dad's job at home out of fear that my sister or I would say something at school and put him in danger.

"I can clearly remember the ceasefire in 1994, I was playing round at my friend's house when there was a newsflash on the radio.

"Then in 1996 we moved to Enniskillen. It wouldn't have been safe for us to live in Fermanagh before the ceasefire.

"It was very different. Ballycarry is very Protestant, big murals of King Billy and all that. But Enniskillen is a very mixed place and I think people rubbed along well, even during the Troubles.

"My sister and I went to state schools in Enniskillen and I didn't have many Catholic friends, but there was never any bother."

Jenny went to study medicine in Great Britain before returning to Northern Ireland to start her career. But, like so many exiles returning to Northern Ireland, she found that the background hum of sectarianism now jarred in her ears:

"After I graduated I eventually got a training post at the children's hospital in Belfast because I wanted to work in paediatrics.

"I'd left Northern Ireland when I was eighteen and came back eight years later. It was a culture shock to start working in Belfast having lived in Fermanagh and then England.

"I felt like an outsider having been away, in the end I left Belfast after six months.

"The hospital course wasn't well organised, there was no set teaching or training. It was about who you knew.

"I was doing shift work at the A&E and I was really being pushed to reveal what side of the community I belonged to. And I don't feel like I belonged to either side, but it doesn't work like that in Belfast. You know, the questions about where you're from, where you went to school.

"I have a Catholic surname but I didn't go to a Catholic school so that confused people. But, when I had to call out the name of a patient with an Irish name, I'd pronounce it wrong and then it was clear to everyone which side I was from.

"There were different friendship groups based on religion and I was frozen out of the Catholic clique. People just want to put you in a box."

Listening to Jenny describe how she left Northern Ireland for a second time, having given it a chance as a young adult, it's impossible not to think of the human capital which is lost because of the benign apartheid of the place:

"I missed the quality of training in England. But I felt like going back home was something I had to get out of my system. I realised Belfast wasn't it's all cracked up to be so I moved back to England.

"We have two kids now – aged six and two. Our six-year-old loves going to Northern Ireland but I'm not sure how much of the Irishness he sees. I tried to disengage fully from the politics of Northern Ireland because it's just depressing."

As the child of a mixed marriage, it's sadly unsurprising that Jenny feels out of place in Northern Ireland and now struggles to think of the place that defined her as home:

"I'd say 'I'm going to my parents' rather than 'I'm going home'. I think I'll forever feel torn. It's still a part of me and I feel nostalgic about the history and the music.

"It's where I grew up, it's a big part of me, but I've lived in England longer than I've lived in Northern Ireland."

Thousands of miles away in Sydney, Eamon Eastwood explains to me that – like Jenny – he struggled to fit in to Northern Ireland's segregated society.

But, while Jenny felt out of place because her parents were from different religions, Eamon's sense that he was a misfit stemmed from his omnivorous appetite for sports.

I speak to Eamon just before lunchtime in the UK, the middle of the evening for him. For some reason I can't quite put my finger on, I had feared Eamon would be a cagey interviewee.

But, as soon as he starts talking, it's obvious he has a lot to get off his chest:

"I've been away for so long, I've had time to reflect. I left when I was eighteen and there's a lot of stuff I need to process about what was going on in my life at the time.

"I've had twenty-five years to think about the environment I grew up in and why I left and never went back. It's something that lingers in the back of my mind – but it doesn't mean that I want to go back."

Eamon goes on to tell me about his childhood in east Tyrone – not the most violent part of the North during the Troubles. But not the least violent part either:

"I was the second of three boys, my brothers are called Cathal and Fergal and we grew up in Cookstown. Mum and Dad are from Cookstown, their parents are from Cookstown. My father was a school teacher and my mother stayed at home on Union Street.

"The Eastwoods are well known in the town for owning businesses, but my grandfather wanted my father to do something that was more stable, less of a risk than business, so he persuaded him to go into teaching.

"It was a very happy childhood and we didn't want for anything. All the doors of the street were open and you ran in and out of people's houses."

Like Liam Devlin in Seventies Twinbrook, Eamon had a happy childhood despite the Troubles. When he talks about the conflict, the memories come flooding out, as does his recollection that his parents tried their best to keep up the pretence that everything was fine:

"Yeah, the Troubles came flashing into your life. One time one of our windows was blown out by a bomb. I remember my mum saying it must've been one of the wildcats on the street who knocked out the window.

"It was too difficult for her to explain what had actually happened.

"I remember Cathal was riding his new bike one day and he stumbled across an IRA ambush and that shook him up.

"And I remember running out of the house in our pyjamas because there was a burning car out the front.

"There was one Twelfth when Paisley was leading the march down Union Street. All the Catholic houses had their curtains pulled. We were peeking out in fear of the Orange march."

When he became a teenager, Eamon started to realise that he didn't fit in to Northern Irish society's conformist sectarian blocs:

"I loved football at school – soccer and Gaelic. At the time there wasn't a soccer team in Cookstown for my age group so I went to play for a team in Coagh, it's a wee loyalist village just outside Cookstown.

"I was the only Catholic on the team but I was oblivious to that, I didn't think to ask why we didn't all go to the same school together.

"There was a picture of our team in the local paper and some of the kids at my school saw it. They gave me shit about it, called me a Brit-lover.

"It brought me to tears, but it also made me more determined that I wanted to keep playing soccer as well as Gaelic. I ended up playing for Tyrone in the Milk Cup[45] at under-16 and under-18 and I went to Manchester United's centre of excellence so, you know, I did alright."

But, once again, the Troubles elbows its way into our conversation as Eamon explains why the number of Catholics on his football team fell from one to zero:

"The atmosphere in Coagh changed. One of the boys I played with in midfield, his father was killed. He was a UVF commander. So there was this animosity in Coagh that there hadn't been before. Plus there was a soccer team that had started in Dungannon so I suppose it just made sense to move."

Just as the Louginisland massacre near her home in Ardglass propelled Tracey Taggart to leave, the Omagh bomb less than thirty miles from Eamon's house in Cookstown crystalised his feeling that his time living in Northern Ireland should come to an end:

"I went to uni in Glasgow and it gave me a feel for being away, for living outside of Cookstown, for opportunities. After I graduated I spent three months working for a tour operator based on the Lisburn Road in Belfast. Then I went out to New York to sell this tour package.

---

[45] A youth football tournament that takes place in Coleraine every summer, attracting some of the biggest future names in the game. For instance, all of Manchester United's Class of 92 played in the tournament in the Nineties. Back then, the tournament featured an eclectic mix of teams from elite clubs, Irish towns, and even entire countries, leading to my favourite scoreline of all time: China 2-0 Ballynahinch.

"I came back from New York in 1998 and I wasn't happy and my mum said, 'you don't seem right'. She didn't use the word 'depressed' but there was something wrong with me.

"After the excitement of Glasgow and New York, I didn't want to settle in Cookstown.

"One day in August I was working in Carrickfergus, laying concrete, when I heard the news coming in about the Omagh bomb.

"We couldn't believe it, we were listening to the radio all the way home. That day was the first time I'd ever seen my father cry.

"It was so close to home, listening to the survivors, they had the same Tyrone accents as I did. That really struck a chord with me.

"Aye, of course, if it had happened in Belfast or wherever it wouldn't have been one bit less terrible, but the fact it was so close to home struck a chord with me.

"I had already bought a ticket to go to Sydney before the bomb, but the bomb was the moment where I made up my mind to go and not come back."

Eamon's determination not to return home hasn't wavered in the quarter of a century since, but it sits alongside a strong sense of Irish identity. He has built a successful career in Australia based on his heritage:

"By 2004 I'd started my own business, importing Irish food and drink for the Australian market. We supply Barry's Tea, Club Orange. Guinness Zero is growing in popularity. Have you tried it, Barry? You should, they've got the taste bang-on, it tastes just like Guinness but without the alcohol.[46]

[46] At the time Eamon and I spoke, I'd never tried Guinness Zero, as any non-alcoholic beer I had ever sampled tasted, well, crap. So, when he made the claim, I hope my face didn't betray my scepticism. A few weeks later I happened to try Guinness Zero. Turns out Eamon was right – it's excellent.

"Aye, young people are drinking less now, it's true. My brother got my nephew a rake of beer for his eighteenth birthday, he barely touched it!

"But Tayto's the biggest seller, we supply 3,000 supermarkets and stores. Sorry, no it's Southern Tayto[47] – Paddy Tayto, not Sammy Tayto as we say. Sometimes when I show a Southerner over here the yellow packets, they think it's an Australian thing!"

On business trips home, Eamon sees signs that a healthier society is emerging:

"I'd go back to Ireland maybe once a year to meet suppliers, go to trade shows and spend time with my family. There's no violence anymore and that's a significant improvement. I think there's more inter-religious marriages now as well.

"It feels like there's less animosity now. I was talking to someone I know, she's a Protestant community worker. She told me how, if she has something that needs sorted, she'll just go to Sinn Fein[48] rather than the unionists, because she knows they'll sort it for her.

"And you see a lot more Irish signs now, it's good to see equality being embraced."

But, like Michael Campbell, Eamon also sees the economic stagnation of Northern Ireland through the eyes of someone who lives and works in a functioning, prosperous country:

"Economically, people are just surviving, Barry. There's only one restaurant in Cookstown, that's shocking. I was in there with my brother and his wife on a Sunday night. There was maybe fifty tables in there but only four of them were occupied.

---

[47] The iconic Irish crisp company based in the small Armagh town of Tandragee. Its signature cheese and onion flavour is sold in yellow packets in the North, but red and blue packets in the South.

[48] Some of the party's early electoral success was built on its members' conscientious constituency work, a legacy which continues to this day.

"The pubs aren't as busy as they were either, I think people just don't have the money.

"And definitely you hear more about drugs, you'd hear that such-and-such has broken up with their partner coz they're on drugs. There seems to be a lot of cocaine."

While convinced he is right to stay away, Eamon is aware that the human cost of this decision can only rise as the years go on:

"My daughters are five and two and overall, yeah, I think they'll have a better life here than back home. My wife's Australian and she had this wonderful upbringing by the beach in Perth and we want something similar for the girls.

"But there's sacrifices, they have all this family in Ireland that they don't see. I missed all my grandparents' funerals.

"I watched my grandfather's funeral on a livestream and I sent a letter over that was read out at the service but, no, it's not the same as being there.

"My father died in February. He'd had dementia so it was a release for the family when he went. I managed to get back to see him a few hours before he took his last breath. I was there for the wake, it was amazing, the number of people passing through the house, bringing back all these childhood memories.

"But can I tell you a secret, Barry? Sometimes, when I'm sitting in the living room on my own at night, I go down a Troubles rabbit-hole.

"I sit there for ages watching old documentaries on YouTube. I don't know why I do it. Is it to reinforce my reasons for leaving in the first place? I just don't know."

Mark Heaney is a similar age to Tracey and Eamon, but his upbringing was more sheltered than theirs, growing up in peaceful, overwhelmingly Protestant towns just outside Belfast.

Sitting at home in Essex, he tells me about his early years:

"I was born in the Ulster Hospital and lived in Ballybeen for the first couple of years of my life, then we moved to Comber and when I was in P7 we moved to Ards. It was a normal childhood, just going to school, playing with my friends. The Troubles just wasn't something that I thought about.

"My dad had played football at a reasonable level. He'd played with Pat Jennings at Newry Town. That was as good as it got for my dad, but Pat went on to slightly better things!

"I remember standing watching my dad playing in a game, I would've been eight or nine. The other team was made up of British soldiers.

"I remember one of the soldiers asking me if I was a Protestant or a Catholic. I didn't know the answer. I was just detached from all of that in Comber.

"My dad was a sales rep for Fisher Price toys, so he'd drive all round Northern Ireland. He got a brand-new company car, a brown Ford Cortina.

"He was driving in south Armagh one day when some boys with balaclavas forced him to pull over. Turned out that his car was the same make and colour as one used by a local police officer. The number plate was nearly the same, just one number different.

"Thankfully they realised they'd got the wrong man before anything got out of hand. My dad went straight home and got the car resprayed red!"

But, as Mark got older, he realised that the Troubles were elbowing him towards the ferry terminal:

"My dad fucked off when I was 11 and left my mum to bring up the three of us on her own. When I got to be a teenager, I would go into Belfast more and you'd realise a bit more about what was going on.

"I studied accountancy at the University of Ulster in Jordanstown from 1986 till 1989. I wanted to work for a business rather than being an auditor and most of the apprenticeships in Northern Ireland were for auditing.

"I got an apprenticeship at Allied Dunbar in Swindon. There was me and another fella from the course, Rodney from Buncrana in Donegal. We were both happy enough to see the back of Northern Ireland."

Like Eamon, Mark's attachment to other Irish people has grown, even as his disenchantment from the country itself has become more firmly embedded with each passing decade:

"I worked in Swindon for a load of years for Invesco, then I moved to PWC and they sent me to Dublin for 18 months.

"I had a flat near Connolly Station and I loved it there, I felt at home. There was healthy banter, like on the Twelfth of July my colleagues put up a barricade at the door of my office and said I couldn't march in there. It was great craic. I never felt unwelcome in Dublin.

"In 2017 I moved to Dubai where there's quite a big Irish community, including English teachers and people working in the construction industry.

"I always felt at home with other Irish people. We didn't get into conversations about the politics of back home, I suppose because the thing we all had in common is that we had all left that behind for a reason.

"I ended up buying an Irish bar in Dubai. I remember one night, I was talking to this young woman and she was quite stridently republican, going on about a united Ireland. She was only in her early 20s but she had the same mindset that I used to hear when I was in my early 20s.

"I just found it...disappointing that there's still young people with that mindset. But I've been away a long time so maybe I'm a bit naïve."

Mark's experience of the Troubles may have been less intense than those of Tracey and Eamon. But his disenchantment with the place seems at least equal to theirs:

"I still feel affinity with people from Northern Ireland. I was at my local Tesco the other day and this fella came up to me and started talking to me about my car. Turns out he was from Northern Ireland, so we chatted about the place.

"I'd say, with people from the South I'd feel an affinity too, but it's stronger with people from the North.

"But I've never considered moving back. The longer I've been away, the more frustrated I get with the place. I'd go back once a year, see my mates, some of them work in the security services.

"But no, there's a whole big world out there and people in Northern Ireland have a small-town mindset, I suppose you'd call it a small-country mindset.

"I think that the DUP and Sinn Fein represent extreme minority views and that boils my blood. I don't think there's a credible opposition in Northern Ireland."

Niki Sweetnam speaks to me from her home in Rome the day before Sinn Fein and the DUP submit themselves to the voters once again in the UK general election.

Drowning in emails about the importance of impartiality, it's a relief to close down my Outlook, open up my Zoom and speak to someone who's removed from the whole campaign, a person who I imagine has never been forced to squander a part of her fleeting time on Earth entering a Lib Dem candidate's name into a spreadsheet that no-one will ever read.

We start by talking about Niki's childhood in County Antrim. Hers was a privileged upbringing, but with that privilege came danger:

"I grew up in a wee seaside village called Whitehead. My dad was a bank manager and we had this big, beautiful house on the clifftop. It was a lovely childhood but all the stuff that wasn't normal, you didn't realise at the time that it wasn't normal. It's only with the passage of time that you're able to look back and you think 'crikey!'

"When I was growing up in the Seventies and Eighties, various terrorist organisations were kidnapping the children of people who had money – or in my father's case had access to money.

"I distinctly remember, when I was primary school age, being told off because I was playing out the front, with a view on to the street, rather than out the back.

"I was told to stay in the back garden because there were kidnappers. There's lots of other stuff – having your bag searched in every shop, the guy who served you petrol having a rifle.

"My mum's from the South so we used to go over the border a lot and – rain, hail or shine – we would always be stopped, we'd always be ordered out of the car so they could search it."

Niki has tried not to think about the Troubles in the twenty years since she left Northern Ireland. But an incident last year at the international school where she teaches brought everything back:

"When I was fifteen I was caught up in a bombing on York Street in Belfast, I remember this almighty explosion. There was a crater in the road, it was only filled in about ten years ago.

"All these things came back to me last year when we had a bomb scare at school. In the end it turned out to be a hoax, but it wouldn't be completely implausible for there to be a bomb at the school, because we have some diplomats' children and people like that.

"So there could have been a motive. As a teacher, you have to control your emotions in the classroom. But inside I was having this awful feeling of a loss of control. I look on that day now as a wake-up call.

“I had put a lid on the Troubles and I didn’t feel like I would have to face it again. I’ve tried to compartmentalise what happened and that’s allowed me to feel safe again in Rome.”

Like some of the other people I interviewed, Niki brought up the daily journey to and from high school as a time of particular danger.

One of the many disadvantages of Northern Ireland’s sectarian education system is that it allows passersby to tell a child’s religion by the uniform they wear.

This was a particular problem for Niki as she attended a school in a part of Belfast whose religious mix had shifted significantly in the years since it was founded in 1785:

“I went to Belfast Royal Academy – BRA – which is a very good Protestant school in quite a rundown Catholic area of north Belfast. We would have to be bussed to school from York Street Station because, if you walked through Duncairn Gardens in your BRA uniform, you would be abused or stoned.

“I had this recurring nightmare of getting lost in the back alleys of Belfast on the way back to the station, feeling trapped among the Victorian terraces and the high brick walls. Trying to run away.

“I had these awful migraines all the way through school. I don’t know if that was the reason – you just never talked about it.”

Niki finished at BRA in 1992, a strange time in Northern Ireland’s history. I’m five years younger than her, but I remember the early Nineties as a period when the faint hope that the Troubles would end struggled against the inbuilt Ulster pessimism that presumed the conflict would go on forever.

The violence was nearly over, though none of us knew that at the time. Either way, Niki was exhausted with the sectarianism and insularity of Northern Irish society:

"When I got to eighteen I wanted to study languages at university, but going to Queen's didn't appeal to me. I didn't want to stay in that Protestant-Catholic binary of Belfast, I didn't want to be closed in.

"I went to Edinburgh and I just absolutely loved it, it's such a wonderful city. I chose not to live with other students from Northern Ireland because I wanted to reinvent myself."

Like Jenny Ryan, who went to university in England and then tried to build her medical career in Belfast, Niki gave Northern Ireland a second chance. And, like Jenny, she regretted it:

"After I graduated, I ended up back in Belfast doing a PGCE at Queen's. Even though I'd only been away for four years, I didn't fell at home at home anymore.

"It was the weirdest sensation. I would go out but I didn't see the need to drink yourself to oblivion, so conversations would get a bit boring after a while. I lost touch with my old friends and I wasn't able to make new friends. I didn't feel like I had a place in Northern Ireland.

"I had a good job, teaching at Wellington College but I just didn't feel attached to my roots in Northern Ireland anymore.

"Because of my language background, I was able to get a job with Horse Racing Ireland that allowed me to travel to France and South America and Scandinavia."

But Niki found that even her gentle Belfast accent wasn't always welcome in the world or horseracing:

"I remember twenty years ago, being in the members' section at Goodwood. And I was all dressed up, as you have to be, but I remember some of the women there, they turned their noses up when they heard my Northern Irish accent.

"They literally wouldn't talk to me. They looked down on me because of where I'm from. But looking back now, it doesn't bother me because it's their problem, not mine."

Unlike the many migrants I spoke to who've made their lives in other English-speaking countries, Niki lives among people who have fewer cultural, historical or linguistic links with Northern Ireland:

"They don't study British history in Italian schools. A lot of Italian people detest the British royal family because they think that royals got their wealth through stealing. I mean, that is true, but it's a very simplified version of history.

"When people ask me about Northern Ireland, I have to try to find a way to shape the story so that it makes sense for them. No-one even knows where Belfast is, so you have to explain that you're from Ireland, but it's the bit of Ireland that is part of Britain.

"I try to point out the grey, rather than think of everything as black or white."

Like Eamon Eastwood and Mark Heaney, Niki still feels affectionately towards Northern Ireland. But, unlike the two of them, she has shed her original sense of national identity:

"I go back home for a couple of weeks each year and I slip back into the old habits of drinking tea and having dinner at half five.

"My mum lives near Bellaghy – my dad passed away recently from Alzheimer's. I read a lot of Irish literature, including Seamus Heaney.

"When you're in Bellaghy, you can see what he wrote about. You can almost smell what he wrote about. When I'm in Bellaghy, when I'm with family, I feel like I'm home.

"But I've been away so long, I wouldn't have the first notion of where's a good pub on the North Coast or a good restaurant in Belfast.

"I follow the political developments from Northern Ireland but in a sort of disinterested[49] way because they don't impact my day-to-day life in the way that Italian politics does.

"I don't really feel Northern Irish when I'm in Northern Ireland. I feel Italian, even though I'm not Italian."

Niki moved to Italy twenty years ago and married a local man. She's improved her Italian from "a smattering" two decades ago to fluency now.

At this point in our conversation, my twelve-year-old daughter Ciara wanders into the room with an urgent question about supplies for this week's food tech class. I apologise to Niki for the interruption, but Ciara's enquiry about plain flour levels in the kitchen inadvertently diverts Niki towards considering her own children's identity:

"It's funny just hearing your daughter's Yorkshire accent. My girls are fourteen and sixteen and they've grown up in Rome so they speak Italian just like anyone else.

"I'm fluent in Italian but I still sound like a foreigner – anyone speaking to me knows right away that I'm not Italian.

"My daughters have spent a lot of time in Northern Ireland over the years so they speak English differently from other people in Italy.

"I can't really describe it, they don't quite sound Northern Irish as such, they just sound different from other people. They don't sound like they're from Canada or South Africa or New Zealand."

Fidelma McCorry's accent doesn't have the same mystery as those of Niki's children's. Even after decades in Australia, her vowels remain uncut Ulster.

---

[49] When I type up my notes of our interview I realise, with a pedant's delight, that Niki had used the term "disinterested" correctly – to denote impartiality rather than lack of interest. I think this was the first time I'd heard the term used in the right way.

She's recuperating from back pain as she speaks to me from Adelaide on a very wet April day for me. But as soon as she opens her mouth, the sound of the rain on my window is drowned out by Fidelma's pure Portadown accent – her decades living in Australia having left no antipodean trace on her voice:

"My parents left Lurgan when I was one in 1973, they moved to Sydney and were staying in a hostel, mostly with Portuguese people.

"A housebuilder paid for them to go on a bus for twelve hours to Adelaide to see their homes in the northern suburbs. They bought a place and soon after my twin sisters were born. Both my parents are from families of eleven so it was a big deal when they decided to leave.

"When I was four we moved back to Ireland, we lived a few streets away from my granny in Portadown. Then when I was eight we went back to Australia.

"Then when I was a teenager we moved back to Ireland. I did my A levels and then went to college in Derry for three years."

Like so many people who lived through the Troubles, the conflict barged into Fidelma's life one awful day:

"I was going out with a guy called Gary Convie[50] for two or three years, then we broke up. But he was very important to me.

"I remember everything about that day. I was up in Derry, in a shared house in Magee.[51] My mum rang and my flatmate Fionnuala happened to answer.

---

[50] In May 1994, Gary was sitting in a car eating his lunch with his workmate Eamon Fox. The pair were about to return to work on a building site on North Queen Street in Belfast when their car was riddled with bullets. Both men were killed. There was not even a pretence that their murders were anything other than sectarian. They were two defenceless Catholics murdered in cold blood by the UVF.

[51] The Ulster University campus in the city.

"My mum told her the news so she would know, then she asked her to call me over and then my mum told me.

"I remember sitting watching the report of the killing on the Six O'clock News. One of my other flatmates, she came home later and noticed the strange atmosphere as soon as she came in the door.

"'Fuck me, did someone die?' she joked. Poor girl, she felt awful when we told her.

"After the funeral I had to put my uni head back on and study for my finals. I passed, so it was a bit of single-mindedness I suppose."

Fidelma still carries much of her Irishness with her through her new life in Australia:

"In 1998 mum and dad moved back to Oz but I'd bought a house, had a boyfriend and all that. But the next year the twins moved out there with them.

"I had a million aunts and uncles and cousins but I wanted to be with my nuclear family. I moved out with my new boyfriend, my future husband, who's from Lurgan. Eventually we settled in Adelaide and had three children

"No matter where I was, I always felt Irish. I've lived in Australia for the last twenty-five years now but people still comment on how strong my accent is.

"I'm involved in all the Irish groups in Adelaide, I run the Facebook groups, one of my daughters loves her Irish dancing.

"But yes, I would still carry the Troubles with me. I remember turning off the road once and this four-wheel drive pulled out in front of me and my heart went like the clappers because it looked like an RUC land rover.

"You don't realise the fear you were living with all that time."

Fidelma also makes an observation that I find depressing no matter how many times I hear it from emigrants, when she notes that she's freer to make friends across the sectarian since leaving Northern Ireland:

"I have a friend here who's the daughter of a Baptist pastor from Portadown. If we both still lived in Portadown, we wouldn't have even met, let alone become friends."

In the years she's lived in Australia, Fidelma has witnessed the attitude to Irish people change – but not as quickly as her impatience with the prejudice that still remains:

"I would have taken the Irish jokes in the old day with just a sarcastic 'ha ha' but I've less patience for it now. When someone makes an Irish joke now I just ask them 'would you say that about me if I was Chinese?'

"When people complain about my accent I just tell them I'll speak really slowly for them as they're obviously thick.

"My mum and dad experienced a lot of hostility in the Seventies because of the Troubles. They would have assumed you either supported the IRA or the UVF.

"My mum and dad would always refuse to go to any NORAID[52] events. But, no, people don't make jokes about guns and bombs any more.

"We're not the outsiders anymore, it's people from the Middle East and South Asia who face that hostility now. We're white and we speak English."

On the other side of the world from Adelaide – the East Neuk of Fife to be precise – Ruth Sanderson explains to me that she has also experienced animosity because of her Irish background, though from a surprising source:

"The only time I faced any hostility was when I was younger. I was going out with this American fella and he took me back to Boston. I met his friends, the Murphys, fifth-generation Irish.

"The first thing they asked me was what religion I was. I explained that it was really rude to ask so they decided I was a Protestant and they gave me a lot of grief about it.

---

[52] The IRA's international fundraising organisation during the Troubles.

"I was really shocked by it, the arrogance of people who've never set foot in Ireland in their life having a perception of what Protestants are like."

I don't know Ruth but, being as we're both Northern Irish, she's a friend of a friend. An experienced broadcaster, Ruth is wonderfully outgoing and positive, as radio presenters tend to be on their good days:

"I grew up in a townland called Ballydown, which is just outside Banbridge. I was the youngest of four kids, growing up in a Presbyterian manse.

"I think I had a great childhood. I was born in 1983 so I had that niche Northern Ireland Eighties childhood.

"My best friend's dad was in the police, he was killed in a bomb when we were one, so she grew up without a dad. But you don't know any different from your own childhood. I felt safe because my parents made me feel safe.

"My parents are from the Shankill and Ardoyne. I was very aware that there were people in my family who didn't feel the way my parents felt.

"They were very cross-community. My father came under a huge amount of pressure from the Orange Order because of it.

"He was persona non-grata to them. He refused to have orange services in his church. When the church was being renovated, he made sure that they didn't hold services in the orange hall while the work was being done."

Like Mark Heaney, Ruth began to appreciate how conflicted Northern Ireland was during her visits to the country's largest city:

"Every Monday we would go to Belfast to see the grannies. I remember going through the turnstiles to get into the city centre and the bomb scares. There were no restaurants – there was the Skandia and that was it.

"I remember the first time we went to Britain when I was a wee girl. I had a toy handbag and I remember going into a shop and opening the handbag to show to a member of staff for them to check. They looked at me and said: 'What are you doing?'

"There were a few bombs in Banbridge but that was just normal."

Also like Mark, Ruth grew up in a middle-class Protestant world where leaving Northern Ireland to go to university in Britain was the norm:

"We were all encouraged to go to uni and there was just this expectation that you'd leave Northern Ireland. My three older brothers all went to uni in Scotland, like lots of Protestants in the Nineties. I decided to go to St Andrew's, I didn't even go to the open day at Queen's.

"It's not that I wanted to leave, it was just what you did. I never felt any hostility in St Andrew's because of where I'm from – there were so many of us there from Northern Ireland."

Just as Adelaide gave Fidelma McCorry the room to make Protestant friends, Ruth was able to mix more freely when she left Northern Ireland:

"Once you're outside Ireland, you're all Irish. My best friend at uni was a girl from Dublin called Grainne. We'd wind up our English friends, telling them that we'd got a grant from the EU to be friends.

"I have a friend over here, Catriona from north Belfast. She's thirty-four and she told me that I'm her first Protestant friend.

"I would still be hyper-aware, that when you meet someone from Northern Ireland, you're always trying to work out their religion – asking them what school they went to, what their surname is.

"Finding out if they're Protestant or Catholic without asking them. It's so ridiculous."

Ruth sometimes struggles to explain Northern Ireland's idiosyncrasies to her English husband:

"I moved back to Northern Ireland after uni and worked for the BBC and then I got a job at Radio 4 in

London. I was ten years there and I met Harry. I got a job producing and presenting for BBC Northern Ireland so we moved back in 2016.

"We stayed for four years and our first daughter was born there. It was really nice to be back, to be close to my parents.

"Harry went to boarding school at seven so he struggles with the Irish attitude, you know, I'd have my mother living next door to me if I could.

"He found it hard to understand a lot of Northern Ireland, I had to explain things to him and there were conversations which he felt he couldn't contribute to."

Like Jenny Ryan and Niki Sweetnam, Ruth left Northern Ireland for a second time – though in her case it appears without any sense of disillusionment with the place:

"We moved to St Andrew's for work, there's just a bigger pool of people over here – Scottish, Northern Irish, American.

"I was heartbroken to leave Northern Ireland. Then our second daughter was born in Scotland. Our older girl sometimes comes out with things that sound like her Auntie Nessie from the Shankill.

"They have an English dad, an Irish mum and they're growing up in Scotland. I don't know if I'd move back, it would depend on work."

But the lingering divisions in Northern Ireland appear to be keeping Ruth anchored on the British side of the Irish Sea:

"It would be great for them to be around their grandparents but...that whole context that we grew up in...it's different now but there's still remnants of it, the identity politics, the religious divisions.

"I don't want my kids to have that, but I do want them to live close to their grandparents.

"There's a sense of place that never leaves you. It's nice to feel rooted in somewhere, even if you don't go back there very often.

"Northern Ireland is still home. It's under the fingernails. If you cut me open I'd have the word 'Banbridge' running through me like a stick of rock.

"I want my ashes to be sprinkled into the Bann at Ballydown, off the bridge at Lisnaree. The view from my childhood home is in my soul somewhere. It's a beautiful place."

When Ruth hears an Ulster twang, her better half knows that the day's plans are now on hold:

"I feel affinity with other people from Northern Ireland, a hundred per cent yes. I want to find out where you're from and then find out someone that we have in common. My husband, who's from the south of England, jokes about this.

"When I meet someone else from Northern Ireland, he goes 'well it's time for the wee chat, we'd better give this half an hour.'"

When Ruth mentions her love of the wee chat, my mind drifts fifteen years back in time and twenty-five miles along the M62.

I hear a Belfast twang calling out across a gloomy Leeds evening: "Could you spare some change, mate?"

I look over to the man crumpled on the freezing ground. Months, maybe years of life on the streets are etched on his face.

But for his accent, I would have breezed past him, as I do so many people begging on the streets. It's not indifference, it's just that I'm, you know, busy. And not that rich either.

I can't be stopping every fifty yards to hand over a few coins to every person misfortune enough to have ended up sleeping on the streets.

But because this particular homeless person is from Northern Ireland, it's time for the wee chat. He's heard my accent now and he's pulled himself to his feet.

We're talking about the old country, the different parts of Belfast we're from.

I had planned to hand over whatever coins I had in my wallet, but he has a story for me.

He needs forty quid to get a coach to Stranraer, so he can get the boat home to see his family. He's already got a ticket for the ferry, you see, he just needs some cash to get over to the terminal.

For a split second I believe him, then my Ulster cynicism clicks in. If I hand over a couple of twenties, he won't be heading to the bus station, he'll be straight down the offy.

But, after realising he's spinning me a yarn, I ask myself why I shouldn't play along, help out another Ulsterman who's fallen on hard times.

There's a cash machine down the road, so a minute later I'm handing him two twenties and wishing him well.

Even in that moment, when I realised he was lying to me, it didn't cross my mind not to help him.

Forty pounds was a fair amount of money for a local newspaper reporter in the Noughties. But it's not like I couldn't spare it, so I thought I should.

And, I'd like to think that if the roles had been reversed, if fate had sent my acquaintance to a life of covering Heavy Woollen Planning Subcommittee and me to an existence of sleeping rough on the streets of Leeds, he'd wander over to a cash machine to help me out.

Three years earlier, it had been me who was the one who needed help.

After a year at Nottingham Trent University, time was draining out of my journalism course and an uncertain summer awaited.

Kicking out time from Fletcher Terrace – our characterful student accommodation about three miles from the city centre – was a few weeks away.

The job hunt was underway, but the news editors of the Nottingham Evening Post and the Worksop Guardian had already proved immune to my charms.

Like any self-respecting student (even a relatively old one of twenty-six) I took time out from the job hunt for some much needed drinking.

My classmate Paul's parents were having a party at their house in West Bridgford, the Ken Clarke suburb of Nottingham just over the Trent from the city centre.

As I arrived that Saturday afternoon I heard a Belfast accent among the hub-bub and wandered over to introduce myself to one of Paul's dad's friends. He had made a success of his life in England having been born, bred and buttered in the rock-hard loyalist estate of Rathcoole.

We reminisced about the old country for a bit and then he asked me what my future held. I explained my looming unemployment and the search for a place to live not, I hope, as some kind of sob story, but just as part of the conversation.

A few hours later Paul, myself and the rest of our classmates decided to head into town to continue the day's drinking with the outside chance of attracting some attention from a member of the opposite sex.

As we were about to get into our taxis, my acquaintance from Rathcoole made a beeline for me and handed me his business card:

"Nice meeting you, Barry. I'm sure you'll be fine but, if you are still looking for a place to live in a few weeks, then give me a call, won't you?

"I know people all over this city, I'll find you a room."

As it was I didn't have need to call my new friend from Rathcoole – a week later I found a room to rent in the home of a barely functioning alcoholic in the less-than-glamourous district of Sneinton.

But his instinct to help someone else from Northern Ireland stayed with me. One day, I thought, it'll be me who could help others.

The guts of twenty years later, my employer decided I was sufficiently long-serving to be trusted with the job of recruiting new staff.

Sorting through the good, the bad and the fictional application forms, the ones from Northern Irish journalists called out to me. Eimear from Newry the first time round, Aine from Belfast during the second recruitment.

My first thought on realising they were from Northern Ireland was: "how do I help them?" I had the chance to shave a corner here or there to help out my compatriots.

One of my fellow panel members looked at my marking of Aine's application form and twigged what had gone on. "Er, Barry, let's have another look at her marks."

Aine still made the cut for an interview, but in the end she landed a better job before getting the chance to sit down with us. Eimear was talented, but her experience was too far away from what was needed for the role, meaning I couldn't help her out enough to get her over the line.

Being from Northern Ireland, I never ask someone's religion, but I always know. Aine and Eimear are from the other tradition.

But this didn't dilute the instant urge I felt to try to help them, my feeling of affinity with them.

Reflecting on this afterwards, I allowed myself a little pat on the back for my lack of sectarianism. But, when I thought about it further, I gave myself a wee tut tut for my partitionist mindset.

If Eimear had grown up a few miles from Newry, across the border in Dundalk, had Aine been born in Dublin rather than Belfast, would I have still wanted to help them?

Yes, I think I would. But not nearly as much. It would be the difference between helping a family member and doing a favour for a neighbour.

Mark Aiken's urge to help other people from Northern Ireland is steadily getting stronger nearly half a century after he left the place.

Speaking to me with a Canadian twang untroubled by Ulster vowel sounds, he explains his handful of fleeting childhood memories of our home city:

"We left Belfast when I was four so I don't have many memoires of it. We lived in Orangefield and I can remember sitting out on the footpath waiting for my brother and sister to come home from school because they'd always bring me sweets from the shop.

"And also I remember falling on to a bit of broken bottle on the ground. I cut a nerve in my hand so even now, fifty years on, if I tap my hand on that spot a shot of pain goes right up my arm.

"My dad was in the RUC and this was 1975, at the height of the Troubles. He was shot by a sniper and injured so my parents decided that this wasn't sustainable.

"We were starting to get to the age where we could understand more about the world around us and my mum didn't want us exposed to all that hatred and vitriol.

"My parents applied for visas for New Zealand and Canada and in the end The they chose Canada because my mum's brother had moved there a few months before."

As John Fitzgerald notes, the Aikens were among tens of thousands of people who left Northern Ireland in the early years of the Troubles:

In the 1970s Northern Ireland experienced its highest rate of net emigration since the early 1920s, amounting to 0.9% of the population each year for the decade.

While the economy suffered a major relapse because of the Troubles, the direct effects of the civil disturbances, causing people to leave Northern Ireland, was probably more important than the underlying changes in economic circumstances.[53]

Settling in to Canada at such a young age, Mark had little sense of his Ulster identity during his childhood years:

"We lived in a part of Toronto called Scarborough and it was very multi-cultural – people from India, the Philippines, Africa. Lots of us were immigrants, it was a real melting pot.

"My dad was from Brookmount Street off the Shankill Road and he'd been an Orangeman back in Northern Ireland but he didn't carry on when we got to Toronto. We didn't go to the Twelfth.

"The Orange Order would've been mentioned once or twice at home but it wasn't front and centre. I knew a bit about my heritage, I knew we supported Rangers and all that, but I never went back to visit Northern Ireland when I was a child."

Mark was well into adulthood before he reconnected with his Orange heritage:

"It wasn't until I was in my early thirties that a friend of mine, who was third-generation Ulster, asked me to join the lodge. And from there my interest started to grow. I was at a march in a little town in Ontario called Bobcaygeon where I met my wife, Amy.

"She was born in Canada but her family was from Fivemiletown in Tyrone and she had gone over quite a bit in her childhood. I saw her standing at the side of the road, she was watching her father and her brothers and sister who were in the band.

"We had grown up four miles apart in Toronto and gone to different high schools. We had some people in common that we both knew but we'd never met.

---

[53] p34, One Island, Two Labour Markets; John Fitzgerald, Irish Studies in International Affairs, 2022

"I found out later that she had been a cheerleader for her school at a high school football game that I had played in, for example."

The Orange Order that had inadvertently helped Mark find Amy was once a prominent force in Canada's politics, providing the country with four prime ministers.

In Mark's adopted home of Toronto, the order's influence on politics would've made the old Stormont regime proud – up to 1972 nearly all of the city's mayors were Orangemen.

But when Mark joined, he quickly discovered that the order's glory days were long gone:

"If you look at Toronto's history, it was basically built by Ulster people and the Orange Order has a long presence here.

"I used to be a member of 292 Royal Black Preceptory in Toronto which, in the early Twentieth Century, had been the biggest lodge in the world – it had 400 members.

"I joined the order twenty-two years ago and every year we'd have a decline in numbers – ten or fifteen per cent each year. I remember asking 'why are people leaving?' but I didn't really get an answer. When I got on the executive I worked hard at it and in my first year we broke even on membership.

"We have membership drives, try to make it more tangible. But you know it's not just us, it's churches, it's masonic institutes.

"It's lot of things, isn't it? People are more insular now, more involved in their online world."

In the years before Covid, Mark's attachment to Orange culture grew into a desire to return to live in the country he can barely remember:

"My parents were always going back and forth to Northern Ireland when I was a child, but I had no desire to go visit.

"I didn't go back until 2018. I was part of the Canadian delegation at an Orange meeting in Edinburgh, and then my wife and I flew over to Belfast.

"I remember on the plane, she said 'wait till you see how green Northern Ireland is' but ironically it was in the middle of a heatwave, it was more than thirty degrees and everything from the plane looked like different shades of brown.

"We went to see my aunt in Ballysillan.[54] At the end of the road people had gathered any old stuff for the bonfire and when they lit it, the fire burnt the asphalt a foot deep. They just left it for the council, or whoever, to repair.

"We went to see the murals on the Shankill Road but I didn't feel any pull. I didn't feel like 'oh my God, I'm home'. It was just disappointing."

But when Mark ventured into solidly Catholic parts of Belfast, he found a community with a post-conflict vibrancy which was absent among his own people:

"I went down the Falls, because I thought 'why would they care? I'm just a Canadian'. You drive down the Falls and everything looks like it should for a main road, for a shopping area, the facades are all well maintained.

"And then you go to the Shankill and there's a hole in the ground and you ask people why it's there and they say 'oh, that was bombed in 1972.'

"So you think 'OK, remember the bomb, but you don't have to live with it.'

"They seem to be much more entrenched in the history than the Catholics are. It seems to be much more part of the identity for Protestants in Belfast, clinging to the horrors of the Troubles."

At this point in our conversation Mark revealed to me that a close relative of his had been murdered during the conflict.

---

[54] A loyalist area of Belfast.

I got the impression that he shared this traumatic family memory with me, not because he wanted my sympathy, but rather to illustrate the pointlessness of the bitterness which he saw in loyalist areas:

"I understand the hurt, Amy's aunt and uncle were murdered in the Troubles. My uncle was murdered.[55] The fact they used a child in the killing too, that always stuck with me.

"My parents had split up a year or two before. My dad had just started to get back to a good place when his brother was murdered.

"My uncle was killed in October and my dad died the following March. His death was unrelated, but you're left wondering whether the shock and the grief over my uncle's death were a catalyst for my dad's health problems.

"So yes, what I'm trying to say is that I could be bitter if I wanted to, but I don't see the point in it."

But, while the open wounds he saw in Protestant Belfast were a disappointment, Mark discovered a healthier Orange culture in the town of Kilkeel, down near the border:

"When we went to Kilkeel for the Eleventh night bonfire we saw a small, family-driven community event.

"We both felt a real connection to the people in Kilkeel. I was Grand Master of Ontario West at the time so I started helping fundraise for a statue in Kilkeel for Robert Hill Hanna.

"He was from Kilkeel but moved to Canada and then won a VC in the First World War. We raised £18,500 in the

---

[55] William Aiken was a taxi driver who received a call asking him to pick up a mother and her child from Belfast's Royal Victoria Hospital on October 23, 1990. When he arrived, the woman asked him to wait a minute before turning away. Two gunmen then approached William and shot him in the head. No group claimed responsibility for the attack, but a British military report on the murder said William was "shot and fatally wounded by PIRA terrorists in an apparent sectarian attack."

end. I remember going over to Kilkeel for the unveiling of the statue, seeing all the Union Jacks and the Canada flags flying in the main square.

"They have pop-up radio station that they run in the two weeks coming up to the Twelfth and we call in from Toronto requesting tunes.

"We went to Schomberg House in Kilkeel where they've got so much information about Ulster-Scots history and culture.

"I was really impressed how the Orange Order in Kilkeel were doing so much outreach work during the pandemic, so much volunteering, looking after old people.

"It's the kind of thing I wanted us to do over here but we didn't really have the numbers to get it done."

Mark and his wife were so taken with life in Kilkeel that they are now preparing to settle in their ancestral homeland:

"In 2019, my wife and I were on the plane home and we just said to each other 'why are we leaving again?'

"We're going to move somewhere in the Mournes, somewhere round Kilkeel. I have a friend from the lodge who's moved back to live in Antrim so he's giving me tips on the admin side of making the move.

"Luckily I'm an IT manager so my skills are transferable, I'm just brushing up on my certifications to make sure I've got the right ones for the UK.

"Most people think we're crazy to want to move back. I know Northern Ireland isn't perfect but there's problems everywhere – the situation in Canada with taxes and inflation is horrific.

"It still baffles me that there's bombers in government now. It's the price of peace, I get that, but I still find it troublesome. You can put a shirt and tie on, but it doesn't make you a good person.

"But more and more Northern Ireland feels like home. The people, the lifestyle, the communities, they align with who we are.

"We'd been up to Ballintoy Harbour, looking out at the water, looking over to Scotland. Your mind can't wrap itself around the fact that what you're looking at is real, that it isn't some sort of CGI image because it's so beautiful.

"And I knew that this is where we're meant to be, that we should move over while we're still healthy enough to make a contribution to all the great things that are going on there.

"I don't see a negative side to moving over there. It's going to be happy and fulfilling."

As we end the call, I wish Mark all the best for his move to Kilkeel.

But I can't help feeling that his optimism about Northern Ireland's future comes in spite of its recent history, rather than because of it...

OUR IMPERFECT PEACE

"Sammy! Good to see you've got your clothes on!"

I don't remember April 1998 as a time of great hope – and not just because I was a nearly nineteen-year-old without a girlfriend.

By then, peace talks were well into their fourth year. In August 1994 the IRA had announced a ceasefire, followed six weeks later by loyalist paramilitaries.

Negotiations on a new peaceful Northern Ireland then got underway with all the urgency of a Jose Mourinho team taking a free kick when they're one-nil up.

After eighteen months of haggling over process, the IRA lost patience and decided to give it one more go at uniting Catholic, Protestant and Dissenter through the reconciliatory medium of Semtex.

Another year and a half passed before the Provisional movement reluctantly concluded that, while postponing the 1997 Grand National had been great craic in how much it annoyed the British, it hadn't infuriated them quite enough to persuade them to withdraw their 20,000 troops from Northern Ireland.

Ceasefire or no, peace talks carried on between the British and Irish governments and those of Northern Ireland's parties not currently supporting killing people.

Walkouts, proximity talks, wrangling over decommissioning weapons, arguments over North-South bodies. On and on it went to the public's general indifference.

The talks were background noise, much more pleasant background noise than the Troubles soundtrack, but no more uplifting.

To put the length of the negotiations into an Arsenal timeframe, the talks started as we basked in the glow of George Graham's supreme achievement of winning the Cup Winners' Cup with superb defensive displays.

By April 1998, Arsene Wenger was revolutionising English football with his swashbuckling new-look team, who were on the brink of wining the double.

But up at Stormont, it might as well have still been 1994.

The previous attempt to negotiate a settlement – the Brooke-Mayhew talks of 1992/93 – did at least have the good grace to fail within twelve months.

Those earlier negotiations had involved four of Northern Ireland's five biggest parties: The Ulster Unionist Party (UUP) and Democratic Unionist Party (DUP), who wanted to maintain the link with Britain; the Social Democratic and Labour Party (SDLP), who wanted eventual Irish unity and Alliance, who were effectively the None Of The Above Party.

There was no invitation for the region's fourth largest party, Sinn Fein, who were licking their wounds after losing Gerry Adams' Westminster seat in the 1992 general election.

This snub wasn't due to the party's dwindling support, but rather because of Sinn Fein's continuing insistence that the IRA's campaign was justified and that the conflict would be resolved when said paramilitary group – to which they definitely weren't linked – managed to kill a few more British soldiers.

However, even with this more manageable cast list, the Brooke-Mayhew talks still failed to win five-star reviews.

The unionist parties had come round to sharing power with the SDLP, nearly two decades after the collapse of the Sunningdale Agreement in the face of loyalist violence.

But the talks failed because the two sides still couldn't agree on an acceptable level of North-South co-operation.

Taken from this perspective, there was no reason to presume that the negotiations which followed the paramilitary ceasefires in 1994 would be successful.

If the parties who didn't approve of killing people couldn't agree between themselves, wouldn't adding in the apologists for loyalist and republican murderers make a deal even more unlikely?

But for once, Northern Irish pessimists were disappointed.

Tony Blair arrived that Easter week, doing a Sigmund when he announced that soundbites could be left at "home" before noting, apropos of nothing, that he felt the hand of history on his shoulder.

By the Thursday – Maundy or Holy depending on your religious background – it was clear that history's hand had a firm grip on Blair's shirt.

On that day, my uncle Bill happened to be visiting from Scotland so we'd all gone out to Aldens, the new restaurant in Ballyhackamore, the not-quite-gentrified-yet area of east Belfast.

After the meal, we piled into the car to drive a mile or two up the road, just to have a look at Stormont as a deal, seemingly, drew close.

Stormont is a grand Georgian building at the end of a very long drive.

Outside the gate on the main road, a gaggle of young loyalists, some of them with Union flags over their shoulders, had gathered alongside senior figures from the DUP, the party which had long since absented itself from the talks.

The DUP's two most senior figures were already in the press Portacabin up the drive, ready to hold a press conference denouncing the unionist parties who were on the brink of reaching a deal.

But we saw the party's middle rank there at the gate with the young protesters – Nigel Dodds, Gregory Campbell and Sammy Wilson. The kind of people who radio producers rang when Ian Paisley and Peter Robinson were busy.

They looked, in the Ulster vernacular, scundered – fed up and beaten.

One of our travelling party, perhaps having overindulged on the wine list at Aldens, yelled out to Sammy that he was glad to see that on this occasion he was dressed – a reference to a picture which had appeared in the Belfast tabloid the Sunday World two years earlier showing the former Lord Mayor of Belfast and his lady friend gambolling naked through a field.

On the short drive home, we listened to further verbal humiliation for the DUP, as Radio Ulster carried their press conference from the Stormont Portacabin.

Paisley, long past his tub-thumping best, was attempting to tar any unionist still in the talks as a Lundy – a traitor about to sell Ulster down the river.

But this time, the bully was bullied.

A group of supporters of the PUP and UDP – the loyalist-linked parties only hours from signing a peace accord – barged into the Portacabin and heckled him remorselessly. "Where are you leading us, Ian?" "Are you going to tell us to go out and kill again?"

Paisley, his booming voice and quick wit failing him, could do nothing more than mutter bitterly that they should go back to their friend Gerry Adams.

Well, that's the DUP's done, I thought. How wrong I was.

Eventually Paisley himself would make friends with Gerry Adams, and chuckle alongside Martin McGuinness, Adams' long-serving deputy in war and peace, who went on to become the old preacher's Deputy First Minister.

But there were nearly ten years between Paisley being heckled in the Portacabin and the DUP leader chuckling along with McGuinness.

It took almost a decade for Sinn Fein and the DUP to come to an understanding.

Their more moderate opponents, the UUP and the SDLP – the two parties whose leaders received the Nobel Peace Prize for reaching agreement on Northern Ireland's future – had by then been banished to the margins.

Firmly established as top dogs, Sinn Fein and the DUP made a second peace. Unlike the Good Friday Agreement, it was a deal untroubled by the need to have endorsement by the people of Ireland, North and South.

In the St Andrew's Agreement of 2006, the two parties tweaked the original deal of 1998 to ensure that every assembly election remained a sectarian headcount.

Crucially, the DUP and Sinn Fein ensured that the rules meant the biggest party on each side – i.e. them – could collapse the institutions and condemn Northern Ireland to a period of no government, regardless of what any other party wanted.

In the years to come both Sinn Fein and the DUP would exercise this power, condemning all of Northern Ireland to years of stasis.

As you'll see in the coming pages, those years of drift persuaded some people to leave Northern Ireland, while for those who had already emigrated, they enforced their determination not to return for anything more than fleeting visits.

Sinn Fein and the DUP established a new duopoly in which, in an unacknowledged way, they needed each other.

In the Noughties, both of them were led by men whose Troubles CVs helped motivate the other party's voters.

Paisley's fundamentalism, his residual bigotry, his long history of stirring up anti-Catholic feeling helped get half-hearted Shinners to the polls. How sweet it would be to see the old man having to play second fiddle in his dotage.

And McGuinness' dark past propelled otherwise moderate unionists into the arms of the DUP. Rather an embarrassing, ageing bigot as First Minister than the one-time Chief of Staff of the IRA.

But my criticism of the St Andrew's Agreement shouldn't be taken as an indication that the original deal on which it was built was a perfect settlement.

In many ways, the Good Friday Agreement is an infuriating document because its strengths are also its weaknesses.

The agreement has worked almost perfectly in the way that matters the most – it brought the misery of the Troubles to an end.

The killing ended because of the breadth of support in Northern Ireland for the agreement.

And the agreement doesn't work – in terms of facilitating stable governments – because of the breadth of support it enjoys, in particular from two parties who insist on retaining their minority veto.

The Good Friday Agreement has saved thousands of lives, and we must always remember this and be thankful for it.

But the agreement is structured in such a way that makes both stability and reconciliation very difficult to reach.

The agreement's imperfect peace allowed paramilitaries to carry on in positions of power within their communities.

Killing people in uniform, or people who didn't share your religion was now very much forbidden and thankfully became extremely rare.

But, as far as the British and Irish governments were concerned, paramilitary violence and intimidation within their own communities was an awkward detail, rather than a deal-breaker.

Paramilitaries – particularly loyalist – remain armed and active. They continue (present tense) to intimidate, to collect protection money, to administer punishment beatings and, above all, to deal drugs.

Dirk Schubotz has studied why Northern Ireland's emigration rate has remained so high during the post-agreement years.

Dirk grew up in communist East Berlin but has lived happily in another deeply divided European city – Belfast – for more than twenty years.

He told me that the Good Friday Agreement's refusal to deal with the legacy of the Troubles plays a part in explaining Northern Ireland's high emigration rate:

"It's in some working-class communities, not in middle-class areas. It's young men who experience drug dealing and punishment beatings.

"The Troubles is a factor in the high level of self-harm and stress. One of the issues is cross-generational trauma."

But Dirk thinks that the impact of the agreement's failings on the Northern Ireland's economy is more crucial in pushing young people out the door:

"Socio-economic background is the main factor. Northern Ireland is more deprived than England so there are more mental health problems. You can compare Northern Ireland to some parts of Newcastle and Manchester – or Blackpool where it's really bad."

Ann Watt works for the Belfast-based thinktank Pivotal. In 2021 they asked more than 300 Northern Irish students who had moved to Great Britain to explain their reasons for leaving.

She told me that Northern Ireland's sectarian divisions – which the Good Friday Agreement enforces rather than confronts – are the key recruiting sergeants:

"It was no surprise that the continuing divisions in Northern Ireland was a big issue for those who'd left.

"Our research backs up all the anecdotal evidence that the continuing divisions are a big factor in many people's decision to leave. They said they were fed up with the ongoing tensions and that they didn't feel a connection to the historical conflict.

"A lot of them expressed a desire to live somewhere that they described as 'normal' – a place where they wouldn't be around people who were making assumptions about them based on their name or where they went to school.

"Northern Ireland pushes people away through continuing divisions.

"And there's also the fact that young people feel that the government isn't concerned about the issues that concern them – job opportunities, climate, mental health.

"They feel that the government is fixated on the past and the constitutional issue."

The main reason that Northern Irish politicians are, in Ann's words, "fixated on the past" is that the Good Friday Agreement has totally failed to deal with the legacy of the conflict that it ended.

In a sense this is no surprise. Look back at that footage from 1998 of George Mitchell announcing a deal and notice some of those who are in the room clapping.

David Ervine, John White, Martin McGuinness, Tony Blair, Gerry Adams. With the exception of the INLA and the LVF, who maintained a forlorn opposition to any peace, all the groups with blood on their hands had supporters in the room.

So it's probably no coincidence that the agreement includes no mechanism for dealing with the past, for providing answers to so many grieving relatives.

And the small, intimate nature of Northern Ireland only makes this failure worse. Perhaps the person who murdered your loved one has just walked past you in the street.

Northern Ireland has had no peace and reconciliation effort, such as the one led by Archbishop Desmond Tutu in South Africa.

Those who killed during the Troubles continue to insist they were right to do so and have, in the last decade, proved depressingly effective at recruiting young people to rhetorical support for a "war" fought before they were born.

Thousands of families are denied the truth of who killed their loved ones, who maimed them, who left them traumatised.

This unwillingness to confront the past has led to the growth of transgenerational trauma (TGT), where those who lived through the Troubles unwittingly pass on their pain to those they love the most – their own children and grandchildren.

Damien McNally is the leading authority on TGT. He speaks to me on a Friday afternoon from his home in Banbridge.

We talk for more than an hour, Damien occasionally scratching his bald head as he goes over how Northern Ireland's awful past affects its still-not-great present. He peppers his answers with my name, saying "Barry" almost as a comma.

Damien begins by telling me about his own father, Paul, who was murdered by loyalists in the Ardoyne area of north Belfast in 1976.

His father was just twenty-six at the time and Damien was only four months old. Like so many Troubles victims,

Paul was an innocent civilian, murdered in cold blood purely because of his religion.

And, like so many of the victims, no-one has ever been tried for Paul's senseless killing:

"Ten years ago people were talking about transgenerational trauma and I thought 'what is this?' so I did research into it, talking to other people who lost loved ones in the Troubles.

"I did that piece of work because my dad was murdered when I was a baby. I never knew him. I was talking to other people who were bereaved as children about how it affected them.

"People were throwing about the term 'transgenerational trauma' without thinking about what it meant. It's not an illness that you can deal with through medication.

"You have to deal with it as a society. I was trying to show at the time that if you don't deal with it now, it will spread into the next generation.

"I talk to student nurses and doctors at Queen's about the Troubles, about how it might be a factor for some of their patients in the future. Sometimes afterwards they'll say to me 'I was aware of someone in my family being killed, but we never talked about it.'"

If the seeds of TGT were planted by the Good Friday Agreement, the government of Boris Johnson sprayed water all over the weeds of pain two decades later through its amnesty plan.

Instead of a South African-style peace and reconciliation process, the UK government moved to simply draw a veil over the Troubles, introducing an amnesty that would make any future prosecutions impossible.

The Tory right was enthused, as this would halt all cases against former soldiers and police officers who served during the Troubles.

The painfully slow prosecution of a handful of individuals – such as Soldier F who is on trial for killings on Bloody Sunday – enraged many British politicians and journalists.

And in one sense they had a point.

A state, even when it's secretive and duplicitous, generates a paper trail. With enough hard work, damming evidence can be uncovered.

Paramilitaries don't take minutes. As long as their ageing volunteers keep their mouths shut, the chances of building a case against those who killed decades ago are slim indeed.

So we're left with the situation that former soldiers and police officers feel victimised, even though they accounted for "only" ten per cent of the killings during the Troubles.

And many of those killings, of armed paramilitaries, took place in circumstances which wouldn't trouble a judge's consideration for more than a few seconds.

But the Johnson government smashed the nut of state prosecutions with the sledgehammer of an amnesty for all.

And, for Damien and other victims, this was a re-traumatisation:

"Amnesty has been another traumatic experience, being told that there won't be any prosecutions, that we're closing the book on the past.

"There's not going to be any justice. So you're not talking about trauma from fifty years ago, you're talking about trauma that's happening now.

"I've been in meetings with the last two secretaries of state about this and I just think 'you couldn't give two shits about us'. It's kids and grandkids going to court trying to find out what happened to their loved ones.

"It was different during the Troubles. If you had a family member shot, someone else would be shot the next day and you'd think 'I'm not that unusual'.

"But now, when you see the news, people are talking about the price of bread, or whatever. And then you think 'what happened in the Troubles wasn't normal'.

"The peace process was great for a lot of people, particularly for young people, but a lot of us are left without answers.

"The peace process was society moving on, but that leaves a lot of us thinking 'what the hell was that all about?'

"The Good Friday Agreement told the victims to step aside because it's too difficult to deal with."

Damien believes that all of us who lived through the Troubles – whether we were bereaved or not – carry some level of trauma from that period:

"We need a process to hear the experiences of people who grew up in the Troubles, those who weren't injured or bereaved. What was it like growing up here?

"We lived in a weird time. There were bomb scares and you couldn't go into the town. How I go into town, where I feel safe in my school uniform, that low-level stuff had a big impact on people's lives.

"It's the normality of the abnormal. It's only after the ceasefires that people had the time to reflect that it wasn't normal.

"There's a lot of people carrying a lot of stuff from our past. It's a big part of who we are."

When Damien talked about how all of us are "carrying a lot of stuff" whether we were bereaved or not, he could've been talking about my friend, Ciaran Tracey.

Ciaran and I met when he joined the 5 Live Breakfast team in 2016.

At the time our editor, Gill, was showing a striking fondness for Northern Irish producers.

I was her gateway drug in 2013, but soon she was hooked, recruiting Ciaran, who's from Lisburn; Claire and Gary from Fermanagh, Jason from Banbridge and Rory from Millisle.

For a few months in 2017 there were six of us – fully a quarter of the round-the-clock team from the same small part of the world.

In an accidental act of perfect representation, Gill managed to recruit three Protestants and three Catholics.

Soon enough this absurdly high number started to dwindle as the others moved on to better things. In Ciaran's case this meant full-time podcasting, a forum that suits his intense, forensic manner.

We meet at Café Expo in Didsbury, a district that would be a notorious by-word for middle-class suburban life if were in London rather than Manchester.

After some pleasantries, and fetching a surprisingly reasonably priced coffee, I ask Ciaran about his upbringing.

I'm shocked that, as he describes how the Troubles affected his first day on Earth, he puts his hand up to his eye to wipe away a tear:

"Bobby Sands died the evening before I was born. Mum was in Lagan Valley Hospital giving birth to me the next day and Dad was trying to get to the hospital but he couldn't get there in time for my birth, he couldn't get out of Andytown because of the rioting.

"Sorry, Barry, sorry...just give me a minute...

"It's OK. Anyway, Mum was a teacher, Dad worked in Ulster Bank. They were new middle class.

"I grew up right next to Thiepval Barracks in Lisburn, which was the base for the whole British Army in Northern Ireland.

"It was a nice part of Lisburn, very middle-class, gentle, green. Childhood was seeing soldiers walking past your door four or five times a day.

"They would let you look down the sights of their rifles. Out of my bedroom window you could see the masts in the base. It was just always there.

"When I was about nine, me and my neighbour, we were messing around with a hose and we sprayed it over the hedge, knowing the soldiers were there.

"My friend was a Protestant, we were just messing about, we didn't do it out of any sense of hostility We ran away through the trees, I remember feeling so scared."

As the conversation goes on and my coffee goes cold, I realise that asking Ciaran to talk to me for this book has given him permission to share feelings he usually keeps hidden:

"I remember at the age of six going into Lisburn and being left in the car on my own while my parents fetched something.

"And I was sitting there terrified that there would be a car bomb. Even today, if I see a car with its hazards on and no-one in it, I don't want to know, I'm gone.

"Granny and Granda lived in Andytown, so we went there a lot and that scared me. Going past Twinbrook, you would see graffiti advertising the IRA's latest upgrade 'Mark 3 Mortar.'

"The thing that really scared me was the corporals being murdered[56], when was it 1988? I would've been seven. That terrified me because it happened in Andytown. After I saw that I was really scared of Andytown.

"But we had a very happy middle-class childhood, we'd go into Lisburn on our bikes."

Despite coming of age in a quiet, middle-class area, Ciaran appears to have had a troubled adolescence, with fears of violence rattling round his head:

---

[56] On March 19, 1988, a car driven by British Army corporals Derek Wood and David Howes ploughed into the funeral procession for IRA member Caoimhín Mac Brádaigh, who had been murdered at another IRA funeral just three days earlier by the loyalist Michael Stone. Fearing another murderous attack, mourners surrounded the car. The two corporals were disarmed and beaten before being shot dead by the IRA.

"I knew if I heard the door being kicked in where I would run to. Why did I come up with that plan? They were never going to kick in our door right next to Thiepval.

"I remember on the way to Belfast, you used to go past the Old Warren estate in Lisburn which was a UDA estate. I remember the graffiti.

"The UVF had a sadism to them that started to scare me.

"I found the early Adair[57] years terrifying – maybe 1992 to 1995. Do you remember that famous quote of his, Barry? He was asked if he'd ever had a Catholic in his car and he said: 'Only a dead one.'

"That was chilling. During the Drumcree[58] crisis I remember oil barrels blocking the road and my dad having to turn the car around."

Ciaran agrees with my observation that he carries a lot of trauma from that time:

"Growing up in the Troubles, it's hard-wired, it's a fear that will never change.

"Caution. Hyper-vigilance. I can't look at an unattended bag, I have to go.

"I remember a few years ago, we went to see one of the Bond films – I think it was Quantum of Solace. I just didn't like the look of some of the people in there, I said to Coletta: 'I'm sorry but I'm going to have to leave.'

"Until ten years ago, if Coletta was away, I would sleep in my jeans with my shoes at the end of the bed so I could get away if the door was kicked in."

Unlike most of the people I interviewed, Ciaran left Northern Ireland at a relatively late age. He was in his mid-

---

[57] Johnny Adair, the high-profile leader of the UDA in the Shankill in the 80s and 90s.

[58] The government decision to prevent Orangemen from marching along the almost entirely Catholic Garvaghy Road in Portadown led to four summers of violence from 1995 to 1998. At some points during those feverish weeks law and order broke down across Northern Ireland.

thirties when he left Belfast behind for Manchester. He was married and had a rewarding, if demanding, job at BBC Northern Ireland.

In other words, he gave post-agreement Northern Ireland a good chance:

"I applied to Coventry, Milton Keynes and Reading but I got into Queen's in 1999. Nortel had just invested in Northern Ireland, so computer science was the thing.

"I used to go to Revelations, which was the first internet café in Belfast. I failed computer science so I studied English instead.

"I got a job at the Integrated Education Fund and then I started at the BBC in 2008. I ended up working at Spotlight, it was an incredibly intense experience.

"My first Spotlight was 'Who Killed Bobby Moffett?'[59] We had to hand-deliver the rights of reply to all the people you read about in the Sunday Life.[60] It was very stressful.

"Coletta and I had been married for a few years when she got the offer to work over in England. I wanted a blank slate, so we moved over in 2016, before the Brexit vote."

Far from facing prejudice in England, Ciaran thinks the fact that being Northern Irish makes his life easier:

"Being from Northern Ireland over here opens more doors than it closes. If you email someone and then talk to them on the phone, they're surprised to hear your accent.

"There's something about our accent, it doesn't sound bolshy. People are more likely to give you a hearing.

---

[59] Bobby Moffett was a UVF member who was shot dead on the Shankill Road in 2010 having fallen foul of other members of the group.

[60] A Belfast tabloid that specialises in reporting on loyalist paramilitaries to such an extent that, when my brother was working in a shop in east Belfast, some men entered and informed the staff that their days of stocking the paper had come to an end.

"It's easy to say that they didn't like me in NBH,[61] but I don't think that's because I'm from Northern Ireland, I think it's because I'm not from the metropole.

"It's not like the 70s – 'no blacks, no dogs, no Irish' – that prejudice is gone."

Like some of the other emigrants I speak to, Ciaran points out the depressing fact that he can express his identity abroad with a freedom which isn't always on offer back home:

"My brothers and sisters live in Northern Ireland. I was over there last week. The dereliction of east Belfast is terrible – it's worse than Rochdale.

"I was in a bar in east Belfast, a craft beer place opposite the Welders Club on the Newtownards Road. Great place, but I felt like I had to keep my jumper on to cover up my Celtic tattoos *(pointing to his arms)* I love it, this is me, these tattoos.

"I can express my affinity with Celtic themes. I sure as fuck wouldn't have got the tattoos done at home.

"I can express my Irishness over here in a way that I couldn't in Northern Ireland.

"My name has a fada, it's actually pronounced 'Keer-awn', that's what people call me when I'm in Dublin. I was never called 'Keer-awn' when I grew up, it was always 'Keer-an'.

"At the BBC you're taught about impartiality so, if you include the fada in your name, you're making a statement in itself. If you add a fada to your Twitter name then it becomes a statement."

Ciaran is emphatic when I ask if he has considered moving back to Northern Ireland:

"Would I like to bring up my children in that atmosphere? Hell no.

---

[61] New Broadcasting House, the BBC's HQ in London.

"It's mono-ethnic and the one ethnicity that's there fights with each other. I don't want to bring up my children against a background of bitterness and petty point-scoring. I want them among different faces, different cultures.

"Are they Irish? I hope so. But I would say I'm Northern Irish.

"Northerners will never be Irish enough in the Republic."

Like Ciaran, Emily Shanks left Northern Ireland at a relatively late age, with Belfast hosting her early adult milestones of career progression and house buying. But, like Ciaran, she grew frustrated with the place before she reached thirty.

Emily begins by telling me of her fond memories of her childhood in Lurgan:

"I was born in 1982 into a big Irish Catholic family. My mum is one of sixteen children – my grandparents have 55 great-grandchildren. I was only one of three, I've got an older brother and an older sister.

"My parents were both civil servants and they both got up every day to go to work, never had a day sick, and they instilled that in me.

"Mum and Dad just wanted what was best for us."

But the north Armagh of Emily's childhood was a particularly violent place, thanks to the long-running parades dispute at Drumcree and the activities of the loyalist killer Billy Wright:[62]

"When I was a teenager, Garvaghy Road was a big thing. There was a lot of rioting in Lurgan around it and you were aware of the heightened tensions each year in the run-up to July.

---

[62] Wright, nicknamed King Rat, was based in Portadown and led a murderous unit of the UVF in the final years of the Troubles.

"The army would stop us on the way to school and look in our bags. I remember them making me empty my milk out of its carton to prove it was nothing suspicious.

"We knew Rosemary Nelson[63] a wee bit, my dad used to drink in the pub with her husband and their house backed on to ours.

"She was well known because she represented some colourful characters, shall we say. I wanted to be a lawyer like her.

"I remember the day it happened, coming home and not being able to get in the house because everything was cordoned off.

"I had to wait in the Woodville pub until mum and dad came back from work. The next day, I looked out the window and the army were crawling around our garden looking for debris because her house backed on to ours.

"I told them to leave but of course they didn't listen to me."

Emily moved to Belfast and enjoyed a contented life there during the Noughties. It was one of Northern Ireland's better decades – admittedly not an especially competitive contest:

"I went to Queen's in 2000 to study law and Spanish. I got to spend a year in Spain as part of the course. I thought it would boost my desire to see the world but for some reason it didn't.

"I felt like I had seen a bit of the world but then I returned to the safety of home. So I qualified as a lawyer and then I was working as a solicitor in Newry and then in Belfast. I was working in the family proceedings court so it was a lot of cases involving parents getting a divorce and arguing over access to the kids.

---

[63] A prominent lawyer who represented several high-profile terrorism suspects. She was murdered in 1999 by a car bomb planted by the previously unheard-of loyalist group the Red Hand Defenders. State collusion was immediately suspected but hasn't been proven.

"At that time there were a lot of new bars and clubs in Belfast, I was in my twenties, I was going out with my mates, we were all qualified solicitors.

"But as I got closer to thirty, it just started to feel so...small, I suppose you'd say. I bought a house in Belfast and then I thought about my future – was I going to do this job for the rest of my life, pump out a couple of kids and go to Majorca for a week every summer?

"I didn't want to think that this is it for the rest of my life, working really hard for very little pay in a very male environment. Dealing with the same kind of cases every week and having to beg for work.

"And law is very incestuous, you know, solicitors marrying each other. I just thought there was no prospects for me.

"No disrespect, but I thought there had to be more to life than negotiating contact between two people who can't stand each other."

Ironically the financial crash of 2008, which brought economic misery to millions, ended up providing Emily with an escape route from the world of Belfast solicitors:

"My sister worked for a financial consultancy called First Derivatives and they needed someone who spoke Spanish. I put my name forward, I didn't get the gig but it put me on their radar and I ended up getting a three-month gig with them in London.

"I had no money saved, so my dad gave me this big wedge of cash before I left. I got to London and the cabbie wouldn't take the money because it was Northern Irish money. That was a great start!

"I went into this wee room they were putting me up in. I was looking at the bed with no bedsheet, thinking 'I'm nearly 30 and I've given up my career and my home in Belfast. What the fuck?'

"But I went to the 24-hour Asda, bought some bedsheets and got on with it.

"I was working for RBS on Bishopsgate and I hadn't a clue that investment banking even existed. But I got my head round it. They needed people with a legal background because it was after the financial crash and they were having to ring-fence their investment banking from their retail bank.

"Then I moved into their sales team because I'm just like my sister – we can talk. I was working in New York and then Singapore. It's funny, wherever I went with First Derivatives, there was always lots of Irish people so the craic was unbelievable. I've never had such a vibe but after a while they had a change of management and the culture changed.

"So I left and I formed my own company, Noviam, we place graduates with banks for eighteen to twenty-four months and then the bank decides whether they want to keep them."

Emily has stayed connected to home – but like Ciaran Tracey and Eamon Eastwood– her trips back to Northern Ireland only reinforce her determination not to return:

"My sister has three kids and my brother has two and my best friends from primary school still live there so I'd go back to Northern Ireland maybe five times a year.

"I always look forward to it, but that's because of the people I'm going to see. But my heart sinks when I arrive.

"Belfast seemed like it was on the rise when I lived there, but it's in decline now. The city centre's very dirty and there are lots of homeless people about, lots of boarded-up shops.

"I actually feel unsafe in Belfast now, which I didn't before. Last time I was there, I saw these two young girls knocking lumps out of each other outside the McDonald's on Royal Avenue while everyone else stood by and watched.

"Because I live in London, I suppose I'm spoiled with transport. So it's a bit of a shock when you come home and arrange to meet up with people and right away they're worrying about how they're going to get the last train home, or if they'll get their husband to pick them up.

"When I'm back home I feel like I'm never out of the car.

"It used to be when I went to buy a round in Belfast, I felt like Rockefeller coz it was so much cheaper than London, but the prices in Belfast are insane now.

"But you know, I'd always encourage people to visit Belfast, to go on the black cab tours and visit the Titanic museum. It's just such an interesting city because of its history and the people are so nice."

As Emily continues talking to me about the frustrations she experiences on her trips home, she stumbles across a great phrase to describe the last decade of drift – "pressed pause":

"Maybe coz of Stormont closing down for all that time, but it just felt like someone had pressed pause and there was nothing really happening.

"Like my old school, St Michael's Grammar, it was closed down and they were halfway through knocking down the old building when Stormont stopped, so it was just left there, half demolished.

"I still care very much about the politics of Northern Ireland. I live in Jeremy Corbyn's constituency so I don't see the point in voting – he's always going to win.

"So I vote back home because I feel like my vote could make a difference."

Emily has the easy articulacy you'd expect from someone who spent a decade in the legal profession. But when I ask her how the Troubles have affected her, she pauses, as if it's a question she's not considered before:

"Er...I've learnt so much about myself since I left Ireland and I've got much more patriotic. I see this resilience in my mum that I didn't notice before, which I think a lot of women developed because of the Troubles.

"I realise now, at my age, what it must have taken for my parents' generation to get through it.

"How does it affect me? I'm not sure. But I feel like I'm good at crisis management. I stay calm and say to everyone 'cool your jets, we'll be grand.'

"I just feel like I'm going to manage and that comes from my upbringing, from my parents who always got up and went to work no matter what was going on."

Like Emily, Jo Gamage also returned to Northern Ireland having lived abroad – but it's a decision she now regrets much more than Emily did.

Of all the people I spoke to for the book, Jo seemed the most on edge, the most disillusioned with post-agreement Northern Ireland.

I'd like to think that everyone I interviewed found it therapeutic to talk to someone who shares their unique background. Contributing to the book is, in effect, permission to talk about things that are usually left unspoken.

But with Jo, I sensed this more than anyone else.

A few other people who contributed to this book, including Ciaran, briefly broke down during our interviews, wiping tears from their eyes and apologising for momentarily losing their composure.

But Jo seemed constantly on the cusp of crying. Perhaps it's because of her circumstances – back in Northern Ireland but desperate to leave again – that she found it helpful to speak to someone else who understood her frustrations.

We talk just before each of us is about to go on the school run. She starts by telling me about her childhood:

"I grew up in a wee village called Annacloy in County Down. I was one of five children. I had a lovely childhood, great parents, school was fun.

"I was always a homebird. I thought I would stay here, that I would look after mum and dad when they got older."

The shortage of university places in Northern Ireland forced Jo out against her will. But once she left, she realised that the inadequacies of third-level education in Belfast had been a blessing in disguise:

"I remember when we were studying for our 11 plus, I heard my teacher talking to the head about who in the class was going to pass. He gestured to the table I was at and said, 'none of them will pass.'

"I got an A and I got into grammar school, but his words stuck with me. I thought I must have just fluked an A on the day, I had imposter syndrome. For the first three years I didn't feel that I belonged at grammar school.

"When it came to uni time, I wanted to study physio and there was only one course in Northern Ireland, at the Ulster University campus at Jordanstown.

"Lots of people wanted to do the course so they just hiked up the grades. You needed two As and a B to get in, which is more like the grades you'd expect for a medical degree.

"Rather than offering interviews for people who wanted to do the course, they just went with grades and mine weren't good enough."

The thinktank Pivotal has found that Jo's experience of effectively being forced out of Northern Ireland by its shortage of university places is very common:

The demand for courses in HEIs in Northern Ireland outstrips supply of places. QUB reports that for every 100 home applicants, there were only 60 places available at Northern Ireland institutions in 2018/2019.

"Restrictions on full-time places do not apply to students from GB and international students who wish to study in Northern Ireland. The grade requirements for students from outside of Northern Ireland also may be different to the entrance requirements for home students

with some programmes accepting lower grades for these students.[64]

But Jo ended up seizing an opportunity which she hadn't really wanted:

"I was forced to leave Northern Ireland to study. I thought it was very unfair, it's a ridiculous system.

"But when I left, I realised it was the best thing for me. I made new friends in England based on who I was as a person, rather than on being someone's sister or daughter.

"It built my confidence – these people liked me for who I am. I went to Leeds and I had a brilliant time there, doing placements all over West Yorkshire.

"So, when it came to finding a job, all my contacts were over there. I was working in Pinderfields Hospital in Wakefield when I met a young doctor called Layan.

"He was from Sri Lanka but had grown up in England. We got together and pretty early in our relationship he suggested leaving for New Zealand because the NHS was going to crap. I didn't really know much about New Zealand but I knew he was the right person for me."

But the young couple weren't destined for a long life together:

"Layan spent five years training to become a plastic surgeon. We had two sons and moved back to England and Layan planned to complete his one-year final training and then we would move back to New Zealand.

"While we were back in England, we found out that Layan had pancreatic cancer. He died in March 2020, just before the first lockdown.

"When he was sick, he told me that I should go back home after he died to get support from my family. We moved back to New Zealand but life became more and more of a struggle.

---

[64] p6, Should I Stay or Should I Go? Reasons for leaving Northern Ireland for work and study; Pivotal, Public Policy Forum Northern Ireland, 2021

"Then my dad got Parkinson's. I would Skype them two or three times a day and I could see how much my mum was struggling.

"You feel so guilty when you're so far away. My brothers and sisters all live in Northern Ireland but they all work full-time.

"I decided to move back for a year because I could work part-time and help mum and dad. I wanted to spend time with my dad while I still could."

Each passing day in Northern Ireland strengthens Jo's determination to leave, particularly in order to limit her sons' exposure to the country's education system:

"My boys are eight and eleven now. The younger one has developed a wee twang from being in Northern Ireland for a bit, but they're both Kiwis.

"I had to convince them to come over here. Neither of them have enjoyed the rigid and strict school system.

"It's horrible to see how much they hate school. There's a group of disruptive kids in school. The whole year group are way, way behind on things like handwriting because they were only starting school when the first lockdown happened in 2020.

"At school it's just work, work, work, everyone sitting at a desk. In New Zealand there's one desk round the teacher where some of the children sit to do a set task, but then it's mats and bean bags.

"It's a much better way for young boys to learn, much more fun. They can't wait to go back to school in New Zealand. We didn't realise how good the schools were until we came to Northern Ireland.

"Luca is in P7 so he did the Eleven Plus practice tests with the rest of the class but he didn't have to do the real thing because we're going back to New Zealand.

"Seeing the pressure the other kids are under, at that young age, to get into a good school. That's just the system here. I'm very relieved that he isn't doing it. I know from my sister that everyone gets a tutor to try to get into a good school.

"When we go back to New Zealand I want the boys to go to the Catholic high school. It's a good school but not one that you have to pay for, I think that's important.

"There's a good social mix of people – white Kiwis and people from Tonga and Samoa who are Catholics. It's not just rich people.

"They go to a Catholic primary school in Crossgar, they're learning a few prayers for confession. There's three schools in Crossgar and the integrated one is the biggest. Things are changing but it will take generations to phase it out."

Jo's affectionate feelings for Northern Ireland are as fleeting as the country's good weather:

"When it's a lovely sunny day like today you think 'I could live here' but most days, when the sun's not shining you think you couldn't live here.

"There's a lot of Irish guilt about leaving your family, even though they're very supportive of me. My other Irish friends in New Zealand feel the same.

"My internal dialogue is going 'thank fuck I don't live here anymore' when it rains. It's so miserable. The fact that politicians couldn't get down to business, setting our own rules for our own society, it was pathetic."

Jo's disenchantment is exacerbated by the failings of the NHS in Northern Ireland, which struggles under the unique double challenge of Westminster-imposed austerity and Stormont-imposed political stasis:

"My job in New Zealand was similar to the one I have here in Northern Ireland so you can really see the difference, how badly broken the NHS is.

"There's a culture of long-term sick over here. People get paid to stay at home for six months when they're stressed and it's the rest of us who have to pick up the slack.

"Living in another country opens your eyes to things you wouldn't notice if you never left. In New Zealand people only phone in sick when they're actually sick.

"I've heard about a lot of suicides since I've been back, people at work talking about people they know who've killed themselves.

"I thought it might just be that people in Northern Ireland talk about it more but then I looked into it and the suicide rate here is higher than New Zealand, higher than England.

"My brother works in mental health up in Belfast. Three suicidal people and one bed and he has to decide which one of them gets it.

"My manager at work, her husband was really sick with chest pain, he need antibiotics. She phoned the GP first thing at nine, she was waiting to get through until 3.30 and then it was 'sorry, there's no more urgent appointments, try again tomorrow.'

"In the end he coughed so hard that he broke a rib and he ended up in A&E for lack of primary care. The NHS isn't responsive to the needs of the people.

"In New Zealand, adults have to pay twenty-five pounds to see their GP so that cuts out all the crap. You get seen that day and you can spend twenty minutes with your GP, maybe talk about other problems you're having. I don't feel safe here – people are waiting nine hours in A&E."

Jo struggles to find a way to share her feelings about Northern Ireland with her friends and family:

"People say to me 'oh you've been here for a year, would you not stay?' And I say something about how I can't stay because my sons are Kiwis, or that I miss the sunshine in New Zealand.

"And that's true, but I can't tell them the rest – the fact that I don't want to stay here because it's miserable. That would be disrespectful to them because they've decided to stay."

But, despite her disenchantment with the post-agreement world, Jo does bring up example of how the Northern Ireland she lives in is clearly better than the one she grew up in:

"I went to the Paddy's Day parade in Downpatrick and it was lovely to see some Protestant bands taking part and to see the different ethnicities – there were Chinese people marching with dragons and Indian people with drums.

"The last time I went to the parade it would have been a hundred per cent white. That was really nice.

"But I just find, you go round the towns and villages and it's depressing. So many boarded-up shops. When I go into Downpatrick, I just go to the Asda and then come straight back, it's so bleak."

Jo is unsure how connected she'll feel to Ireland once she returns to New Zealand:

"Next year is my mum and dad's fiftieth wedding anniversary. I don't know...it's ten K just for the flights. It would be better to save the money in case my dad goes downhill and I have to come back to help out.

"Growing up here, everyone I know was buried because we're Catholic but I'd rather be cremated. Layan was cremated.

"I'm going to get his ashes made into diamonds so the boys can use them in their wedding rings if they want.

"I don't want to be scattered in the sea, no, put me in an urn. If one of the boys decides to go off to Ireland, or wherever, the two of them can split me."

When she returns to New Zealand, Jo is looking to reconnecting with her Irish friends:

"I met a woman from Dublin at my swimming class and I bonded with her more than with any of my Kiwi friends. Whether you're from the North or the South, we're all Irish.

"I'd look after her kids, she'd look after mine. There's that bond with other Irish people abroad because they miss their families too, they're feeling guilty too."

I finish our interview by asking Jo – as I ask all the people I speak to – if she still considers Northern Ireland to be "home". I hope it's a good way of persuading the emigrants to explain their complicated feelings about our complicated homeland.

When I ask Jo this question, she pauses and takes a deep sigh before answering:

"When I'm in New Zealand I would say 'we're going home in the summer to see my family'. Now that I'm in Northern Ireland I would say 'I'm going home on August the second.'

"I remember a few years ago, we landed back in New Zealand and there were people walking around barefoot and I thought 'I'm home'.

"I think of Northern Ireland as the place I come from, I'm Irish but I'm also a Kiwi. When Ireland play the All Blacks, I would cheer on Ireland.

"I love Ireland, I had a great childhood but...yeah...it's not where I choose to be anymore. I feel like an imposter in Northern Ireland, I don't fit in, I don't really belong here.

"It's complicated isn't it, Barry?"

Many of the emigrants I spoke to shared – as I do – Jo's feeling that they don't fit in. This sense of being an outsider helps turn a vague thought of leaving home into the purchase of a plane ticket.

But that feeling that you don't belong doesn't drift away when you step into the arrivals lounge in Austin, Auckland or Adelaide.

It doesn't disappear the minute you get to Liverpool, Stranraer or Heathrow. Because now you're really an outsider – an export from a society which is conflicted in a unique way.

No other nominally Christian society in the world is divided in the way that Northern Ireland is. Nowhere else in the world has Protestant areas and Catholic areas overseen with peace walls.

No-one else has the unwritten codes we use to determine someone's religion without ever asking. Failure to fit in to a society which itself stands isolated in the world can be a lonely experience.

One person who I'm surprised to discover shares this feeling of being a misfit is my old friend Pete Devenney.

When we speak we're at opposite ends of the week. For him, it's six thirty on Monday morning and, like any self-respecting small businessman, the working week is already underway as he drives to his first meeting of the day.

For me it's half five on Sunday evening, I've been up since three in the morning (my fourth pre-dawn start of the week) and I'm sipping red wine, toasting Arsenal's six-nil thrashing of West Ham.

We briefly turn on Facetime Video and I see his face for the first time in ten years. Pleasingly, he's as grey as me, but annoyingly he's markedly less bald.

Pete and I met in South Korea in 2004 where we both worked as English teachers. Twenties Pete was gregarious and quick-witted.

Forty-five minutes into 2005 he reached across the bar table and asked if he could have one of my cigarettes. When I said yes, he took one, lit it, exhaled and sighed: "Well that's another new year's resolution fucked, Barry."

But when we start talking twenty years later, he begins by telling me that younger Pete was not so carefree. In fact, my native city kicked the craic out of him:

"I grew up in Portrush, I lived there for the first seven or eight years of my life and it was the happiest of times.

"Then we moved to Belfast and it was harsh and pointy, there was an edge to it that wasn't present in Portrush.

"I was this happy-go-lucky character but Belfast changed me very quickly. I went to Inst[65] but I don't ever remember being happy there, I just wanted it to be over.

"Before Inst, I had a primary school teacher whose husband was from Australia and I just wanted to go to Oz, to see the beaches and the happy people."

Like Ciaran Tracey, Pete brings up the televised lynching of the British corporals as a moment that lives with him:

"I remember sitting in the living room with its beige walls listening to – what did you call your woman? Pamela Ballantyne, that's it. Listening to her telling me about the latest tit-for-tat killing.

"I remember the corporals being killed in Milltown. That solidified it for me. I thought 'that's crazy.'

"That was the last straw for me. A few years later I remember going to Leeds and Glasgow to look at unis and noticing that there was no army on the streets.

"I chose to go to uni in Glasgow. Yeah, there was a sectarian edge to Glasgow, but it was Belfast Lite. I would go drinking with friends who supported Celtic and I would go drinking in a loyalist bar next to Ibrox.

"But I always felt their sectarianism wasn't my issue, it was just a Glasgow thing.

"Then I went to live in Leeds, where they hate southerners. I suppose you've got to hate someone!"

Pete returned to Belfast but, once again, felt that he didn't fit in:

"I moved to Oz and then in 2002 I moved back to Belfast. I was working in customer service for NTL for nine months, getting enough money together to go travelling again. It was the honeymoon after the Good Friday

[65] The Royal Belfast Academical Institution (RBAI), Belfast's second most self-important school.

Agreement, there was a construction boom, but I felt aloof from it all.

"The place was small-minded, people were always reminding you about things you did years ago.

"I moved to Korea and I loved it there, I met like-minded people who I could learn something from.

"Northern Ireland is all about schools and systems and jobs where you have to wait for the person above you to die before you get their job. New Zealand's not like that."

When I ask Pete if he's experienced prejudice against people from Northern Ireland, he struggles to think of any examples:

"People have always shown an interest in Northern Ireland when they realise that's where I'm from. They ask me about 'the situation' and my experience of it.

"But there's been no overt hostility. Except for maybe once when I was at university. My Scottish girlfriend's mother said she felt sorry for me as I had no prospects because I was from Northern Ireland and had a shaved head.

"Yes, I think you're right, that was more anti-Pete sentiment than actual prejudice."

Having settled in New Zealand, Pete has become more aloof from Northern Ireland and is no longer a fan of the wee chat:

"My attitude when I meet people from Northern Ireland now is very different from what it would have been in the past. I treat them the same as I would treat anyone else, I don't go looking for conversation with them, looking for commonality.

"When I was younger and I met someone else from Northern Ireland, I would want to know where they're from.

"When I meet younger people from Northern Ireland through work they're the same as I was, they make a beeline for me. They want a sense of family, the safety of the group.

I no longer feel that affinity, that need to bring people into the group.

"I'm as comfortable now talking to someone from South Africa or China as I would be talking to someone from Northern Ireland.

"As I've travelled more my worldview has changed and I've become more comfortable with who I am. Your job, your family defines you more than your background.

"So when I meet someone from Northern Ireland I don't feel that sense of commonality with them anymore.

"But I do have a couple of friends from Northern Ireland and we get together and have a few drinks and a bit of craic. They have the same brutal sense of humour as me, which is different from the New Zealand sense of humour."

But, despite Pete's ears no longer pricking up at the sound of an Ulster vowel, he's adamant that Northern Ireland has shaped him for the better:

"I carry my Northern Irish identity with me, very much so. The world the two of us were brought up in was harsh. There was the Troubles, there was a lot of things happening that other people weren't exposed to.

"And I spent my teenage years living on the Upper Malone Road, near the Mary Peters track, so I'm not giving you a personal sob story.

"I carry that past with me and I don't really understand why people are depressed.

"I live in a beautiful part of the world but I deal with twenty-five-year-olds who are constantly depressed.

"We all have problems, but I just think 'you're lucky.'

"My experience wasn't terrible, but the Troubles were just ever present. I think my black sense of humour comes from that."

Pete and his partner Amanda endured New Zealand's notoriously intense Covid lockdown. He's one of several people I know from Northern Ireland who say they found the restrictions of that era easier to bear than others.

I took to lockdown like it was an old pair of shoes. For those of us who lived through the Troubles, the privations of the pandemic were faintly familiar.

Both demanded a constant vigilance in order to reduce your chances of death. This wariness sat alongside the knowledge that, no matter how cautious you were, through no fault of your own, you could end up dead.

And the pandemic, like the Troubles, disrupted normal life each and every day. No-one who endured, for instance, the breakdown of law and order around Drumcree in the mid-Nineties would be overly fazed at being unable to go to the pub for a few months.

When I point out the similarities to Pete, he's intrigued by the comparison:

"I would say, out of everyone I know, nobody enjoyed lockdown as much as me. Coz it was a bit like the Troubles? I hadn't thought about that, but maybe you're right.

"It was before Jack was born, so it was just Amanda and me. I thought it was one of the best times of my life – I thought to myself that this must be what retirement is like. Amanda hated it but I loved it."

With the pandemic over, Pete is now free to return to Northern Ireland whenever work and finances allow. But he seems resigned to slowly drifting away from his homeland:

"Amanda's from a small village called Palmerston. Her family had a small farm. It was a poor upbringing, but a very happy one.

"We've been together for ten years and we've been over to Northern Ireland. She's done the black taxi tour and found the whole thing incomprehensible and laughable.

"I used to be passionate about the political situation but now I just distance myself from it.

"Ireland won't be a big part of Jack's life. I enjoy visiting Ireland but I don't have fond memories of it. I had a good childhood but I don't remember enjoying it. I was pretty eager to leave.

"I won't be making a big deal of his Irish heritage. When I meet someone who's very nationalistic I just think 'it's just an accident of birth.'

"If you walked into my house you wouldn't think 'this guy's from Ireland', I don't have the paraphernalia up on the walls.

"I would follow Ireland in the rugby but I wouldn't be passionate about it. If they win, that's brilliant, but it's not going to ruin my day if they lose.

"I would still refer to Northern Ireland as 'home', I would say 'I'm going to go home this year.'

"But I'm fairly confident I'll spend the rest of my life in New Zealand, unless I do something stupid like retiring to Bali.

"Northern Ireland will always be home because that's where I grew up. But New Zealand is the place that feels most like home.

"I would move back if Amanda and Jack wanted to, or if one of my parents was very ill and needed looking after.

"Amanda has talked about moving to Ireland to give Jack a new experience. Northern Ireland isn't the place I grew up in, it's changed, but not enough. I wouldn't rule it out, but I wouldn't be overjoyed at moving back."

When I ask Pete if he feels any guilt for missing family occasions, his answer reminds me of my own period living many time zones away from home.

I knew something was wrong the minute I heard my dad's voice on the other end of the line. I spoke to my parents for about half an hour each Sunday, just after the Archers omnibus finished at a quarter past eleven in Belfast, seven fifteen in the evening in Taipei.

If he was phoning outside this time, it could only be bad news. "I'm afraid your gran's died."

There was sadness, but no shock, she had been drifting towards the end for some years. Earlier that year, when I said goodbye to her before moving to Taiwan, I knew there was a good chance I would never see her again.

We bury our dead quickly in Ireland, normally within three days. For financial and work reasons, there was no way I would be able to make it back for Gran's funeral.

There was no chance to join the family farewell to someone who had been present for every one of my twenty-three years, playing the old piano in our front room as I sang along, handing over the big tin of chocolate biscuits when we visited her house on the North Road.

And in her later years, sitting in the front room of her little flat on Kincora Avenue, reminiscing about the old days, using Ulster phrases like "this long time" that were going to die with her generation.

Missing births, deaths and marriages weighs more heavily the further you move from Northern Ireland.

People like Pete, who've settled in New Zealand, feel that guilt far more heavily than those of us who are only an hour's flight from Belfast City Airport:

"I've missed everything – my sister's funeral, my grandmother's funeral. These days, I could afford to fly back to Belfast, but five years ago I couldn't.

"My big concern now is my parents, they're in their late seventies. Mum came out last year and Dad's coming this year.

"I see them about once every five years so I might see them two or three more times before they die...that's pretty hard to sit with.

"When you're younger you don't think about these things. I've chosen the furthest place from Northern Ireland to build a home and that means sacrifices for me and my parents."

Pete pauses for a moment, slips into cliché and then apologises for being trite:

“It is what it is...sorry, Barry, I hate that statement.

“Jack’s not going to see his grandparents much and when he’s a teenager he won’t see that side of his family but that’s to do with my age, I’m an old dad.”

When I ask Pete if he’s thought about his funeral arrangements, I’m expecting him to say no – he never struck me as the morose sort.

But I’m surprised by his emphatic response:

“I’ve chosen somewhere. I’ve known all my life that I wanted to be buried there. There’s a cemetery on a hill overlooking Portrush.

“I was so happy there. And so sad in Belfast.”

Elsewhere in New Zealand, that same sense of guilt is also on the mind of Jen Carswell, who grew up in the County Down seaside town of Bangor in the 1980s:

“When someone dies, you’ve only got three days to get home or you miss the funeral. Both of my grandparents have died since we moved out here and I couldn’t go to either of their funerals.

“It’s very difficult...funerals are a very important part of the grieving process. You think that your family’s thinking ‘why’s she not here?’

“My dad posted me a DVD of gran’s funeral and that helped.

“You dread that phone call. My mum accidentally Facetimed me last week in the middle of the night. My heart jumped when I saw her name on the screen.

“If it was one of my parents who died, we’d have to go, just use the credit card and go.”

The evening sun shines through Jen’s window in Wellington and dawn has just broken in Yorkshire as she tells me how she came to leave Northern Ireland.

Like Jo Gamage and Ciaran Tracey, Jen recalls a feeling of not fitting in, despite a happy childhood:

"My older sister went to Jordanstown but I wanted to go away to university, I was the black sheep. I don't know why, I think maybe I found Northern Ireland too insular.

"I studied speech and language therapy at Reading and I've worked in that field ever since. I applied for a few jobs in England but I was ready to go back home and I ended up getting a job in Cookstown.

"I hated it. Cookstown is so small and, if you don't want to go to the pub, there's nothing to do in the evenings. After a year or two I bought my first place in Glengormley, just outside Belfast. That felt like I was back in civilisation.

"I grew up Christian but I dropped out of the church at uni. Then I started going to a church in Bangor and that's where I met Ben, who's from Yorkshire.

"At first I thought: 'Oh no, this means I'll end up back in England' because I was settled in Northern Ireland. But Ben was offered a job in New Zealand.

"I'd never been to New Zealand, we had a lot of discussions about moving there. When we went in 2008 I didn't think I was leaving for good, but I'm still here 16 years later and we've got three children.

"There's no hostility here, maybe a wee bit towards English people, but not to us. Ben sometimes tells people he's married to an Irishwoman because that helps him. People will tell you about their great grandfather who was Irish."

Like Pete Devenney, Jen's attachment to Northern Ireland has waned the more she becomes accustomed to living in a functioning society:

"I really struggled in the first few years, I didn't want to put down roots because it felt like I was betraying my family.

"I remember when we visited, my grandmother said, 'maybe you'll stay there for good' and that annoyed my mum. I kept referring to Northern Ireland as 'home'.

"It's only when my kids came along that I started to think of New Zealand as home. Never say never, my parents are getting old and it's not fair on my sister. I think it's only family health that would bring us back now.

"We last went back in 2022. It was depressing, people are a bit moany, no government, Brexit, covid. I think the pandemic made Northern Ireland even more insular, people weren't venturing out."

When a Northern Irish émigré becomes a parent, the already difficult job of child-rearing is complicated by considering how to explain their conflicted homeland to their offspring.

I've tried to describe to my children why, when we go into a restaurant or a cafe, I can never sit with my back to the door. But I'm not sure that they understand.

Jen has also wrestled with the problem:

"I haven't really explained the Troubles to the kids. When they tell me about earthquake drill at school, I tell them that we used to have bomb drills in school.

"Kiwis ask me if I grew up somewhere like Derry Girls, but no growing up in Bangor wasn't like that.

"We've got a fourteen-year-old son, a twelve-year-old son and our daughter is nine. I got my sons to watch the film Belfast and I think they understood it. 'For the ones who stayed, the ones who left and the ones we lost' that stuck with me, it made me cry.

"My kids don't have their aunts and uncles and grandparents in their lives.

"After lockdown in New Zealand there was all this coverage of family reunions and I remember thinking: 'You haven't seen your mum for six weeks? I haven't seen mine in four years.'

"It's hard but it was our choice."

Jen is one of many Protestant emigrants I speak to who feels more open to the Irish part of her identity since leaving Northern Ireland:

"My daughter does Irish dancing. My grandfather was an Orangeman, he'd be turning in his grave. It's weird having to explain to people over here that we didn't do Irish dancing at school, we did Scottish dancing.

"I just say I'm Irish now. I got an Irish passport right after Brexit, I want my kids to be able to live in Europe if they want to.

"I don't think I would be against unity, I'm not massively opposed to it."

Rev Glenn Chestnutt is another Protestant who's moved towards a position of agnosticism on Irish unity.

He spoke to me for longer than anyone else I interviewed, spending and hour and a half explaining his life story in a gentle north Antrim burr unaltered by nearly a decade in Canada.

When Glenn appears on the Zoom screen from his church office in Montreal, I reckon he's mid-forties like myself.

But when he starts telling me his life story I quickly realise he's nearly a decade older than me – his youthful appearance a good advertisement for the long-term benefits of a healthy Presbyterian lifestyle:

"I was born in Ballymoney in 1970 and I grew up in a wee village outside the town called Dervock. It was a Presbyterian home, a Presbyterian environment that I grew up in.

"My family owned the local shop, we'd owned it for several generations so we'd be well known in that part of north Antrim. I was one of three children. I've a brother who's also a Presbyterian minister in Ballymena and my sister, she also lives in Ballymena.

"There was a real mix of people in the village, there was even a safari park at the other end of Dervock, believe it or not. I just remember it as a lovely home.

"But yes, of course I remember the violence, the fortifications everywhere. Dervock would be predominantly unionist, if not loyalist.

"That's the way north Antrim is, the villages would tend to either be Protestant or Catholic. But I went to Dalriada School in Ballymoney and there was a good mix of Protestants and Catholics there.

"I made several friends who I didn't realise were Catholics until after we became friends. What I mean is that their religion didn't occur to me when I got to know them.

"In the late Seventies and the Eighties I became more conscious of what was going on in Northern Ireland.

"I remember I was at the church badminton club and the fella who ran it, he rolled up his trouser leg and told us 'there's were I was shot.'

"And I remember us all gathering round to look at the scar. He'd been in the UDR[66] and he'd been ambushed somewhere out in the country. He'd been shot two or three times.

"And then, when I was fifteen or sixteen there was the Anglo-Irish Agreement[67] – are you old enough to remember that, Barry?[68] I remember there was a riot in Ballymoney, people fighting, plastic bullets being fired. And my dad telling us it was time to leave.

---

[66] The Ulster Defence Regiment, the British Army's Northern Irish regiment during the Troubles. Its members, many of whom were part-time, were often targeted by the IRA while they were off-duty.

[67] Signed in 1985 between Margaret Thatcher and her Irish opposite number Garrett Fitzgerald, the agreement gave the Republic a formal consultative role in Northern Ireland for the first time. Unionists, having wrongly assumed that Thatcher was on their side, reacted with fury and campaigned for years against the agreement.

[68] Not quite. But I do remember seeing the "Ulster Says No" banner that unionist councillors hung at the front of Belfast City Hall in the years after the agreement.

"And other things stick in my mind, you know, like the mortar attack on the police station in Newry[69] and of course Enniskillen.[70]

"I was at a youth group in Bangor that day. I remember us going back up to Ballymoney in a Bedford van with the radio on, listening to the news from Enniskillen."

Glenn explains how two visits to prison, separated by two decades, brought home to him the sheer length of the Troubles:

"I visited Magilligan twice, but twenty years apart. The first time would have been 1975 I think. My mum was driving a woman and her two kids up there to see her husband, their dad.

"I came along and I remember being jealous because the other two kids had been given presents and I hadn't because my dad wasn't in prison, he was at home.

"And the second time would have been in the mid-Nineties. I was a primary school teacher in Derry stroke Londonderry, you know call it what you want. But I was starting out as a minster then and I was invited to got to Magilligan again. I remember going into this Portacabin to take the service.

"I suppose the thing that struck me was how long the Troubles went on. The first time I went, the prisoners were all my dad's age. And then when I went for the second time, they were around my age."

---

[69] On February 28, 1985, the IRA launched nine mortars at Newry police station. One of them landed on a Portacabin where officers were eating at the time. Nine of the officers were killed and another 37 wounded. It was the RUC's biggest loss of life in a single incident during the Troubles.

[70] In what was probably the most notorious attack of the Troubles, the IRA bombed the Remembrance Sunday service in the Fermanagh town. Twelve Protestants – many of them pensioners – were killed and 63 more were wounded.

Glenn chose to go to Queen's but – like many Protestant students in the Eighties and Nineties – his university years weren't full of carefree tolerance:

"In 1988 I went to Queen's to study chemistry. The students' union was very militant then. I was staying in halls and I was the only Protestant on my floor. It was the first time that I'd felt like a minority.

"I remember I had a bottle of Kia-Ora in my cabinet in the kitchen. And someone had ripped open the door and written 'you Orange bastard' on the bottle.

"There was another fella in the halls, I remember him on the phone finding out that his – sorry I can't remember if it was his uncle or his cousin – but his relative who was in the UDR had been killed.

"When other people in the halls found out, I remember the roar of applause in the canteen."

Glenn's career as a Presbyterian minister eventually took him to the west of Scotland – Pete Devenney's "Belfast Lite" – the part of the world that most resembles Northern Ireland, whether through its sectarianism, its ship-building heritage, its dreich hillsides, or its residents' fondness for alcohol:

"I was a teenager, I was interested in girls and ska. It was only later, when I was teaching, that I decided to become a Presbyterian minister. That allowed me to go to Princeton to study, I was there from 2000 to 2004.

"I had always wanted to study overseas and I thought it would be great, which it was, but then I'd go home and be a minister in the Presbyterian Church in Ireland.

"But when I was at Princeton I met my wife, she's Canadian. We lived in Canada for a while and then we moved to Scotland where our son was born.

"I was the minister at St John's in Gourock in the west of Scotland, we had a congregation of about 500. Gourock is quite similar to Northern Ireland, it was a former shipyard area so it still has a strong sense of identity, of everyone looking after each other, very family orientated.

"But in other ways it was very different from Northern Ireland. I mean Northern Ireland is very different from anywhere else in the Western world.

"The independence referendum in 2014, that was heated, as in sometimes there would be heated debate, but there wouldn't be violence or rioting.

"In the church there would be ministers who supported the SNP and others who were Labour or Conservative. They wouldn't say it openly but you would know by comments they made. And there would be tension in services when we played the national anthem, some people would sing and some wouldn't.

"But for me the big difference was that everyone started from the point of view that they were Scottish, either they were Scottish nationalists or they were Scottish unionists.

"And in Northern Ireland we don't have that because unionists have always struggled with the idea of calling themselves Irish."

Glenn's next calling was to another conflicted society, though one whose similarities to Northern Ireland are less direct:

"In 2016 we moved to Montreal. It's a very cosmopolitan, sophisticated city, it's like a smaller version of New York.

"The church was built in 1931 by Anglo Montrealers and it has close ties to the Black Watch Regiment, we hold a service for them every year.

"John McCrae, who wrote In Flanders Fields, worshipped at our church. We have a service called National Sunday where the flags of all the countries of our congregation are flown.

"We had twenty-three this year including Ukraine, Pakistan, Indonesia. We have twenty people who've applied to join the church, from Kenya, France, Nigeria,

Korea. Most of our liturgy is in English but we do have some Francophone members as well.

"There's a woman who comes every Sunday, she's Greek Orthodox so she calls me 'father' and reaches out and kisses my hand. And we have some other Orthodox people who've come from Ukraine since the Russian invasion.

"But again, like Scotland, there are similarities with Northern Ireland.

"I was speaking to an Anglo-Quebecer the other day. She's lived in Montreal all her life but she's planning to leave, to go to Alberta, which is where her husband's from.

"Anglos are leaving Montreal, they feel prejudice coming from some French speakers. All the laws and regulations are in French, so English-speaking lawyers and accountants end up leaving.

"When immigrant children come to Quebec, they have to go to a French-speaking school. But the real hardliners are in the Quebec countryside, not here on Montreal Island."

Perhaps because of his upbringing in Northern Ireland, Glenn is able to see the nuances in the divided society where he has made his home:

"I have a French O Level and I did a French immersion course when I got here so I speak a bit, I do some parts of my services in French.

"Generally we get along, when I meet someone new they'll say 'bonjour, hi' and I'll reply 'bonjour' and they'll realise right away that I'm an Anglo, so we'll speak in English after that.

"And I understand where the Francophones are coming from. Back in the Fifties and Sixties they couldn't get jobs if their English wasn't good enough.

"And when you talk to Francophones now, many of them will say 'you have to understand, we're the last French nation in the whole of North America.'"

On his returns home, Glenn sees a society still uncomfortable in its own skin:

"Have you seen the end of Derry Girls? Obviously it's a comedy, but it captures really well the excitement and the exuberance after the Good Friday Agreement.

"But that doesn't exist anymore. Who in Northern Ireland is actually striving for the common good?

"All the peace lines are still up in Belfast. In South Africa they had a model of reconciliation, if it was the right way of doing it, I wouldn't know, but they had the idea of talking to each other about the past to find a way to work together in the future.

"I don't see that in Northern Ireland."

Despite his thorough Protestantism, Glenn is one of the growing number of Protestants more comfortable with a sense of their Irishness:

"I think Brexit was a big mistake. I went in to the post office in Ballymoney to get an Irish passport form but I hesitated because I knew the woman behind the counter.

"She asked me what I wanted and eventually I told her I wanted to apply for an Irish passport and she said 'sure, take a few forms.'

"My goodness, how things have changed! I didn't think anyone from my village would ever entertain the notion of becoming an Irish citizen.

"But yes, I got an Irish passport for myself and my son."

Protestants becoming more comfortable with their sense of Irish identity is one of the positive aspects of the last twenty-five years of peace.

Which is not to say that Glenn Chestnutt necessarily supports a united Ireland because he now has an Irish passport, or the fact that Jen Carswell takes her daughter to Irish dancing classes shows she's determined to end partition.[71]

We don't know if Eamon Eastwood's friend in Dungannon – the Protestant community worker who gets help from Sinn Fein – agrees with that party on the pressing need for Irish unity.

For all we know, the Protestant band members that Jo Gamage saw playing at the St Patrick's Day parade in Downpatrick might just have come along for the craic.

But all these little gestures suggest a society becoming more comfortable in its own skin.

Without the daily violence and the constant vigilance it demanded, people have the room to re-evaluate their worldview, if they wish.

But still, in the main, having spoken to the people quoted in this chapter who grew up in the Troubles and left after the peace was secured, it's impossible to look back on twenty-five years of peace and not think what might have been.

What should have been.

It's now more than a quarter of a century since that night at Aldens, that drive up to Stormont to catch a glimpse of what I thought was the demise of the DUP.

But they, alongside Sinn Fein, have dominated the politics of Northern Ireland in the years since the agreement.

They set up the system which gives each of them a veto over the formation of any government, despite neither party getting more than thirty per cent of the vote.

Political dysfunction, institutionalised division and economic decline have followed, as night follows day.

---

[71] You can find out what Glenn and Jen – and everyone else I interviewed – thinks about a united Ireland in the final chapter. But please don't skip ahead. I have loads more interesting emigrants I'd like to introduce you to first.

And all of these structural failings encourage the young people of Northern Ireland to head for the ports and airports.

Everyone I spoke to in this chapter grew up in the Troubles, as I did. And, like me, they all left after the conflict ended.

We all experienced Northern Ireland at its worst, but found that the improved version was not enough to convince us to stay.

But the generation who came after us who, thank God, only know about the Troubles from their parents' stories, are equally likely to leave.

Why has Northern Ireland not built a better society for its ceasefire babies?

GENERATION BETRAYED

"There was one school year we buried five of our mates."

I hadn't met Alana Cahoon before we speak on the phone, but I had made assumptions about her.

I found her through an interview she gave a few years earlier for the Financial Times. Before we spoke I listened to her soft Portadown accent on a podcast. Then I noticed that she was a member of the Ulster Unionist Party.

Along with the SDLP, they had dominated Northern Irish politics during the Troubles. And, like the SDLP, they were sidelined after the conflict ended in part because they were too middle-class.

Putting these snippets of information together, I assumed that Alana had a similarly comfortable upbringing to my own.

But when I start the interview by asking her what she's studying in Glasgow, I realise instantly that I've got the twenty-one-year-old totally wrong:

"Oh well that's the thing, Barry, I've dropped out of uni. I had been studying politics and economics at Strathclyde.

"In my first year I got a government grant and a bursary because I'm the first person in my family to ever go to university. But those payments stopped in second year and I hadn't been made aware that they were going to stop.

"I found out in September that I was going to get £1,200 and then nothing until January. The average rent here is £500 to £600 a month. I asked if I could have a wee bit of help, but they said I couldn't because I was working, so I did have money coming in.

"I needed to prove to them that I was broke. I tried to keep going, but I was working 30 hours a week as well as studying so I dropped out in November 2023.

"It's gutting because I'm passionate about politics and I was enjoying my degree, but I just couldn't afford to do it anymore.

"It was embarrassing to tell people here what had happened. So many of the people I know here are well-off. Some of them are getting £400 a month from their parents. My mother would send me fifty quid every now and again."

Alana explained that she's determined to get back to university as an adopted Scot:

"The Scottish grant is £500 a month minimum. I was on the Northern Ireland maximum of £300 in second year, so I had to drop out. You have to have lived in Scotland for three years before you're eligible for the Scottish grant, so I'm going to work until I've lived here for three years and then I'm going to apply for the funding and go back to uni.

"I was working in a hotel bar, now I'm working in a cocktail bar. I'm still living with a friend of mine from uni. It's a tenement flat about 20 minutes from the city centre – one of those places with lovely high ceilings, but it gets freezing in winter."

Alana's childhood in post-agreement Northern Ireland was far tougher than mine:

"There was one school year we buried five of our mates. Road accidents. Drugs. Suicide.

"I went home for a funeral during first year at uni. When I came back here my friends asked me 'was that your first funeral?' I said 'No, it's the sixth or seventh I've been to for someone of my age.'

"I know a couple of lads from Northern Ireland over here and they said the same. There's lots of drugs in Portadown, lots of ecstasy.

"I remember I got a job in a bar in Portadown. On my first night working there, there was a guy killed. It was a one-punch situation. It was shocking but at the same time, it was just something that happened. There's so much tragedy that goes on 24-7.

"But I had a happy family life. I was one of the very few people that had two parents who were still married. I was the only one in my friendship group."

When she tells me why she chose Scotland over Belfast, I feel seen. As I suspect would my old school friends turned student flatmates, Andy, Ian and Malcy:

"I didn't even apply for Queen's or Ulster University. There's all that stuff about Queen's being a cold house for unionists but it wasn't so much that.

"I wanted to meet new people. The people I know who went to Queen's are living in houses with the people they went to primary school with. It's a small-town mentality.

"I chose Glasgow because I'd been here a few times on the ferry. I didn't get a chance to visit the uni or the halls because of Covid. I moved here completely blind."

Despite her financial struggles, Alana seems determined to make a new life in a functioning Scotland, rather than her dysfunctional homeland:

"Would I move back to Northern Ireland? Never. There was a lot of death around me in Portadown. Everyone I know from back home is either addicted to drugs or has left.

"What am I going to do if I go home? Sit in the house all day and not know anyone.

"I've met so many people over here through work. I have more of a community in Glasgow after two years than I had in 19 years in Portadown.

"I've a small family – Mum, Dad, my sister and Granny – that's it. My mum wants me to come back but she knows there's no incentive for me to come back."

We talk during one of the Stormont Executive's lengthy down-times. There is much wrangling between the political parties about how to dress up the Brexit trading arrangements in a suitably acceptable way to the DUP so that they bring the ball back out and let everyone play.

While these talks go on there are no locally elected politicians working as ministers, striving to improve the life chances of young people like Alana.

She sees the contrast with the SNP-led Scottish Government. Of course, that administration is sometimes a long way south of perfect, but Scottish ministers do actually have to govern:

"Everyone in Scotland who's under-twenty-two gets free bus travel, so it doesn't matter that I live outside the city centre. Why don't we have that back home?

"Scottish people are so much more open about things like mental health. We're quite repressed, we just deal with our own problems.

"I'm still active in the UUP from afar. I had a girl contact me recently because she wanted to talk to me for her PhD. She said, 'I can't find young women to talk to me about unionism.' There isn't a lot of young women in unionism. I feel a wee bit out of the loop, but I try to read as much as I can.

"I feel slightly optimistic about Northern Ireland but I need to see the executive last, because a broken executive is all I've known for how many years."

Alana would have every right to be bear a grudge against a society which gave her so little, which forced her to grow up so quickly.

But, unlike most of us from Northern Ireland, she seems to have been near the back of the queue when God was handing out the bitterness:

"I don't miss Northern Ireland but every time I hear the accent my ears prick up. I do try to be friendly with them.

"I think we all have a similar personality in a weird way, we're quite laid-back. We all had an upbringing that was different to people over here.

"It's nice to have people around you who understand the things you've been through. I remember watching Blue Lights[72] with my friend from Edinburgh and she was like 'surely this is from years ago' but I told her it wasn't. I mean, it's fictionalised but it's based on reality.

"I used to live with a girl from Letterkenny, a Catholic guy from Coleraine and an English girl. She didn't understand that we had different flags.

"I still refer to Northern Ireland as 'home' when I'm here in Glasgow. But when I'm in Northern Ireland I'd say, 'I'm going home tomorrow' and it upsets people.

"I have two homes. Northern Ireland will always be home but I'm building a new home for myself here."

And then we say goodbye. I'm angry that Alana is having to run so hard to get the things in life that are a gentle walk for many people, myself included.

But I'm also struck by her positivity and resilience. She'll get to where she wants to go.

And Northern Ireland – stoic, stubborn Northern Ireland – put her on the path to success. But it also repelled her.

Alana grew up in an entirely peaceful Northern Ireland, too young to remember any part of the Troubles.

But, as we saw in the last chapter, she also came of age in a dysfunctional sectarian society.

Before hearing from other people who grew up in post-agreement Northern Ireland, it's worth taking a moment to consider why the last decade has been so frustrating.

As explained earlier, after the Good Friday Agreement came the St Andrew's Agreement.

---

[72] The excellent BBC drama set in a contemporary police station in Belfast.

But the governmental structure was becoming so moribund that the Northern Irish parties sat down once again in 2020 to reach the New Decade New Approach (NDNA) compromise – effectively Good Friday 3.0.

It was an attempt by all parties and the two governments to restore Stormont on a more stable footing after Sinn Fein collapsed the executive in 2017.

The New Approach lasted two years into the New Decade before it tumbled over again, the DUP the party to pull the plug this time.

Looking back now at the priorities spelt out in NDNA, you see hints that Northern Ireland's high emigration rate is a problem, but without a specific acknowledgement:

Investing for the future to ensure Northern Ireland is equipped to harness opportunities and drive sustainable productivity, including opportunities for future trade as we leave the EU. The economic context has changed considerably in the past three years. A top priority of the Executive will be to develop a regionally balanced economy with opportunities for all. [73]

The other part of the NDNA which could help persuade young people to stay in Northern Ireland is its commitment to address the why-is-nobody-shocked-by-this-anymore issue that Northern Ireland's second city, Derry, still doesn't have a university.

The unionist-dominated Stormont government infamously snubbed the mainly Catholic city in the 1960s, deciding that Northern Ireland's second seat of higher education should be established in mostly Protestant Coleraine, despite the town having only a quarter of Derry's population.

Sixty years on, the University of Ulster is now Ulster University but it is still headquartered in Coleraine.

---

[73] New Decade, New Approach, HM Government, p8

However, a commitment to expand the university's campus in Derry does feature in NDNA:

The Executive will bring forward proposals for the development and expansion of the UU campus at Magee College, including the necessary increase in maximum student numbers to realise the 10,000-student campus target and a Graduate Entry Medical School. [74]

A fine ambition, but one that has yet to be realised. In fact, since the NDNA was signed in 2020, the number of students at Magee has fallen.[75]

While there's no explicit acknowledgement in the NDNA that thousands of Northern Ireland's young people are fleeing the economic basket-case that their home has become, there is plenty of attention paid to the pressing issue of language in one of the most solidly monoglot parts of Europe.

Seven pages of the 62-page document are dedicated to outlining how the new Stormont government will ensure "rights, language and identity."

This includes creating an Irish Language Commissioner, to protect the rights of people who speak Irish (all of whom also speak English fluently).

While the focus on the importance of Irish seems odd, given Northern Ireland's more pressing problems, Irish is at least a language.

The same can't be said of Ulster-Scots.

Realising that the Irish language generated funding and esteem for nationalism, some unionists decided a few decades ago that they needed a language too. And so Ulster-Scots was born.

---

[74] New Decade, New Approach, HM Government, p40

[75] https://www.belfasttelegraph.co.uk/news/education/student-numbers-drop-at-magee-despite-countless-commitments-to-expand/41307118.html

As the NDNA gives Irish its own commissioner, of course Ulster-Scots must have one too, working closely with the "Boord o Ulstèr-Scotch" on the best way to promote a language which has no native speakers.

People from Northern Ireland do indeed speak a distinct dialect of English whose relation to Scottish English is obvious to even a casual listener – we sometimes affirm with "aye" rather than "yes" and we've been known to describe something small as "wee."[76]

The North of Ireland has been intertwined with the West of Scotland since long before the Plantation, indeed since long before Christianity.

That history is obvious every time a Northern Irish person opens their mouth. During my six years working at the Huddersfield Examiner, people returning my calls referred to me as "that Scottish reporter" more times than I can recall.

I was always amused, but never offended, because there's nothing wrong with being Scottish and centuries ago my family were Caledonian.

Perhaps they spoke a little like me.

In my entirely biased opinion, people from Northern Ireland speak one of the most beautiful versions of English in the world.

But the beauty of Ulster English is not the fleeting, vulnerable beauty of a butterfly.

Rather it's the strong, confident beauty of a tiger.

Ulster English will continue to thrive, to evolve, to delight and to confuse without any taxpayers' money.

It needs no boord to protect it.

---

[76] In fact people from Northern Ireland often use the word "wee" when it doesn't seem to denote smallness.

For instance, a shop worker, having taken your money, will often ask: "Would you like a wee receipt?" Don't be fooled, intrepid visitor, the receipt you're being offered is a normal-sized one.

After New Decade New Approach's long sermon on the importance of Ulster-Scots comes a brief nod to the importance of improving infrastructure, including a fleeting mention of the A5.[77]

This is the road that connects Northern Ireland's second biggest city, Derry, to the island's capital through the border town of Aughnacloy.

Despite linking two of Ireland's major conurbations, much of the Northern section of the route is single lane, a factor in some of the crashes which have taken fifty-seven lives on the road since 2006.

For economic and safety grounds, any functioning government would prioritise upgrading the road to a dual carriageway – and indeed such a plan was announced way back in 2007.

But, at the time of writing, the A5 upgrade remains in limbo. The UK taxpayer has spent £110 million preparing for an improvement that may never happen.[78] Shovels are not yet in the ground and may never be.

Since 2007, there have been interminable delays exacerbated by the fact that, for much of that time, there's been no functioning executive.

How many of those fifty-seven people who died on the A5 would be alive today if Northern Ireland had a healthier political system?

It's impossible to come up with a precise number, but it also seems fair to assume that, whatever the figure is, it wouldn't be zero.

Whenever I hear coverage of more A5 delays, I can't help thinking back to my first ever visit to Galway, more than ten years ago.

Arriving at Dublin port, our sat nav (it was the early Teenies) confidently informed us that the journey right

[77] New Decade, New Approach, HM Government, p52

[78] https://www.bbc.co.uk/news/articles/cp333p76l2go

across the middle of Ireland from east to west would take three hours.

Just two hours later Jenny and I were at the B&B. The ageing technology of our sat nav had not kept up with the Republic's improving infrastructure – in this case, the fact that Dublin and Galway were now linked by a motorway, one of many which the Southern government built in the Noughties.

"Oh, it's great, isn't it?" remarked the B&B owner when I explained why we had arrived sooner than expected.

Over in New Zealand, Rory Hughes has endured a more stressful journey home to speak to me.

We've had to push our Zoom back by half an hour because his bus journey home from work took much longer than usual:

"We live in this wee place called Tauranga. There's only one arterial road and it was closed for roadworks so we had to go the long way round. It's usually a fifteen-minute ride but it took forty-five minutes. Even the Kiwis were getting mildly annoyed."

Rory is a little older than Alana and grew up in less stressful circumstances. But as our conversation goes on he reveals that he is – he thinks – paying a physical cost for a conflict he never experienced:

"I was born in 1996 so that makes me a ceasefire baby, doesn't it? I grew up in leafy south Belfast. Mum and Dad were working class but we grew up comfortably middle class.

"I grew up off the Ormeau Road, have you seen it now? It's been so gentrified, the number of cafes is ridiculous."

Rory's school life was marked by the peculiar geography of south Belfast, in between Catholic and Protestant, working class and middle class:

"I went to primary school two streets away at Holy Rosary. My childhood was grand, no big political moments, but our primary school was petrol bombed twice.

"To be fair, I think the second time was an accident, I think they tried to put the petrol bomb through someone's letterbox but couldn't get it in so they just threw it into the school instead.

"It burnt down my classroom that I was about to go into for P4, so we were in one of those mobiles for two or three months. The novelty of that wore off when it got cold.

"The kids in school were more deprived than we were. I remember in P6 the teacher got me to help some of the other children to learn to read. That was very weird.

"Then I went to Aquianas Grammar School on the Ravenhill Road. And that was the opposite, it was a proper middle-class school, you know, other kids going on ski holidays and we couldn't afford to go on ski holidays.

"Aquianas was grand, no petrol bombs, just a load of awkward kids.

"I used to play football when I was twelve or thirteen and you'd go into these estates. You know the ones, flags on all the lampposts and it looks like a Vinnie Jones movie."

Unlike Alana, Rory chose to stay in Northern Ireland for university – but the appeal of post-agreement Belfast eventually wore thin:

"After school I went to Queen's studying history and social anthropology. It's a way to spend three years learning how to write essays and argue with people.

"I know Queen's is only round the corner from where I grew up, but it just seemed like the best option. What was the Lib Dem leader called? Nick Clegg, aye. He had said he was going to scrap tuition fees and then he tripled them in England.

"So I think it was more than 8K over there, or £3,300 a year at Queen's.

"After graduating I worked at PWC in Belfast for nine months, then I did a master's in media and broadcast production at Queen's.

"Then I went to Glasgow, it's six years ago now. Glasgow is like Belfast but bigger, you know, the same friendly atmosphere where people will stop in the street and chat to you.

"My partner is a doctor and we wanted to go somewhere else and experience new things. I felt like I'd done Belfast, there's not a lot of things to do there. We moved to New Zealand a year ago.

"You know how New Zealand is two islands? Well Tauranga is on the right-hand side of the top island. It's not a big city, more like Lisburn than Belfast."

Having left Glasgow, the city that most closely resembles Belfast, Rory finds it a struggle to explain a homeland about which he feels ambivalent:

"When I meet Kiwis, I try to explain that I'm Northern Irish by saying that I'm Liam Neeson Irish, rather than Cillian Murphy Irish and they get it.

"I don't think we've met anyone else from Northern Ireland, but we've met people from the South – Cork, Kerry, Sligo. Aye, they joke about us being British or about us not being Irish enough but that gets my hackles up.

"I suppose I would say I'm Irish-leaning Northern Irish. It comes and goes. I'd like to call myself Northern Irish but what is there to be proud of from Northern Ireland? Rory McIlroy maybe, but that's it."

For Rory's generation, the Troubles are something that their parents lived through. But the conflict has left its mark on him:

"I remember being aware of the Troubles when I was a child. My dad told me about going to school. He grew up in south Belfast but he went to that school in west Belfast, the one with the green and gold badge. St Mary's I think.

"Anyway, first day of school, he got his head kicked in on the bus because it was obvious he was a Catholic. The rest of the time, he went to school on the bus with his tie in his pocket and his blazer in his bag, looking like the youngest office worker in Belfast.

"I have ulcerative colitis – it's a bit like IBS. You have to take mediation for it, I have to pay for it here in New Zealand, but back home we've got the NHS so we don't have to pay, which is great.

"Anyway, no, there is a point to this, Barry. My dad has ulcerative colitis and so do I and so does my brother. But there's no other trace of it in the family. His brother left Belfast when he was quite young and doesn't have ulcerative colitis.

"I think it's a manifestation of the trauma from the Troubles, all that unprocessed stress. I think he's passed that on to me and my brother.

"But you don't know, you couldn't prove it.

"When we go to a bar or a café, I always let him sit down first, he's only comfortable if he can see the door.

"My dad's a sixty-five-year-old man from Belfast, so who knows what's going on in his head? But that's his belief."

Rory's reluctance to return to Belfast, to start a family there, is strengthened by the fact that his wife does not fit into the binary identities that define Northern Irish life:

"We're moving back to the UK in the summer, maybe spend three weeks seeing our families and then settle back in Scotland.

"Why not move back to Northern Ireland? Lots of reasons really. I mean maybe if we have kids it would appeal, you know, having all the family there for childcare.

"But for now, it doesn't appeal. My partner's of Indian heritage, she moved to Antrim when she was eight. When we walk down the street in Belfast, she's usually the only brown person, but that's not the case in Glasgow.

"If we have kids, they'd be mixed race so they'd face difficulties in Northern Ireland.[79]

"And there's other things. My best friend is gay and he told me how it works if he meets someone in a bar in the Gay Quarter in Belfast.

"They go out of the bar holding hands, but as they carry on walking and they get closer to the city hall, they feel like they have to let go of each other's hands and walk a bit apart.

"And there's work too. I work in the media so it's better to work anywhere other than Northern Ireland. I don't want to be a producer on the Stephen Nolan Show.

"And my fiancé wants to be a psych doctor so you need to be in a big city for that."

But even if he never returns permanently, Rory retains an affection for home:

"The way we swear makes me homesick, I liked the way you were using swear words just there, Barry.

"And the black sense of humour. I make jokes about anything because my mum and dad always make jokes about anything.

"And the pubs, I miss the pubs. In New Zealand it's all 'come on in, it's quiz night' or 'wings for twenty dollars tonight' you know all commercial.

"But pubs in Northern Ireland are third places. You've got home and work and then you need a third place, somewhere where you go and take things slower. Pubs in Northern Ireland are just places to go to unwind.

"And I miss the bread. The bread here is awful.

"But there's things I don't miss. Like vowels. The way we use vowels is terrible, it's like they're bumps in the road.

---

[79] Some other emigrants I spoke to noted, with pleasure, that Northern Ireland is becoming more ethnically diverse. But it's growth from a very low base. The 2021 census found that 96.5% of the Northern Irish population was white. In England and Wales the figure was 82%.

"I watched Derry Girls the other day and I had a wee cry, but I don't really feel homesick for Northern Ireland. It's only my family that I miss."

Unprompted by me, several of the people I interview bring up the name Matthew O'Toole as one of the few politicians in Northern Ireland who are concerned about the high emigration rate.

Perhaps his concern comes from knowing he is part of a small group of people – those who left Northern Ireland and came back.

He grew up in south Down during the final years of the Troubles. Matthew's family ran the Heights Bar in Loughinisland, scene of the final sectarian massacre of the conflict – though, at the time, none of us knew that it would be the last.

He left Northern Ireland for London where he rose quickly within the civil service before returning to Belfast. His ascent there has been similarly swift, co-opted by the SDLP into their Assembly seat for South Belfast and becoming leader of the opposition just three years later.

We talk on a Friday morning. I try to separate my book interviews from my day job as much as possible. But when a senior politician offers to give you forty minutes of their time, you don't haggle over the timings.

So, as Matthew drives to work in Stormont, I slope away from my desk and take a seat in the BBC Green Room where I once met Julian Clary.[80]

Matthew agrees that the main problem for Northern Irish society is that he – as someone who left and came back – is the exception. People like Alana and Rory, who emigrated with no desire to return, are the rule:

"There are definite reasons for leaving and they align with the different problems they cause. The Republic has

[80] He was very civil, not always the case when a celebrity has to make small talk with a producer.

had periods of high emigration, so it's part of a general Irish problem.

"But the problem in Northern Ireland is that a large number of school leavers and graduates leave and they don't come back."

The fact that so many graduates don't return to Northern Ireland, locks the place into a self-perpetuating loop of economic decline.

Northern Ireland's schools are often excellent, its culture stresses the importance of education. It has the most numerate and literate primary school children in the English-speaking world. But 20 years later, many of these bright young people are lost:

"The economic issue this causes is that it reduces the proportion of graduates and apprentices that this place would otherwise have.

"We export, in inverted commas, a university-worth of young people at the start of each academic year. A very high proportion of these people never come back, or only come back much later in life because of family circumstances, rather than for economic reasons.

"This reinforces the low productivity in Northern Ireland, which is already lower than the UK average and way, way, way behind the South. If you're exporting a significant proportion of graduates they will create value and economic activity elsewhere."

But Matthew agrees that Northern Ireland's anaemic economy is only one of the factors pushing the post-ceasefire generation to the airports and ferry terminals:

"Young people are frustrated at the dysfunction at Stormont and continuing sectarianism. It's an incentive to leave, that's my personal experience from other Northern Irish people I knew when I lived in London.

"Even if these problems didn't feature in their thoughts when they decided to leave, after they leave they crystalise. When they're living in Manchester, or Leeds, or London, they think: 'There isn't this focus on identity. No-one cares where I went to school, it doesn't matter.'

"Fewer curious young people means fewer people to challenge the tribalism of Northern Irish politics."

When Matthew brings up transgenerational trauma, I'm surprised by the example he uses:

"There's the unresolved trauma around the Troubles. I left twenty years ago, but it wasn't like I was living in New Zealand, I would come back over the summer, I'd be working in pubs.

"What struck me when I came back was that there was still a significant amount of division in this society, even long after the Troubles ended.

"There are definitely young people who weren't even born when the Good Friday Agreement was signed who are carrying the trauma of the Troubles from their parents and grandparents.

"It comes up a lot – their concept of themselves is that they come from traumatised communities and that's very striking after twenty years.

"When you look at young people in Belfast, Carrick and Larne burning buses over the protocol, it's hard to believe that thirteen- to-fifteen-year-olds could be so angry about custom movements and additional health rules that now apply at Larne port. I think it's a form of trauma.

"And the same up in Creggan,[81] people are cosplaying as dissidents and bringing misery to the people there. Other people look at that and they want to leave."

Matthew only became leader of the opposition because the voters decided that that is where they would like his party to be – the twelve seats they had in the previous assembly was enough to secure one Executive post.

The eight seats they managed to hold on to in the 2022 election entitles them to nowt.

---

[81] An estate in Derry where dissident republicans are particularly prominent.

Matthew believes that the larger parties – who the electorate have trusted with power – are unconcerned about Northern Ireland's high emigration:

"I don't think Sinn Fein or the DUP particularly want to talk about emigration. Sinn Fein want to talk about emigration from the Republic – Mary Lou McDonald goes to Australia and says, 'we want you to come back' – but they don't talk about emigration from the North.

"One of the things keeping people away is an exhaustion with tribal politics."

Matthew believes that the path to reversing the emigration rate runs to Northern Ireland's two cities:

"We need a structural change in Northern Ireland so it isn't a place that ambitious people want to leave. We need to create more university places, how we pay for that is an issue because I don't want to jack up fees.

"And there's a big issue in Derry, which for more than sixty years has had a very legitimate complaint that it doesn't have a university. It's the only city of its size in the UK and Ireland that doesn't have a university. People may well want to stay here for family or financial reasons but they end up going to uni in Southampton or wherever because there's no place for them here.

"People want to live in cities so we need to focus on making Belfast the most exciting medium-sized city it can be. We need to rebuild Belfast's relationship with Dublin. Dublin is overheated, it's unfeasible for many people in their twenties, thirties, forties to live there.

"How can Belfast absorb some of those people and develop its own buzz? We need to make much better use of the vacant premises in the city centre to make Belfast a much more attractive place for people to want to stay in after they graduate.

"It's got a strong cultural scene at the moment but we need to get people living in the centre of the city."

Matthew admits that the agreement – his party's crowning achievement – has been implemented in a way that only encourages emigration:

"I think our public life needs to have a purpose beyond simply managing division. That doesn't mean we shouldn't have a view of the constitutional future, but it does mean we need a shared sense of overcoming division.

"The First Minister and Deputy First Minister have set a positive tone at the minute. Public life here can be so negative and so defined by division that it puts young people off.

"It's just about how we carve up the post-Good Friday Agreement pie. Being a civil servant in London was a prestigious job, but in Northern Ireland the civil service is seen as stagnant and ageing – which it is, to be honest.

"One of the problems of the post-Good Friday Agreement is that people have misunderstood that the aim was to get people working together so that, what Mark Durkan[82] calls 'the ugly scaffolding of unionism and nationalism' will fall away."

Matthew believes integrated education can help – but he goes on to explain that he struggles to decide how to explain the conflict to his young children:

"Our first son was born in England and we've had another son since we moved back and they go to an integrated school. Most schools in south Belfast are mixed whether or not they're integrated.

"The Executive's just been cutting funding to integrated schools. Integration in education needs to be matched by a much broader sense of sharing.

"I still think about our sons – do I want them to be as defined by their surname as I was? I haven't yet started talking to them about this stuff."

---

[82] Leader of the SDLP from 2001-10 and one of the key architects of the Good Friday Agreement.

Matthew tries to end our interview on a positive note – but the frustrations of his job won't quite let him:

"The worst thing about this place is the politics. There are great upsides to living here, it's better than it was in the Nineties or Noughties, there definitely has been progress.

"But when people move away they become aware of how abnormal this society is.

"I remember in the Assembly, Sinn Fein put down an amendment about increasing support for 'upland' farmers. Then the DUP said we needed more support for 'lowland' farmers.

"Because I'd been away, it took me a while to twig what was going on. It's Protestant farmers on the lush pasture land with their cattle and Catholic farmers in the uplands with their sheep.

"There was an additional layer to the debate that wasn't about farming. It's only when you've been away that you realise how strange it is."

Marc Strathie shares Matthew's cautious optimism that Northern Ireland's high emigration rate can be reduced.

As Senior Policy Advisor for Devolved Nations at the Institute of Directors (IOD) he understands how the high number of young people leaving has become a vicious circle:

"Northern Ireland is the least productive part of the UK and that has a massive impact. It leads to economic inactivity, of which Northern Ireland is also the worst in the UK.

"The workforce is ageing and people are not moving to Northern Ireland from other parts of the UK or from the EU. The birthrate is stagnant as well, so you've got this kind of perfect storm.

"We speak to people who were born in Northern Ireland but now live elsewhere to try to get them to move back, to invest. We know there are people from Northern

Ireland living in the US, in Australia who want to come back.

"But the three fundamentals we need to get right are education, housing and childcare.

"A few years ago we had a cyber-security company who were very interested in investing in Belfast. But when they looked at it in detail, they found that the skilled workforce, the infrastructure, it just wasn't there. So they invested in Dublin instead. It's a struggle to get investment."

Marc hopes that the restored executive can put right some of the damage to Northern Ireland's reputation during the two long periods of no government:

"The lack of a government was a really big problem for both business and society. There was no policy discussion, no fresh insights, it was a real period of stagnation. No-one wanted to invest.

"Stability is key for investors. The period without a government eroded trust in the business community because there wasn't a partnership approach.

"Who would want to invest in a place that had no functioning government that you can talk to about roads, about agriculture?

"Hopefully now that's changing – Conor Murphy[83] launched our report earlier this year. We've had more engagement in the last few months than we had in the previous three years.

But Marc warns that Northern Ireland's brain drain could get dramatically worse in the coming years:

"At present, 5,000 young people aged sixteen to twenty-four leave Northern Ireland every year – most of them to go to university elsewhere. But by the end of the decade we're expecting this to double to 10,000. The number of courses being offered at UU and QUB is being cut and this will have a serious impact.

---

[83] Sinn Fein's Economy Minister in the current Executive.

"The opportunities in higher education are shrinking and the other routes to form a business, or to get a vocation haven't arrived. There has to be a greater emphasis on retaining people, on Northern Ireland being a good place to do business.

"There's an opportunity with the new Labour government. They want to reset relations with the EU and Northern Ireland can be a bridge between the UK and the EU because it has a foot in both camps.

"We feel that the schools system is pretty disjointed and that hampers business growth. Young people come out of higher education unprepared for what it means to work in business in Northern Ireland.

"But we also need more vocational training and more entrepreneurial routes so that young people aren't just pushed towards higher education.

"Businesses need to take a more active role in schools, we want teachers to come and spend some time with businesses and then take what they've learnt back to their schools, work it into the curriculum."

Marc goes on to use two examples of the demands on government funding to demonstrate the difficulty of managing a deeply divided society:

"If the UK government bails out Harland and Wolff, that will annoy one section of the community. And if money is poured into Casement Park, that will annoy another section of the community. That's the kind of thing that holds back investment."

Harland and Wolff, the shipyard where the Titanic was built, is totemic to Belfast Protestants, a central part of our identity.

It's currently looking for government support to refinance £200m worth of loans. Its collapse would be a moment of real sadness for most Protestants.

For many Catholics – whose ancestors were either excluded from or discriminated against within Harland

and Wolff's walls – the shipbuilder's demise would be met rather differently.

Casement Park in west Belfast was for many years the home of County Antrim's GAA teams. It closed in 2013 and has become derelict.

But, in what one might call an ambitious move, an unbuilt new Casement was selected as Belfast's venue for the 2028 European Championships, which will be hosted by Northern Ireland, the Republic of Ireland, England, Wales and Scotland.

All that was needed was for the UK government to commit the lion's share of the £400 million needed to build a new Casement Park big enough to host five matches – Northern Ireland's national football stadium at Windsor Park being too small for UEFA's standards.

Nationalist politicians thought this money should be committed. Unionist politicians felt it shouldn't.

Shortly after Marc and I spoke, a new Labour government was elected and quickly decided that the funding would not be forthcoming.

While the rest of these islands will welcome European football fans in the summer of 2028, Northern Ireland will miss out.

No European Championship matches at the Catholic stadium. And none at the Protestant stadium either.

Perfect post-agreement parity of esteem.

When I speak to Tim Wilson, his mind is on rugby rather than football though, being the open-minded type, I try not to hold this against him.

It's Saturday afternoon, and he's just about to sit down with his family to watch Ireland win a second Six Nations championship in a row.

But soon enough in our conversation, he explains to me that the ugly scaffolding of unionism and nationalism is encouraging him to leave Northern Ireland for a second time:

"In 2015 our daughter was born and we wanted to be closer to one set of grandparents for her sake.

"As Corina's from New Zealand, it just seemed to make more sense to move back to Northern Ireland. I got a job at a company called PRM in Lisburn and we moved to a wee village called Glenavy in 2016.

"After fifteen years away,[84] it wasn't the differences that I noticed, it was the lack of progress. You turn on the radio and they're arguing about the same old stuff. There's no sense of moving on, of being open-minded, there's so many groups with their head in the sand.

"I used to come over for a week here and there to go to the NW200, ride on my motorbike. Because I was only over for a few days, the political situation didn't bother me that much.

"But now that I live here again, I've realised that the whole place is stuck in a rut. It grinds you down, you get tired of if after a while. There's so much effort concentrating on the past."

Tim makes an oblique reference to the Casement Park row as he pours out his frustration at Northern Ireland's benign apartheid:

"It's that whole attitude 'well the GAA are getting money for something, so we need an awful lot of money for something that's ours.'

"When the census came round a few years ago someone I know, who I respect a lot, said to me: 'Make sure you tick

---

[84] I know what you're thinking: "How can someone who left Northern Ireland as an adult well over 15 years ago possibly count as a ceasefire baby?" Tim is not a young emigrant – in fact he's even older than me. But, as you'll see, as someone who's returned to Northern Ireland, Tim's frustrations are frustrations with post-agreement Northern Ireland. The things that are driving him away are the same things that are forcing younger people out the door.

Ulster-Scots on the form to look after our side and get money for us.'

"I don't speak Ulster-Scots. The person who urged me to do that, they wouldn't know the difference between Ulster-Scots and Klingon. There's just too much of that 'them and us' mentality.

"When I lived in England, Northern Ireland was the centre of the universe. It was home – the accent, the food, the scenery, the humour. I would always be telling English people 'oh, Northern Ireland's better.'

"But when I moved back here the rose-tinted glasses came off. A lot of my friends have moved on, I've got a good friend in England, another one in Scotland. All I have here now is my parents in Belfast and some work acquaintances. Northern Ireland is part of me but I won't let it define who I am. We've got options now."

Unlike other emigrants, Tim doesn't see Northern Ireland's sectarian education system as a reason to leave. In fact, despite growing up in an overwhelmingly Protestant part of Belfast, he welcomes living in a much more religiously mixed part of rural County Antrim:

"Our kids go to a very good primary school, and it's a Catholic school. They put education first and nothing else really matters. We're Christians and there are one or two things about the school I wouldn't agree with, but mainly it's no bother."

Tim's second emigration appears more political than his first, which was driven by economics:

"I was born in Belfast and brought up in Braniel until I was eleven, then we moved to the Old Holywood Road. I went to Inst, came out of there in 1990 and then I went to Jordanstown to do a degree in transport and logistics.

"I ended up working for a warehousing and transport company called TDG. I ended up working in sites all over the UK from Cumbernauld to Swindon. I bought a house in Northampton and then I met Corina and we got married in

2014. I was managing up to 900 staff, so it was firefighting all the time.

"Shifts that were supposed to be eight or nine hours ended up being twelve to fourteen hours because you didn't want to leave your colleague who was picking up from you in the poop."

Feelings of being an outsider appeared only fleetingly for Tim:

"In England you would get the odd joke about the stupid Irish but you just end up being another part of the team. But your accent makes you stand out.

"When I lived in England, a friend pointed out to me that when I sit down in a pub or a restaurant I would always sit facing the door so I could see who was coming in. I hadn't realised that I do that, I don't know why I do.

"Nobody ever told me to do that during the Troubles. There was one time when I sat with my back to the door on purpose to see what it felt like. It just didn't feel right...I don't know why."

Above all, Tim believes that his daughters will have a better life in New Zealand than Northern Ireland:

"In 18 months' time we'll be getting a one-way ticket to New Zealand. It's not a decision we've made overnight.

"The weather in Northern Ireland is shockingly shite[85]. We bought a couple of tins of fence paint last May. It said on the tin that when you apply the paint, you need two dry days. We weren't able to use the paint until the start of September.

"Our girls love being outdoors but it's as if the weather is keeping them prisoner. You wrap them up in more layers than an onion, then say, 'off you go, have fun' and five minutes later they want to come back inside.

"I've only done 1,000 miles on the motorbike in the last two years.

---

[85] It's just a beautiful alliteration, isn't it?

"This is the best time to go for the girls, before they go to secondary school and develop long-term friendships. They can adapt very quickly at the age they are. They have tonnes of cousins in New Zealand and they've never been there.

"I want to give them the option when they're older that they could live in Europe or New Zealand.

"Everyone will want to be their friends at school, they'll be a novelty, people will be asking them 'what's a dander?' We're learning Māori, we can count to ten and I know a few phrases now.

"The hard thing for me was telling my parents, it took me six months to do it, I mulled it over and over.

"Then one day I took them out for lunch, we had a very nice meal and then I said: 'Just so you know, in about two years we're going to move to New Zealand.'

"There was silence for about a minute and then my mum said: 'I hope you realise we'll miss you.' That was six months ago and they haven't mentioned it since. They haven't changed in terms of visiting more and I haven't brought it up.

"It's a mindset of people in Northern Ireland...it isn't healthy."

Like Tim, Annmarie McPolin has two young daughters. And like him, she thinks their future will be better in New Zealand than Northern Ireland.

As she explains her upbringing, she juggles her five-month-old on her knee while keeping a keen eye on what her two-year-old is up to across the room:

"I grew up in a village called Hilltown, which is near Newry. It was the nineties so you'd still have the usual patrols but it was a happy childhood.

"There was myself and my two brothers, one older, one younger and our grandparents lived nearby. At one point my parents bought a pub in Donegal so we lived there for a few months but then we moved back.

"I went up to university in Belfast to study quantity surveying. I'd be up there during the week and then come home at the weekend."

After three years at university, Annmarie was confronted by an age-old Northern Irish problem – an education system that far outstrips the economy into which its graduates emerge:

"I graduated in 2011, in the middle of the economic crash. I still remember what our professor said to us when we graduated: 'There's 120 of you in the class and there's four jobs available in the whole of Northern Ireland.'

"He felt bad for us because there was no hope for us to work in our chosen profession in our own country.

"So we scattered across the world. I emailed however many companies in Northern Ireland, offering to work for free. No-one even bothered replying. Eventually the old guys in these companies are going to retire and there'll be no-one coming through to replace them.

"I chose to go to New Zealand and I landed in Auckland just after the earthquakes. I spent two weeks there and I realised that it rained all the time.

"So I went down to Christchurch and I just fell in love with the place, everyone's so friendly, it's nice and spacious and you're so close to the outdoors.

"There was a great demand for quantity surveyors. You could pretty much go into a pub and have a pint and you'd end up with a job by the time you'd finished your drink.

"There was literally nothing to stay at home for, but I'm quite glad that the economic situation was not great because I always thought from a young age that I wanted to travel.

"I remember when I was 19, I was going out with a fella from Hilltown and he was building a house. He asked me 'where do you want me to put the front door' and I said 'why would I care?' and he said 'because it's where we're going to live'."

Annmarie struggles to reconcile her Irish identity with her strong desire not to return to the country that defines her:

"I don't think I'll go back, the lifestyle and the weather are good here. I used to go home about once every two years and I'd find that everyone feels so negative all the time.

"I ring my mum most days. I missed the funerals of both my grannies. That was hard, watching the ceremony on a webcam. When you emigrate, grief hits you differently. You're grieving for the time that you didn't spend with them before they died.

"I started working on a project for my daughters, I'm doing them a book on their mother's lineage. I think it's going to be weird for them being first generation, they're not going to feel Irish or Kiwi.

"Before the kids came along I wasn't as keen to mix with other Irish people in Christchurch. I wanted to meet people from other countries, not just stay with other Irish people.

"But after we had kids, that changed.

"Probably it's still home. Growing up in Hilltown, my family would be quite nationalist. But I remember thinking that our phone numbers were British and our postcodes were British.

"Being from Northern Ireland is quite a complex identity. From quite a young age, I felt like I wanted something different."

But despite her disappointment on her trips home, Annmarie echoes a common sentiment from emigrants I spoke to – that a childhood spent in Northern Ireland prepares you for whatever life might throw at you:

"I'm quite grateful for the environment that I grew up in because it did shape me. I think people from Ireland, from Scotland, we have a tenacity, a work ethic.

"I don't know why that's the case that we all work so hard, but we definitely do.

"I've noticed when I go home, sometimes you'll drive past this big new house, with a wee house, almost a shed next to it. And the shed is where the grandparents lived.

"That's where our work ethic comes from – our grandparents who were working just to survive. Irish people have always gone out in the world and we probably always will."

Louise McCloskey grew up in a similar background in the town of Dungiven in south Derry:

"I was born in 1988, the youngest of four girls. It was a traditional Irish background – Dad was a farmer and Mammy was a nurse before my sisters were born. A big Irish family – my dad's one of eight and my mammy's one of nine so I'd have more than 50 cousins all over the place.

"It was a happy childhood, you know, Gaelic games at the weekend and things like that. My sisters are quite a bit older than me – ten, nine and seven years – so I was very much the baby of the family.

"I suppose I have some traits of an only child, wanting to be in charge, always taking on the organisation of things."

Although she is too young to remember the period before the 1994 ceasefires, Louise has a vivid memory of the final – and worst – atrocity of the Troubles four years later:

"I can distinctly remember the Omagh bomb. There was a wee shop we'd always go into and I remember seeing the paper on the counter a few days after the bomb, with all the faces of the people who'd been killed, just so many faces.

"And the mother who was killed when she was pregnant, that stuck in my mind.

"I can remember the adults talking about the Good Friday Agreement and I remember some of the prisoners being released.

"But in my teenage years I wasn't political. One of my sisters works as a journalist at Stormont and she was horrified that me and my friends weren't interested in the politics of Northern Ireland. She thought we needed to know about our history but I always found it upsetting. Even now when you watch the news from Northern Ireland, it's depressing."

Like the other younger emigrants I speak to, coming of age in Northern Ireland's most hopeful era did not persuade Louise to stay:

"I went to the University of Ulster in 2006 to study accountancy and I had a really good time, you know, living in the Holylands.[86] Two of my sisters lived in Belfast by then – the one who worked at Stormont and another who worked as a radiographer at the Mater Hospital.

"I suppose it's because of them that I saw more of Belfast than I would've, we were always going to gigs and exhibitions. But I also knew that there were parts of Belfast that it wasn't safe to go to, both from a religious perspective but also from being female.

"After uni I was offered a job by a chartered accountancy firm in Coleraine. I'd wanted to leave but I felt guilty because I'd been offered this place when some of my other classmates hadn't, so I stayed in Northern Ireland for another two or three years.

"Then one of my sisters got married in 2012 and another got married the following year, so I thought I'd stay for the weddings but then I'd go.

"So that was me, off to Sydney for six months and then Melbourne. My partner – now my husband – he's from Dungiven too and we've lived here ever since. We have a wee boy who's going to be two on Wednesday."

Having become a mother, Louise is now thinking about how to explain her conflicted homeland to her son:

---

[86] An area near Queen's well-known for its raucous street parties.

"I've been watching the news from Palestine and thinking about how I would explain this to my son if he was old enough to understand. I would try to explain the context to him, that not everything is black and white.

"I still call Ireland home, people at work would comment on that. But I'm conscious that when my son gets older, I'll have to stop doing that because it's going to be strange for him. First-generation migrants like him face challenges around their identity.

"In my heart I'll still think of Ireland as home, but I probably will stop calling it that for his sake."

But, despite this, Louise seems comfortable being Irish in Australia:

"We live on the western side of Melbourne and most Irish people live on the eastern side but I'm involved with Irish associations.

"I went to a meeting of Mná le Chéile – it means Women Together – and I ended up joining the committee. It's really nice to be surrounded by Irish people, to have that feeling of community, especially since Covid. I still feel like I have a Northern Irish mentality.

"I tell you a thing that I think is Northern Irish is that I can be quite defensive. I get really frustrated if I think someone's misquoting me. We just say what we think, don't we? So, I don't like it when someone twists what I said.

"I've not been back since 2019, and my husband he hasn't been back since the year before. It's definitely hard to miss family occasions.

"My coping mechanism is to try to stay detached from it. But you know, I miss the little things maybe more than the big family landmarks.

"Popping round to your mate's house for a cup of tea after work, that sort of thing. I'm lucky so far in that I haven't had to deal with the death of anyone close to me yet since I moved here.

"But in the back of your mind, you know that it's going to happen."

Unlike some older emigrants, Louise has never experienced prejudice because of her Irishness:

"It's really nice to be living in a country where you're seen as the 'fun' immigrant. Because I'm white and I speak English? Not so much that, I think it's just that Australians love Irish people.

"When they hear your Irish accent, they think you're great craic and that you fit in well with their culture.

"But I know that other immigrants' experience can be very different so, that anti-immigrant rhetoric that you got around Brexit for example, that upsets me."

Louise is one of many emigrants I spoke to who brought up Brexit unprompted.

As things stand, the UK leaving the European Union has left Northern Ireland – which would rather have stayed in – more isolated than before.

But John Fitzgerald points out that, with the right Executive leadership, Brexit could give Northern Ireland the chance to reverse the drain of emigrants:

Students who graduate from Northern Ireland institutions are more likely to work in Northern Ireland than those who study abroad.

However, research by Pivotal shows that the factors causing so many Northern Ireland graduates to live in GB go beyond the issue of wage rates and standard of living, requiring a wider solution to the problems that Northern Ireland faces.

If policies were successful in attracting back graduates from GB to Northern Ireland, this would make Northern Ireland a much more attractive location for investment by foreign multinationals.

If the Brexit protocol provisions bedded down and were seen to be permanent, Belfast and Derry /

Londonderry would be in a position to compete for foreign investment with other cities on the island.[87]

As things stand though, Northern Ireland continues to lose young people, pulling it into a downward spiral, as those young people who remain feel lonely.[88]

It's something that Grace Farrell brings up when I speak to her in Chicago:

"In 2021 to 22 I was back in Northern Ireland. It was during the pandemic and I didn't leave the house much except to walk the dog.

"I would go to the pub once a week with my aunties, but there wouldn't be anyone else there under-forty. I'd Facetime my friends in Dublin and London and think that that was where I'd love to be.

"There were no new people to meet in Rostrevor, no new experiences to have. Even going out to have a coffee with someone, you'd need to find someone to give you a lift to the café."

As Grace talks to me about the frustrations she faced after returning home to County Down, I can't help noticing how curious her accent has become.

Her voice is like a calm American lake, until she gets to words like "now" when her Ulster vowels bubble to the surface.

Like Liam Devlin feeling out of place in Twinbrook, or Jo Gamage considering herself an outsider in Annacloy, Grace feels a sense of guilt at not fitting in among her large, loving family:

"I had a lovely childhood growing up in Rostrevor. It's a wee border village about twenty minutes from Newry. I

---

[87] p57, One Island, Two Economies, John Fitzgerald.

[88] There are parallels with the next chapter, which looks at the experience of gay people in Northern Ireland. The more gay people who emigrate, the harder it is to build a scene in Northern Ireland, thus making it more likely that those who are same-sex attracted will leave, sometimes more from boredom than because of prejudice.

have two siblings but a load of cousins – 50 in all. My family is very into the Irish language and singing in the Irish language.

"Growing up life was really nice, I'd say it was perfect.

"I was born in 1998, the year of the Good Friday Agreement and I know my parents would've struggled during the Troubles.

"Since I was ten, I wanted out of the North. I always felt very different.

"I didn't play football, I didn't have a lot of friends, I would spend a lot of time reading in my room. I would watch TV shows form England and the US and want to move there.

"There was nothing for me to do. I'd still say that now, there's nothing for me in Northern Ireland except my family."

Like many children who feel out of place, school for Grace was a trial rather than a refuge:

"I went to the Catholic girls' school – though I didn't know anyone at school who went to Mass. These days it's just something for older people, maybe you'd go to Mass the odd time just to have a pint with your mates afterwards.

"Sex education was up to each school and now, as I look back, I ended up in some unsafe situations because of my lack of sex education.

"I would love to have kids and move back home. But I don't want them to sit in school – like I had to – listening to some talk about how having an abortion is wrong."

Grace feels far more at home outside of Northern Ireland:

"I went to Trinity and it felt so diverse compared with Rostrevor. I wouldn't want my children to only have friends from the same background as theirs. It's not healthy, it's not how the world is.

"Then I moved to Boston. I loved the city but the job was pretty boring.

"I find making new friends in Ireland quite hard but it's really easy here, people are really enthusiastic.

"My visa runs out in a few weeks so I'm doing a bit of travelling before I have to go back – going to see my friends in Chicago and Texas.

"I have to go back next week. Hopefully I can settle in London – both my siblings are there and I have three or four cousins there as well."

Like many older emigrants, Grace finds trips home of more than a few days only reinforce her determination to stay away:

"I like to visit home, but it's depressing when you live there. Seeing you family is fine for the first three days but then the place starts to drag you down.

"I think of Rostrevor as my home, but I don't think of Northern Ireland as my home – I've never even been to Derry.

"If I was thirty-two with a partner and a child, I'd move back so they could get a good education.

"It is beautiful there. But it's the same patterns on repeat at Stormont. When there is progress it's superficial, Stormont was designed so that nothing really progressive can happen.

"When you give so much power to the DUP then I don't feel welcome."

Eimear Willett also feels unwelcome in conservative Northern Ireland. As she explains her background, I understand why she struggled to fit in.

She starts by explaining that everyone in Northern Ireland thinks that, because she's called Eimear, she must be a Catholic.

I give a little disapproving shake of the head at my countrymen's latent sectarianism, without having the heart to tell Eimear that I had assumed exactly the same thing myself:[89]

"I grew up in Derry, although my Daddy is actually Australian and that has really influenced my perspective. My mum was born in London and moved to Derry, but I've never had any contact with her. I was raised by my dad and I wasn't brought up Catholic or Protestant.

"My brother's called Kelan – which is also a Catholic name – but he used to go to army cadet training at Drumahoe, which is a wee loyalist village just outside Derry.

"I had quite an exposure to both sides during my childhood. There were Catholic and Protestant people on our estate.

"I went to integrated primary school and secondary school which has had really big impact on how I view things now. At the integrated school there were Buddhists, Seventh Day Adventists, the emphasis was on finding similarities rather than differences.

"I've never looked at my friends and thought what religion are you? People think I'm Catholic because I'm called Eimear, I get this all the time.

"I've got an Australian passport, I don't vote Sinn Fein, I'm not a Catholic."

Like Jenny Ryan, who moved to Belfast from easy-going Enniskillen, Eimear found Northern Ireland's capital city a much more openly sectarian place than her hometown:

"When I went to Queen's it was a real eye-opener, the whole Catholic-Protestant thing.

"I was there from 2019 to 2022 doing international politics and there's all this division on campus, there's this

[89] And I'm a Protestant with a Catholic-sounding first name, so I really should've known better.

whole idea that it's a cold house for unionists and this problem with people wearing GAA jerseys.

"Students who had gone to schools of one religion or the other were defined by that."

Since moving to continental Europe, Eimear has had the occasionally frustrating experience of explaining Northern Ireland 101:

"I spent a summer in the US and then when I graduated, I did a Masters in the Netherlands, and it had a year in the Czech Republic. People in the US and the Netherlands have said to me 'you guys blow things up all the time' and then you have to explain how it's a bit more complicated than that.

"When I got here to the Czech Republic, I had to have a big argument with the uni. They demanded I pay UK tuition rates and I eventually persuaded them that I didn't have to because I've got an Irish passport, so I only have to pay the rate for EU students.

"I tried to explain the conflict to my professor and it took him ages to get his head round it. But Northern Ireland is not a big place, it's not significant in terms of European history.

"I definitely miss home a lot, I've noticed my Irish identity has become stronger but I try not to stick to Irish people, I try not to go to Irish bars because I want to meet different people.

"I've gone from telling people 'I'm from Northern Ireland' to 'I'm from the North of Ireland' and that doesn't come form my upbringing – my brother lives in east Belfast these days."

When I ask Eimear if she ever thinks about returning to Northern Ireland, she's one of several people who pull out a Bill Murray reference to explain why she has no plans de-emigrate:

"I don't want to go back home, moving back to the North would just feel like Groundhog Day. Nothing changes, it's the same shit over and over again. There's still no change, still no money, Lough Neagh has literally turned green.

"Part of me feels guilty because I want to go home and help change things, but it's such an uphill battle.

"The course is coming to an end. The other people on the course, they'll go to work for their governments, in Italy, Spain, the Netherlands. But that opportunity isn't there for me.

"I've just found a job in Madrid teaching English. I'll stay in Spain until I can get a job in Dublin or Brussels. I can't see myself moving back to the North. I'm not aligned with any party in the North so I don't see what I would do.

"I was sixteen when Brexit happened. I remember hearing the result and thinking 'this is so bad.' I'm so glad I've got my Irish passport because it allows me to live and work in Europe. I'm looking out the window at a blue sky (*chuckles*).

"Northern Ireland doesn't work, it's a failed project. Stormont, the Executive, they've failed.

"The whole thing entrenches division. I don't want to be part of it."

Like Eimear, Katherine Parke grew up in Derry at the end of the Troubles. But, unlike Eimear, she has returned to her native city.

Katherine explained how, as someone who is hard to pigeonhole as either Catholic or Protestant, she never truly felt she belonged in Northern Ireland:

"I grew up outside of Derry in a place called Eglinton. My dad was a Protestant from England, mum was a Catholic from a rural background.

"Daddy came over from England in 1971 to work for Littlewoods, he met my mum and that was that. I was born in 1994 so I have no memory of the Troubles but my parents would have spoken about it to us in our teenage years.

"My mum told me about the time she was working at Littlewoods in town and a gunman came in. He fired a shot over her shoulder aimed at a soldier who was on the other side of the square.

"Mummy came home and sat staring at the fire, not knowing what had happened.

"When they were first married, they lived in an area which is popular for people from mixed marriages. But even then, some of them had been attacked in their homes.

"My parents were lying in bed one night and somehow this cat had got in the house. In the middle of the night, it grabbed the blanket on their bed and tried to pull it off. My parents woke up, they thought there was someone in the house, until they saw that cat, they thought their time was up.

"They had a good friend who was lifted by the IRA because they thought he was a British agent. It's only when the other workers vouched for him that they released him.

"It's stories like that which would come out."

Just like Grace Farrell, a Catholic education was hard for Katherine:

"I went to a Catholic secondary school and I felt out of place. There weren't many people from a mixed background at the school.

"We had a language assistant who was from a republican background. I remember in one of the classes, telling him, in Irish, that my father was Protestant.

"He pulled a strange face like he wasn't prepared for that.

"I didn't want to stay so I went to uni in Liverpool. I wanted to broaden my horizons, go somewhere where you're not defined by your background."

Katherine loved Liverpool, despite a few unpleasant moments:

"I was doing French and Irish Studies and I thought it was perfect, this is what I want to do. But still there wee moments. I remember when I first got to halls and some of us were sitting round drinking, getting to know each other.

"One of the girls said 'How did you get to uni? Aren't you a Gypsy?' I was taken aback, but I looked at her and said 'no, I'm not a Gypsy, but why would it matter if I was?'

"But in Liverpool as a whole, people love you if you're Irish and people were very open and interested to hear about Northern Ireland.

"I had a bit of a breakdown in Liverpool. I didn't have a job and the lease on my house was running out so I came back to Derry to recover to try to get back on a solid footing.

"When I came back, a cousin of mine, his mother makes kitchens and they were looking for someone to work in the office and I've been there ever since. I do admin, payroll, banking, design work. It's nothing to do with my degrees.

"So I haven't given up the idea of moving away again. But my parents have both got health issues so I've stayed.

"My mother has mild dementia and my father has chronic heart failure. My mummy can't make dinner anymore. My brother's settled in Liverpool so I can't leave my parents."

While far from dismissive of Derry, Katherine is clearly remaining in the city through a sense of family duty:

"I was away from 2012 to 2019, mostly in Liverpool but a year in France as well. I'd leave again if I could.

"After Derry Girls and the City of Culture,[90] you could see tourism becoming more important. I'm sitting on the walls now talking to you and people are just walking round me having a good time. There's a lot more life in Derry now,

---

[90] Derry was the first-ever UK City of Culture in 2013. Jenny and I visited the city with our two very young children that year – it was genuinely excellent. In particular it was great to see how the city's small Protestant minority really embraced the festivities. While on a visit to the Apprentice Boys Memorial Hall I saw their banner proudly hanging on the wall celebrating "Londonderry, UK City of Culture 2013". A less emotionally dead man than me would have wiped away a wee tear at such a thing.

more restaurants and coffee shops. There's a god arts scene, a good music scene.

"But I've got itchy feet, I would like to go abroad again.

"Derry is home, I love it but I'm also frustrated by it. There's so much potential here but it feels like it's being lost."

A little later in the day I speak to Ciaran Ferrin over in Belfast. He has also returned home, though he seems happier than Katherine to have come home and more optimistic about Northern Ireland's future:

"Now that I'm back in Belfast, I have a better appreciation of the place. I actually quite like it. Before, when I saw tourists in the city I'd think: 'Why are you here?'

"Things have got done with the infrastructure – the new central station opened today. We've got a good arts scene, lots of good companies making waves. We should focus on that rather than old grievances."

Ciaran grew up in one of the most deprived parts of Northern Ireland, with the Troubles a background hum rattling round the heads of the adults around him:

"I was born and brought up at the top of the Falls Road. There's me, my sister and my mum and dad. We have big families on either side, my grandparents are from the Falls, Ardoyne and Belleek in Fermanagh.

"We weren't well off financially, but we managed to get by and we lived in a community where people always looked out for each other.

"I'm twenty-six so I've no memory of the Troubles but my parents would tell me random stories about it. You can't change it and I don't think it's anything to be ashamed of."

I'm struck by the next thing Ciaran says, the comparison he draws swirling round my head for the rest of the day. Not because I disagree with the parallel he draws as such, but more because I'd never thought of the conflict in the way that he presents it:

"The Troubles are something of interest to study, how paramilitary gangs emerged in so many areas. But it's something that's been going on for centuries in Ireland, going back to the time of clans and chieftains.

"I think we can learn from that period but, if I'm going to be upset about the Troubles, I'd need to be upset about all those earlier things too."

Ciaran goes on to explain why he's spent most of his adult life outside of Northern Ireland:

"I went to Queen's and then I went to work in different places – I did Camp America, I went to Colombia for three months, then a month in Mexico. Then I went to Thailand for three months. Now I'm back in Belfast and looking to stay here for a wee while.

"I'm looking to earn as much money as possible and keep working on my Spanish – and my Irish. The dream would be to be able to do a remote job and live in Spain – either in Bilbao or Barcelona."

Spending time in so many countries – most of which don't share a common language with Northern Ireland – has led Ciaran to think more about his identity:

"If you're from Germany, or the Netherlands or wherever, and someone asks where you're from, you can just give a one-word answer. But we can't do that. You have to explain you're from Belfast, Ireland, Northern Ireland, the North of Ireland.

"Some people in South America would ask if Northern Ireland is part of Ireland or the UK, if I identify as British or Irish so you take time to explain it.

"I definitely think that humility is a good Belfast trait. We have a very good sense of self-deprecating humour.

"I also think we have a good sense of optimism through tragedy. We're good at picking up other people up when they're down."

Although he's from a very different background to Ciaran's, Matt Thompson tells me from his London flat that he sees similar traits in Northern Irish people around him:

"I like the ease with which people from Northern Ireland talk to people. You end up having a ten-minute conversation with the person behind the counter at Tesco. I think people in England think you're a psychopath if you want to have a conversation with a stranger.

"We don't allow people to get notions. A lot of the people I've worked with have notions of themselves.

"I've dealt with a lot of tyrants and divas and I just want to tell them to wind their neck in."

As Matt describes the family situation he left behind in Belfast, it strikes me that he's a member of a certain type of middle-class, east of the Bann, Protestant family for whom emigration has reached a critical point for ageing parents:

"I was born in 1987 and I grew up in Cyprus Avenue, of Van Morrison fame. My parents were university educated professionals, they had Catholic friends. My best friend when I was growing up was called Niamh.

"The Troubles were there in the background but it wasn't the defining characteristic. I remember stuff like being on the bus into Inst, going past the Short Strand interface after there'd been rioting and seeing the clean-up effort.

"But yeah, coz I grew up in a Protestant area, my first memory of violence would be running away from gangs of spides[91] who wanted to beat me up.

"My dad has four brothers and they all left Northern Ireland, two of them to England, another one went to the Caribbean. Mum has a brother who left to go to England. So all my cousins are English.

---

[91] The Belfast equivalent of "neds" in Scotland or "chavs" in England. I'm sure Welsh people also have a term for their aggressive teenaged boys, but I don't know what it is. Sorry.

"When Nana was getting old and couldn't look after herself anymore -you know needed help with the shopping and stuff like that – there was only my parents around to help her.

"And me and my brother were the only grandchildren she'd see regularly coz the rest were in Manchester or London.

"Now there's me, who lives in London and my brother works for Amnesty International, so he lives all over the place – he was living in Kyiv recently.

"So yeah, that weighs on me, because, as it stands, my parents will have no-one to look after them when their health fails.

"My parents are only 68 and hopefully they've got a good few years left. But what happened when they're 80 and there's no-one around to look after them?"

Matt followed his aunts, uncles and cousins across the Irish Sea, almost because it was just the thing to do:

"It was just expected that you'd leave Northern Ireland. I got into Cambridge to study French and Spanish. I always thought of myself as British, but then you get to England and you're known as 'Irish Matt.' It wasn't said in a hostile way but it took me a while to get my head around it.

"After uni I went backpacking round South America with my girlfriend, who's now my wife. Then in 2011 I moved back to Northern Ireland, for want of anything else to do.

"I was living with my parents and working in various bars and at the Odyssey. I spent six months in Belfast and I found it had radically changed – it had the Cathedral Quarter, the Titanic Quarter.

"Ballyhackamore, which is round the corner from where I grew up, was gentrifying. It had a Thai place, boojoo cafes. The only café in the Hack when I was a kid was a place called Mon In!

"But the jobs that came up weren't in Belfast so I ended up getting a job with the BBC."

After a period at the Beeb, Matt moved on to Sky News, doing a job that requires a lot of travel.

With a lack of grandparenting help in London for their fifteen-month-old, he and his wife are weighing up whether to relocate to his native city, or to hers:

"We're thinking of moving back to Northern Ireland because we find it hard without any grandparents for childcare. We've got a two-bed flat in London and we'd need a bigger place if we have another child. So it would be between Belfast and Edinburgh, where my wife is from.

"She works in TV as well and I think we'd end up in Edinburgh. There's a big BBC presence at Pacific Quay in Glasgow and a whole ecosystem of independent production companies. That just doesn't exist in Belfast."

But Matt's reluctance to move back to Belfast goes deeper than Northern Ireland's economic shortcomings:

"There's also the culture. London is such a cultural centre so we might struggle with Belfast. Whereas Edinburgh has the festival, it's a very cultural place.

"My wife has this slightly unfair idea that Northern Ireland is a cultural backwater and I keep telling her it's not.

"But she's also nervous about what our children would learn if they grew up in Northern Ireland. The fact that the schools are effectively not integrated, she finds that strange.

"She doesn't like the idea of Protestants going to one school and Catholics going to another."

Despite his misgivings about the old country, when I ask Matt if he still thinks of Northern Ireland as home, he immediately turns round and points to a picture on the wall behind him:

"Yes, a hundred per cent it's still home.

"Look, there's the picture I keep on the wall. It's the Mournes. My parents live in Dundrum now. I'd like to have my ashes scattered there."

The concerns which Matt's wife has about the segregated education system in Northern Ireland would only be heightened if she had the chance to speak to Emma Rooney, who explains that she was almost an adult before she made any Protestant friends:

"I was born a couple of days after the Omagh bomb and the same year as the Good Friday Agreement. I grew up in peace and my parents, they were born in 1967, they told me to appreciate what I had. But I suppose you don't really understand that.

"I grew up in Warrenpoint, which is a wee town near Newry. Being from a border area, you're clearly aware of the conflict, but I had a very happy childhood.

"My parents would tell you little stories about the Troubles. Like my mum went into Newry for a job interview and had to park in a control zone[92] or she'd be late for the interview and she nearly had the car towed away.

"I remember the Newry courthouse bomb in 2010[93], which was a big thing for me but I suppose it would've seemed normal to my parents.

"I'm from a nationalist background and, funnily enough, I can remember the first time I heard the word 'Protestant.' It was something that was mentioned on

---

[92] Control zones were common across Northern Ireland during the Troubles, typically in areas around police stations. Motorists could park in these areas, but only if they left someone in the car while going about their business. Any car left unattended would be assumed to be a car bomb and dealt with accordingly.

My dad would sometimes bring me along on his errands to "ride shotgun", something that sounded more exciting than what it actually was – staying in the car while he nipped into this or that shop.

[93] On February 22, 2010, a Real IRA bomb exploded outside the court in Newry. No-one was hurt or killed but the court and other surrounding buildings were damaged.

Radio Ulster, I would've been seven or eight. I remember exactly where I was – I was round at my gran's house.

"I asked my parents: 'What's a Protestant?'[94] and they explained it to me.

"My parents wouldn't allow us to have a sectarian outlook. But I went to Catholic school, so I didn't get to know anyone of a different denomination until I was sixteen or seventeen. I got involved with a couple of youth groups at that time and I got to meet some Protestants my own age.

"I was all excited at first, but lo and behold, they're just people like us.

"My friends thought it was wild that I knew some Protestants. I went to Queen's and I made some Protestant friends. My flatmates were studying Irish so, they wouldn't have had the chance to make Protestant friends so much.

"One of them wanted to put a tricolour up in the living room and I asked her not to, because it might make my friends feel uncomfortable, but she just said 'my house, my rules' and went and put it up."

Emma, who like Matt Thompson took part in the Washington Ireland Program during her time at university, moved to Dublin to work for European Movement Ireland.

She's the kind of twenty-something who another Matt – O'Toole – told me he would like to see moving up to Belfast to take advantage of cheaper housing.

Emma brings this up as an option – but the familiar problem of an anaemic economy weighs heavily on the other side of the scales:

"I have this debate with myself about whether I could go back to the North. But I don't think I could. Dublin is

---

[94] I was the same age when I came home to ask my parents what a Catholic was. But, being from Belfast, "Catholic" was not the actual word that I had overheard in the playground.

much more advanced and European than Belfast, I just can't see myself moving back for job reasons.

"I'm sad about that, I loved living in Belfast. I loved living down at the bottom of the Ormeau Road at uni. I love going back to Belfast, I love talking to my friends about the place. I had this vision that I'd be a young professional in Belfast, get a place on the Lisburn Road.

"I wanted to be one of those people who stayed but...I don't want to say I lost hope but...if I had wanted to get a job at Stormont, the whole thing was frozen at the time.

"The standstill did put me off Stormont. When I was coming up to graduating, there just weren't a lot of opportunities in public policy jobs in Belfast.

"The politics of the North really does get you down. It was so embarrassing last year, when the eyes of the world were looking at us for the twenty-fifth anniversary of the Good Friday Agreement and we didn't have a government.

"But the relationship between Emma Little-Pengelly and Michelle O'Neill[95] is very refreshing and I think the executive is now making a genuine effort to build positive relationships.

"If I was to try to buy a house in Dublin, well that's not a runner unless I won the Lotto. It's either rent for the rest of your life in Dublin or move to the North.

"Come back to me in ten years and I might be happily living in Belfast. But at the moment I feel guilty, I feel like I took advantage of growing up in Northern Ireland – the great education – and then left."

When I speak to Emma, it strikes me how the two Irelands drift further and further apart with each passing year and, by extension, how complicated Irish unity would be, should that day ever come.

[95] The DUP Deputy First Minister and Sinn Fein First Minister.

For people on each side of the border, the other state becomes more and more “a far away place of which we know little.”

For Nordies in the South and Mexicans in the North this point is driven home on a daily basis:

“It shocks me sometimes how little people down here know about the North. You meet people who’ve been to Bali but have never been to Belfast.

“No-one’s called me a Nordie to my face yet! But they do ask me to speak slower.

“I try to go back every other weekend and my family tease me that I drink fancy coffee now and that I’m pronouncing some words differently.”

Emma, speaking to me from her office, doesn’t have a visual representation to demonstrate her affection for Northern Ireland in the way that Matt Thompson did.

But her attachment to their shared home place is equally strong:

“I do think of Northern Ireland as home. I was up there at the weekend and when I got back down to Dublin, I texted my mum and dad saying ‘I’m home’ and then I felt bad about it, saying that Dublin is home.

“But I’m really proud of Northern Ireland and I’m really proud of my strong accent! Northern Ireland is home and it always will be.”

Like Matt Thompson, Nadine McGarry is considering moving back to Northern Ireland.

But, like Emma Rooney, she’s concerned about her potential children growing up in a society where they wouldn’t have the chance to make friends with kids who aren’t Catholic.

Both women grew up in a Northern Ireland that was peaceful, but it was also a society defined by a benign apartheid:

“I was born in 1994 and I grew up in Crumlin, near Lough Neagh and the airport. I have three brothers and we lived in the same house all through my childhood. It was a very happy childhood. I went to primary school in Crumlin and then high school at Rathmore in Dunmurry, which is closer to Belfast.

"I grew up in a Catholic household, my parents are fairly religious. We went to Mass and mum would read at Mass and Dad played the guitar.

"Two of my brothers played Gaelic football and I would have played too, or at least did my best to.

"We wouldn't be a political family, talking about a united Ireland round the dinner table, but my dad would sometimes talk about the Troubles.

"He went to St Malachy's in west Belfast so he would have been caught up in a lot of bomb scares and in one case an actual bomb went off near him, which had a big impact on him.

"But my mother wouldn't talk about the Troubles at all.

"When I was eight my school was involved in a cross-community thing with a Protestant school so once a week we'd go off in the bus to do a thing with the Protestant children. I didn't understand it at the time, I just thought 'great, we get a day out of school'.

"But looking back now, I didn't have any Protestant friends.

"Everyone I knew was Catholic, I went to a Catholic school, all my family were Catholic."

Nadine takes a moment to stir the soup she's making for lunch before telling me how her career has taken her from Liverpool to London to Sheffield and now – potentially – back to Belfast:

"When it came to uni, I went to Liverpool to study law, I didn't even think about Queen's or Ulster because I wanted to get away. Not, you know, get away from my family, but get away and live in a different city.

"I didn't realise till I got there that every other person in Liverpool is Irish.

“When I graduated I went back to live with my mum and dad for a bit, earned some money and then went travelling. Then I thought ‘right, time to get a job’ and I ended up getting a job in London. I was there five years.

“It was immigration law, some of it was human rights and asylum but some of it was getting a visa for some rich entrepreneur who wants to settle in the UK.

“In the end I didn’t like the vibe at the place. There were a lot of people from Oxford and Cambridge at the firm and a lot of ‘you need to bill this client this certain amount so you can get a bonus.’

“So a year ago I moved up to Sheffield and now I work in the public sector helping victims of domestic and sexual abuse.”

Emma sees the shoots of hope when she returns home:

“I go back to Northern Ireland five or six times a year. I think the place has changed a lot since I left twelve years ago. Belfast has become a much more diverse place, which is appositive thing.

“And religion is becoming less of a way of life than it was before. When I was nineteen or twenty I wouldn’t think about moving back to Northern Ireland, but now I very much hope to.

“I think I need a couple of years more experience at work and then I’d like to move back.

“My partner’s English so there’d need to be a bit of convincing. He’s been over a few times and he thinks the people are really friendly and more into a community way of life than people over here.

“But he thinks the politics is fucked up and he was flabbergasted seeing the flags on the lampposts. I think he’d be anxious about things like that.”

I admit to Nadine that I’m surprised to hear her say that she’d like to move back to Northern Ireland. The only other emigrant I’d spoken to who expressed a strong urge to return was Mark Aiken and there aren't many similarities between the two of them.

Nadine is in her early thirties and keen to return to a place she knows well. Mark is in his fifties and enthusiastic about building a new life in a country he left as a young child.

But then I feel guilty at expressing my surprise to Nadine because she's exactly what Northern Ireland needs – an early-career professional returning home to build her life there having been blessed with the perspective of living in a more "normal" society.

But, despite her enthusiasm to return, Nadine does go on to identify the two things which are giving her pause for thought – our old friends segregation and small-mindedness:

"When you start talking about your upbringing with English people you realise that it's different.

"Our school had a convent, our principal was a nun. That's your normal, but when you explain that to people they look at you like 'so, there was a nun walking round your school?'

"When you talk about the sex education you got at school you realise the difference. We were taught that abortion is a sin and, at that age, I probably believed that purely because I was being told it by a teacher who I respected.

"If we did move over there and we had a family I'd want our kids to go to an integrated school.

"Northern Ireland is a sexist society, there have been six femicides there in the last four weeks and I don't think people are concerned enough about domestic violence.

"And also, I've though about going into a workplace and being met by that close-mindedness that you get over there. That worries me a bit."

Just as Protestants were the exotic other to a young Nadine, so Catholics were a mystery to Natalie Cooke as a child. Speaking to me from Bristol, she explains how growing up in rural County Antrim – the heartland of Paisleyism – was a stifling experience:

"I was born in 1992 and I grew up very much in the countryside, abut 30 miles from Belfast. The nearest village was fifteen minutes away, a place called Straid, which is near Ballyclare.

"I grew up surrounded by farms. It was the normal that I knew, but I think I was naive. Some of the people I went to high school are paramilitaries now, which I think shows how sheltered I was from all that.

"My high school was extreme, it was so religious. There were so many rules that were very unforgiving of anyone who didn't conform.

"The view of women was very old-fashioned, I was told by a teacher that I should become a teacher until I got married, as that was the best job for a woman. We weren't encouraged to learn in the way that the boys were.

"I remember when I was doing my GCSEs, there was the debated about abortion in the case of fatal foetal abnormality, when the baby has no chance of surviving – it's going to be born and then die an agonising death.

"When I brought this up, my teacher told me: 'Well the church's position is that the alternative to abortion is adoption' even though, in this case, there was no prospect of adoption as the child wouldn't live more than a day.

"I felt in the minority, I didn't run with the popular crowd. I feel like, if I went there now, I'd end up getting suspended.

"I never really felt like I fitted in. I felt like I was constantly having to hold my tongue because Northern Ireland is much more conservative than me."

Norther Ireland's homophobia – which we'll look at in the next chapter – was one of the reasons that Natalie felt uncomfortable, even though she isn't gay herself:

"I don't understand why people were so against same-sex marriage. I remember singing in some groups that were welcoming to same-sex couple and I remember thinking it's so stupid that they don't have equality.

"I hadn't got married and I hadn't had kids and people were asking 'what are you doing with your life?'

"I don't feel like that in Bristol – no-one cares about that."

When Natalie talks about her upbringing and compares it with her new life in Bristol, it's impossible to avoid thinking of her journey from Northern Ireland as an escape:

"I had got it into my head that I should be a teacher but then I did some shadowing when I was seventeen. The children's behaviour didn't match the behaviour of the children in my head, so I thought I'd better find something else.

"I did marketing at Ulster University and I eventually applied for an MA in Bristol in 2017. I went on the Washington Ireland Program in 2018, though I was one of six people who got t placement in New York.

"I was working community volunteer in Harlem, working in the part of New York with the highest level of gun violence, helping make lunches for hundreds of people in Harlem. It was really cool.

"I eventually got a job in a family law firm and I qualified as a solicitor just last week – I think my first email reply to you had 'trainee solicitor' on it but I've taken 'trainee' off it now. I love it here.

"My partner is Welsh so it makes sense to stay here in Bristol as it's close to Wales."

For Natalie the residual sectarianism of Northern Ireland is reason enough not to return home to start a family:

"I can't see myself putting my kids through the school system in Northern Ireland. The environment I grew up in was quite anti-Irish, anti-Catholic. The things I heard about Catholics when I was growing up was all bad.

"When I go to see my parents – they live in Broughshane now – I look at what's up on the walls in the street. There's all these posters about the Irish Sea border, all this graffiti saying 'Taigs out' and I'm thinking it's bad enough that someone wrote that, but it's worse that no-one removes it, that it just stays there.

"Things are ingrained in your head and you have to check yourself. For instance, you know how Protestants say 'aitch' and Catholics say 'haitch'? Aye, so if someone over here in Bristol happens to sat 'haitch' when they're spelling something out to me, there's a bit in my head that thinks 'they must be Catholic.'

"My brain still puts them in a box, it takes a split second for me to realise that they just happen to pronounce it 'haitch' it doesn't indicate anything about their religion."[96]

Perhaps because of her sense of alienation, when I ask Natalie if Northern Ireland is still home, her answer is much more ambiguous than other emigrants of her age:

"I have a debate with myself, whether Northern Ireland is home. When I'm back there, I say 'I'm going home to Bristol tomorrow'.

"I suppose I think of both of them as home, but Northern Ireland isn't the place I want to live in anymore.

"I don't know...it's possible that it was a disadvantage growing up in Northern Ireland. I had a lovely childhood, I loved going on holiday to Fermanagh, I didn't want for anything.

"But the disadvantage come from the segregated education system and the worldview that a woman should be a mother.

---

[96] Same.

"Where I grew up, you sweep problems under the carpet and don't talk about them. I don't think that's healthy."

My chat with Natalie takes place amid a clatter of interviews with younger people, sometimes three on the same day. Many of the interviews were thanks to the efforts of Caoimhe Ní Mhaolagáin from the Washington Ireland Program, who connected me to some of the former students who've taken part in the course.

Talking to these bright, positive, articulate young adults, I'm struck by how much Northern Ireland is missing out on.

Its culture venerates education and hard work. Its awful history equips young people with a sense of perspective and an inner resilience.

Four big ticks for any future employer.

But then Northern Ireland's economy and its society dispatches so many of these young people to enrich other societies.

This strikes me again when I talk to Owen McMeel, who's swapped County Antrim for Stockholm. Now in his thirties, when I ask Owen about his childhood, he reflects on the central role of education:

"I grew up in a wee place called Moneyglass which is near Toomebridge in mid-Ulster. It's a very small village about halfway between Belfast and Derry. You could take Moneyglass and put it anywhere else in Northern Ireland and it would look pretty much the same.

"I was born in 1990, the eldest of three children, I've a sister and a brother. We grew up close to my grandparents – my parents had built their house on my grandparents' land.

"Dad worked at the Ulster Bank in Andersonstown and Mum worked at a hairdresser's in Castledawson. My mum's from Bellaghy, which is a very republican village, but my mum would never have anything to do with that.

“I don’t think my parents were particularly affected by the Troubles. I suppose I remember things like, if I was going into Ballymena, my mum would always make sure I wasn’t wearing a Gaelic football shirt.

“I remember it as a very happy childhood. I went to St Mary’s Grammar in Maghrafelt and the most important thing for me was playing Gaelic football, getting as good as I could at it.

“Do you know, Barry, I’ve never been asked about my childhood before. Thinking about it, the thing I’m most grateful to my parents for was that they encouraged me to get educated.”

Owen explained how he ended up spending time in Sweden:

“I studied economics and engineering at Queen’s until 2013, then went to the US and India for a bit. Then, when I was looking for a job, a friend of mine referred me to First Derivatives in Newry. So I was there three weeks and then I got to go to London.

“Then we had this really good client in Stockholm, so I got to go for six months in 2015. Up until then I hadn’t even thought of Stockholm as a place I’d go to on holidays. But after six months, I loved it and I wanted to go back.”

But before he got the chance to move back to Sweden, Owen worked for six months in Dublin. While not quite as scathing as Liam Devlin – who considered the city “Dickensian” – Owen was certainly in no rush to settle in the Irish capital:

“I’d always wanted to live in Dublin so I’m glad that I did it. But I didn’t like it there. Life in Dublin was hard, it was a big effort. I ended up walking to work every day – it took forty-five minutes but it was quicker than getting the bus.

“Plus, I was there from October to March, so I didn’t get to see the best of Dublin weather-wise.

"Eventually I got a job with Swedbank and moved back to Stockholm – it's the biggest mortgage provider in the Nordics. Now I work for Klarna doing financial planning.

"I met my partner five or six years ago and we've got an apartment in Stockholm. Her brother has young kids so I'm learning Swedish with them, but everyone speaks English here.

"I cycle to work in ten minutes so, compared with Dublin, I really like the comfortable life we have.

"I think I'm quite outgoing as a person because I'm from Northern Ireland. But Swedes are a little more insular. My neighbours won't say 'how are you?' when you get in the elevator with them."

Owen remains highly engaged in the politics of Northern Ireland, though as with many of us emigrants, you do wonder if this abiding interest helps or harms his mental health:

"Radio Ulster is my alarm clock and I have it on for fifteen to twenty minutes while I'm having a shower and getting ready for work.

"Poor Cecilia also gets to hear Radio Ulster!

"When I first moved here I would only visit BBC Northern Ireland for the sport but now I look at the news on there too – especially about Lough Neagh as I grew up near it.

"It's Groundhog Day. The only part of Stormont that's excelling is the PR department, because every six months there's another big presentation about how wonderfully they're doing."

When Owen takes a cold, hard, private-sector look at the performance of the Northern Ireland Executive he doesn't like what he sees:

"At Klarna, we're judged on five or six Key Performance Indicators – KPIs. So, is the balance sheet stable, growth in assets etc. Where's the KPIs for Northern Ireland? We don't see them and if we did, they wouldn't be brilliant.

"Any progress is very slow. There are only 1.8 million people in Northern Ireland – why does it take so long to get anything done?

"In the private sector, I don't think any of those politicians would be keeping their jobs.

"They'd have to sharpen their pencils.

"In Northern Ireland it's green and orange. A unionist voter isn't going to switch to a nationalist party and vice versa.

"There has to be power-sharing of some kind but how long do we continue with it when it's not delivering for the people of Northern Ireland?

"I want Northern Ireland to be the best place it can be and for that, I think you need the ability to change government.

"I heard Michelle O'Neill on Radio Ulster talking about the Programme for Government and the number of adjectives she used to describe how wonderful it was was amazing. But I'm not sure that it's delivering.

"I go back about four times a year. I don't think it's changed much in the last ten years. There's a lot of nice cafes and restaurants and there's some areas that have been rejuvenated. But the attitudes haven't changed and the politics hasn't changed.

"In terms of moving back – parental leave would be a big thing as I hope to become a parent in the next five years.

"And the infrastructure isn't there. As an example, the first train from Belfast gets into Dublin at ten past nine in the morning. Why can't there be one getting in at ten past seven or ten past eight so you can get to Dublin in time to start your day at work?"

Owen is frustrated at the amount of time politicians spend arguing about how to deal with the past – legacy as its known in Northern Ireland – but he acknowledges that fate has allowed him to take this dispassionate view:

"Arlene Foster's family[97] experienced things in the Troubles that I didn't – and there's other politicians you could say that of. But I think we have to move on. I'm not a big advocate of inquiries into the past – there was wrong on both sides.

"We have to move on, we can't let these memories haunt us forever.

"But, if my father had been shot in both knees, maybe I'd have a different opinion."

But his frustration with Northern Ireland serves only to focus Owen on the things he likes about the place:

"I'm very proud of coming from Moneyglass and the school I went to, the football team I played for and I don't see that feeling leaving me any time soon.

"But because I live further away, I don't see so much of it anymore. I've lost touch with some of my friends. I live in Stockholm now and hopefully we'll have children one day.

"But I don't see Sweden as home."

Catherine Craig left Northern Ireland long before Owen. But, when she breaks down in tears at the end of our conversation, it's obvious that the place still forms a key part of her identity:

"I was born in 1988 in Holywood – which I always tell people is the home of Jamie Dornan and Rory McIlroy. My brother's five years older than me and he lives in Australia now. I did American Studies and International Development at Ulster University in Coleraine.

"I spent a year of my course in Vermont, I went on the Washington Ireland Program in 2010 and then I started a master's at the University of East Anglia, but I couldn't

[97] The former DUP leader grew up in Fermanagh in the Seventies and Eighties, a time when the IRA was pursuing a relentless campaign of ethnic cleansing against her Protestant community. Her father was shot in the head in front of her and one of her classmates was seriously injured when a bomb went off on their school bus.

really find anything to do in Norwich so I ended up back in Holywood for a while.

"Then I left for Canada in 2014, I started working at the University of British Columbia in Vancouver. I used my British passport for one visa and my Irish one for the next. One of the best things about being from Northern Ireland is that you can have two passports!"

After a decade in Canada, Catherine has decided to take the plunge:

"I got my Canadian citizenship in April. My granny's ninety so she writes me letters. After I got my citizenship she wrote 'that's it' – as in she knows I'm not coming back now.

"I just did it for paperwork purposes really, it makes things easier. But it does mean I can vote. I haven't voted for ten years and I have to do my homework on Canadian politics before the next election. I don't take it lightly because there are plenty of other immigrants in Canada – from places like Syria and Afghanistan – who never had the chance to vote before they came here."

Even as a Canadian citizen, Catherine finds that her vowels betray her:

"I just did a presentation on Sunday and someone asked: 'Where are you from?' I was told when I was sixteen that some of the things, I say are really hard to understand – any word with 'ow' in it for instance.

"I've had to learn to say 'towel' as two syllables rather than one. 'Eight', that's another word that it's hard for Canadians to work out."

Unlike some of the emigrants I spoke to, Catherine has tried to mix with people from different backgrounds:

"I made a conscious decision when I cam here to try not to mix just with other Irish people because I saw how, when foreigners came to Belfast, they would stick together. What's the point of going to a new country if you're just going to mix with people from your country when you get there?

"My partner's Chinese-Canadian, his parents came here from Hong Kong and I have a bunch of English friends.

"I used to go back home twice a year before Covid. I really like spending Christmas there. When my partner came with me to Belfast, it was his first-ever time visiting Europe. We took him on the black taxi tour, which was really interesting.

"And yeah, it's changed a bit, there's a sushi shop, a bubble tea café. And there's an influx of people from other countries, not everyone in Belfast is white any more, which is very interesting."

Throughout our conversation, Catherine has seemed calm, speaking with a melodic rising tone. But when I ask her if she considers Northern Ireland to be home, she starts to wipe away tears from her eyes:

"Northern Ireland is home. I know that sounds weird. I would always say I'm Northern Irish.

"I say it's home because my family live there...sorry, Barry, sorry...just give me a second...I've had a lot of opportunities for work here, I've experienced things I wouldn't have been able to experience in Northern Ireland.

"But thinking about that makes me sad, because Northern Ireland is still my home.

"It's something I have struggled with for years."

As our conversation comes to an end Catherine apologises profusely for briefly losing her composure. I tell her never to worry.

After saying goodbye and clicking "end" on the Zoom, I reflect on Catherine's tears.

Maybe her emotional reaction is an example of the way in which many of us emigrants – whether we left during or after the Troubles – struggle with the question of whether we still consider Northern Ireland to be our home.

But there's one group of emigrants who struggle with that question more than rest of us.

A group of people who've never been allowed to feel fully at home in Northern Ireland...

THE MOST LIKELY TO GO

"I never thought the therapy would make me straight."

Northern Ireland has always been a cold house for anyone who is same-sex attracted.

When you speak to someone who's subjected themselves to conversion therapy because of the homophobia of the place, you realise just how chilling their home truly is.

Gareth Patterson talks to me from London on a rainy Monday afternoon, reminiscing about his childhood in a religiously conservative part of Northern Ireland. Despite the prejudice he's faced, I'm struck by Gareth's abiding affection for a society which has never accepted him:

"I grew up in Annahilt, which is a wee village just outside Hillsborough. There's me and my twin brother. Mum was from Ballysillan in north Belfast and Dad's from the countryside outside Lisburn. We were a reasonably evangelical family, you know, church-going Presbyterians.

"There was a great sense of community through the church and my family. That's one of the great things about Northern Ireland, I think.

"My early childhood was a happy one but that changed when I was twelve and my parents separated. Then it became more challenging.

"When I was a teenager, I was so quiet and anxious because of what I was."

Gareth was well into his adult life before he came to terms with his sexuality:

"I went to Queen's to study medicine and I graduated in 2012 and by 2017 I'd finished my GP training. I became a partner in a GP surgery and I bought a house in east Belfast.

"It was only then, when I was twenty-seven, that I started to understand myself more. Up until a year or two before that, I'd been active in the church. But then I started to question my sexuality more.

"I went into conversion therapy for a few years after I heard Iris Robinson[98] talking about it on Radio Ulster one Sunday."

In common with some other emigrants I spoke to, Gareth mentions a painful part of his life in passing and moves on with his answer, just as Mark Aiken did when he talked briefly about the fact that his uncle had been murdered by the IRA.

So I actually have to interrupt Gareth to ask him to tell me more about how the conversion therapy progressed:

"It was one-on-one sessions first, maybe five or six of them. Then there were group sessions. The majority of the participants were gay, but there were a few straight men too, people who were struggling with their masculinity.

"It was mostly men who were older than me but there were two or three my age. We talked about my relationship with my parents and how their divorce supposedly had a part to play.

"Then we talked about my difficulty in creating friendships with other men and how this had led to me developing a sexual interest in men.

"I went for three years and there was some of the teaching that clicked with me, that made sense in a twisted, manipulative way.

"It was definitely a caring environment; it was never aggressive and I didn't feel traumatised by it. He had a soft

---

[98] The DUP MP for Strangford and wife of Northern Ireland's then First Minister Peter Robinson. In 2008 she said that she worked with a man who she claimed could steer gay people away from the "abomination" of homosexuality and towards a straight life.

way about him and I think he genuinely believed in what he was doing.

"But I never thought the therapy would make me straight.

"I kept at it because of the shame I felt at being gay. It was a slow process of realising that the therapy wasn't for me."

Realising that conversion therapy was hopeless, Gareth knew he had to find a way to explain his sexuality to his relatives:

"My family and the majority of my friends were Christian so it just wasn't possible to escape religion. You have this idea about coming out like it's one moment, but in my case, it wasn't, it was slower than that.

"Eventually more people knew, but I still sat in a lot of shame. I didn't feel prepared to own my sexuality. By the end, everyone around me knew I was gay but I didn't feel I had people around me who could support me.

"I wouldn't say that anyone was aggressive or cruel when they found out I was gay, but there was a lot of talk about eternity and damnation.

"Some people wanted to be involved, but their love was conditional. I wouldn't call myself Christian anymore."

Having come out Gareth, like many gay people in Northern Ireland, became frustrated with the smallness of the scene:

"As I came out in my mid-twenties, there was a little bit of going out in Belfast, but I didn't really have friends in that community.

"I had two boyfriends in Belfast but I was new to the scene and I wasn't comfortable in myself as a gay man. I probably still carry shame with me.

"I had been over to London a few times for friends' birthdays and stuff and I just remember that sense of escapism, of being anonymous. It gave me the freedom to be myself.

"That planted a seed in my mind. I would have loved to be stronger, more forthright, more confident. I have some friends who, after a particularly bad experience just thought 'that's it' and left Northern Ireland.

"I wasn't that type of person. Covid was a good excuse to stop going to church and then when lockdown ended, I didn't go back.

"I had thought about going to Melbourne but that seemed too far, so in the end it was between London and Dublin. I didn't need any extra qualifications to work in London, so I moved over here."

Gareth seems to be much more at ease with his Northern Irishness in London than he was in Belfast:

"I love hanging out with other Irish people here. I'm mates with a guy and a girl here from Friends.[99]

"There's something special and unique when you meet someone else from Northern Ireland. You have a sense of something shared, it definitely resonates with me. I've reconnected with my first girlfriend who lives over here. We get animated when we talk about home, the jokes, the positive things, the laments.

"We have a shared experience that people from anywhere else can't relate to, even people from the South. It's a unique place with a unique history.

"A few days ago, my boyfriend and I were at a spa. One of the staff tripped and a bit of the drink they were carrying splashed onto a customer. I think if that customer was from the south of England, they would've got annoyed, you know, maybe angry about it.

"But the person happened to be from Northern Ireland so they just said: 'Ach, never worry, I'm going in the spa in a minute anyway.'

"It was lovely, you know. We've no notions of ourselves, we're very humble people – which has its positive and its

[99] The high school in Lisburn, rather than the Nineties sitcom.

negatives – but it's very endearing and I don't see it in other people here.

"And we don't want to upset people, don't want to ruffle feathers. That's not often the best quality but it is a Northern Irish thing. My partner's noticed that I don't like to create a fuss."

But, despite his obvious affection for his homeland, Gareth can't see himself returning there:

"When I go back to Northern Ireland, I enjoy the best bits of life there and then I leave. For me, I can't see going back there to live. I have a complicated relationship with the place.

"My parents have a lot of their own history and traumas. When you add the layer of spirituality it becomes more complex.

"I still think of Northern Ireland as home.

"The idea of what home is changes through your life, but it's definitely where my heart is."

Unfortunately, Gareth's experience of homophobia is far from unique. In 2021, the charity Just Like Us found that a shocking eighty-two per cent of gay teenagers in Northern Ireland have contemplated taking their own lives.[100]

That's way above the figure for their straight classmates (23%) but also higher than gay high school pupils in England (67%), Scotland (79%) and Wales (73%).

Thinking about even the "better" figures here – that one in four straight teenagers in Northern Ireland sometimes feels so low that they want to end it all – furrows the brow of any parent reading them.

But the eighty-two per cent figure, if it's even vaguely accurate, is scandalously high.

Is it really surprising though?

---

[100] https://www.justlikeus.org/blog/2021/11/25/lgbt-youth-northern-ireland-suicide/

In 2013, the UK parliament voted overwhelmingly to legalise same-sex marriage in England.

The devolved parliaments in Edinburgh and Cardiff soon followed suit.

Stormont did not. In 2015, the Northern Ireland Assembly, during one of its fleeting periods of actually operating, voted fifty-three to fifty-two in favour of letting gay people get married.

The DUP used the machinery of the Good Friday Agreement to frustrate the narrow will of the assembly as well as – according to polls – the much wider will of the Northern Irish public. They used the petition of concern – a safeguard designed to protect one religious bloc from discrimination by the other – to override assembly vote.

As ever in Northern Ireland, nothing happens quickly, but by 2020 same-sex marriage was made legal by Westminster.

And, behold, the sky didn't fall.

Straight people carried on not getting married to people of the same sex.

Churches continued refusing to marry anyone who displeased them, whether because they were homosexual or for some other reason.

Some gay couples in Northern Ireland got married, while others continued happily living in sin.

But what are young gay people in Northern Ireland to make of the debate over whether they should enjoy the same rights as everyone else?

Is it a surprise that they would follow the debate on same-sex marriage and conclude that some of those in power in Northern Ireland would rather they started checking ferry and flight times?

The Belfast-based academic Dirk Schubotz[101] found that gay young people are more likely to want to leave than their straight peers by 62% to 38%. And they're significantly keener to never return, by 20% to just 5% for straight emigrants.

Dirk explained to me how he discovered this startling statistic nearly twenty years ago while trying to find out if, as was claimed at the time, young Protestants were abandoning Northern Ireland more than their Catholic peers:

"It was at a time when unionist politicians were talking about a Protestant brain drain. It was relatively early in the peace process and there were stats coming out that universities here were becoming more and more Catholic.

"Queen's had a Catholic majority for the first time, having historically been a Protestant institution. Students from Protestant grammar schools were going to study in England, getting a foothold there and not coming back.

"There was a level of threat to the Protestant identity."

But when Dirk analysed the figures he found a more complex picture than one of Protestants from east of the Bann moving to GB rather than spending their student years in Belfast.

In fact, he found that the key factor was a sense of not fitting in to Northern Ireland's conformist society.

It's an observation that was backed up by many of the emigrants I spoke to – regardless of their sexuality – a sense that they didn't fully belong:

"I wanted to have a look at it. I found that the young people who were most likely to say they would leave were those who felt estranged from the Protestant and Catholic communities.

[101] https://www.community-relations.org.uk/files/communityrelations/media-files/Is%20there%20a%20protestant%20brain%20drain%20from%20northern%20ireland.pdf

"It was the people who felt they didn't fit in – especially people who were same-sex attracted. I wanted to make that clear because I felt the public conversation over this wasn't accurate.

"It wasn't Protestants who were the most likely to leave – it was the people who didn't fit in.

"Northern Ireland back then was quite a heteronormative society. Same-sex attracted people didn't fall into those two camps of Protestant and Catholic because their religion told them they shouldn't be the people that they were."

Although his way of recording evidence has changed in the intervening two decades, Dirk said the pattern of emigration remained stable:

"We haven't asked those same questions for some time but we have studied the sense of belonging among young people.

"It's still the same – the ones who stand out as having the least sense of belonging and are the most likely to leave are LGBT people and people who don't associate themselves with being Protestant or Catholic.

"What has changed in the last twenty years is that young people are more willing to say that they're different, to say that they're LGBT.

"We haven't seen improvements that we wanted since the Good Friday Agreement. Schools, sports clubs and housing are still arranged around religious belonging.

"People who don't feel Protestant or Catholic can feel that Northern Ireland isn't the place for them."

I was particularly keen to get the views of Tom Hulme on the issue of gay emigration.

Firstly, because he's studied the history of homosexuality in Northern Ireland more closely than anyone else.

But secondly, because, as a gay Englishman living in Belfast, he has a fascinating perspective on the level of homophobia in Northern Ireland.

When he emails me his thoughts, he includes the startling observation that Northern Ireland became *more* homophobic as the Troubles wore on.

Throughout the Seventies and Eighties, Great Britain became markedly more accepting of homosexuality. Pride marches grew bigger and more mainstream, while Britain's laws (and its newspapers) slowly became more tolerant.

But across the Irish Sea, progress on gay rights was a victim of the Troubles:

"I think it's still worth saying that being gay in Northern Ireland was not just harder than elsewhere, but indeed *got worse* towards the end of the century. Remarkable as it may seem, Northern Ireland in the 1960s and 1970s was much more tolerant than it was in the 1980s and 1990s.

"There was little to no policing of sex between men, the churches mostly stayed quiet (embarrassed about the topic and lacking understanding), and I think there was more of a curiosity about homosexuality than outright condemnation.

"Ian Paisley's Save Ulster from Sodomy[102] really poisoned the well of public debate from 1977 to 1982, and then tabloid journalism – particularly *Sunday Life* – dredged the barrel into the 1990s.

"The result was a moral panic about homosexuality in the region and increasing police stings/operations in really innocuous places (woods, grounds of castles etc, not just public toilets, and way beyond Belfast).

"You would not believe the state of some of the reporting of the 1990s especially – men's names dragged

[102] The DUP leader's ultimately failed attempt to prevent the decriminalisation of homosexuality in Northern Ireland. Local gay rights activists responded with an unimpeachably brilliant counter-slogan: "Save Sodomy From Ulster."

across the front page of tabloids for something as innocuous as a blowjob in a public toilet.

"Not surprisingly, there were murders and suicides that followed these outings. This situation only really changed in the mid-2000s, with a shift towards a less aggressive style of policing and press coverage."

But, as Tom explains more, perhaps we shouldn't be surprised that the Troubles made Northern Irish society more homophobic and gay people more likely to leave:

"Paramilitaries, naturally, are intensely heteronormative and lean towards homophobia, but any sign of cultural divergence within sectarianized communities could either be punished or weaponised by the police. They threatened to out people to their families, for example, and lots of suggestions that the intelligence forces used the same method of blackmail.

"We can also see other ways that certain types of homophobia have lasted here much longer than they have elsewhere.

"Northern Ireland is in many ways the hotbed of conversion therapy practices, usually from the evangelical Protestant direction, and the region is constantly politically behind when it comes to voting through progressive reform.

"It's telling that the decriminalisation of sex between men was rejected here in the 1960s and 1970s, and only happened from the outside force of the ECHR in 1982; and the same thing happened again for gay marriage in 2020 – forced onto the region by Westminster.

"I think there has also been a double bind with gay emigration. Because so many people left, it made it harder to sustain the gay rights movement back at home.

"There are constant complaints in the magazines and periodicals of the gay rights movement here at the time that people leaving was making it harder to create a scene."

Now that gay people in Northern Ireland are on the same legal footing as their peers across the Irish Sea, Tom sees some ground for optimism. But he believes that Northern Ireland remains the most homophobic part of Britain and Ireland:

"I moved to Belfast in 2016 when I was twenty-nine, after living in London. I was immediately shocked by how few people were willing to show their face on apps like Grindr – worse even than the small town in Derbyshire where I grew up.

"I found it hard to make gay friends here – there was a hookup culture, and small groups of friends, but lots and lots of gay men who were not out at work or to their families – even in ludicrous cases where they were as camp as Christmas and their family surely knew.

"Northern Ireland is so family orientated and networks of friends and family so large that I think people know that if someone sees you on a gay app, it really would not take long for it to get back to your folks.

"That said, I have seen huge changes even in the few years I have been living here. The Pride parade gets bigger every year, there are loads of happy and out kids in my classes at university – which was not the case in Leicester when I was a student from 2005 to 2008.

"And I think there's an interest in gay history really growing, that was not evident when I started here."

The happy out kids in Tom's class are free(ish) to be themselves in Northern Ireland because of trailblazers like Brian Gilmore.

Now in his seventies and speaking to me in a halting voice from his home in Belfast, Brian recounts how he came to terms with the fact that he was gay. And how he then made Northern Irish society come to terms with the fact that he was gay.

He and his gay peers of that era achieved great change. As he described wearing his 'Yes, I'm homosexual' badge in

1970s Belfast, my mind goes back to one of his contemporaries, the late PA Maglochlainn, president of the Northern Ireland Gay Rights Association.

I met PA a few times and had a couple of conversations with him. And he occasionally shopped in the little Co-op which I worked in on the Lisburn Road, while making my way through undergraduate life in the late Twentieth Century.

When he walked into the shop, PA would always *always* be wearing a T-shirt with a slogan loudly proclaiming the fact that he was gay.

Such is Belfast's intimate geography that, had he decided to pick up his groceries at a shop one main road up, on the elite Malone Road, or another arterial route further on, along the cosmopolitan Stranmillis Road, his attire would have raised no eyebrows.

But the Lisburn Road back then was poor, scratchy, quite loyalist. I'm sure PA got his fair share of hostile looks and comments while proudly proclaiming his sexuality.

I'm equally sure that PA wouldn't have cared less.

Brian, like PA, grew up in Northern Ireland in the post-war years, a time and a place with literally no out gay people:

"I was born in south Armagh in 1950 and I knew from a young age, maybe eight or nine, the people that I was attracted to.

"But it was a very taboo subject, it would have been insane to even mention your feelings to anyone. There was no opportunity to meet up with other men, it was just something that existed in your head.

"I went to Queen's when I was eighteen and I would come home at the weekends. There was a young female teacher who I used to go to dances with.

"In those days women couldn't go into pubs, it was seen as inappropriate. But it was OK for women to go to dances, so I would go with her as a friend. I had no interest in the women that I danced with, it was just going through the motions.

"In Belfast, in a sense, you were freer because you were an independent individual, you could walk down the street and no-one cared who your parents were or whether or not you went to church.

"But there wasn't a gay scene there either. I was a conservative Catholic at the time, I wore my Pioneer badge and I didn't drink.

"But one day I was invited to a party by a man called Jed Cunningham. He started chipping away at me, offering me a can of beer. Eventually I relented and started to have a drink and we got talking.

"At the end he just asked me 'are you homosexual?' and I said 'no, but I'm bisexual' – which was a lie.

"Jed was straight, but he introduced me to a friend of his who was gay and I found out about Belfast's only gay bar, which was on Rosemary Street in the city centre."

Brian quickly became active in Belfast's very small gay scene:

"Things changed from then, I went to parties and met other gay men, had relationships. I went to the first meeting of the Gay Liberation Movement at the students' union.

"We became involved in different campaigns and we used to advertise our meetings in the papers. The Newsletter, they would take our ads but the Irish News[103] wouldn't touch them.

"We started having gay discos in the students' union. It was the early Seventies, Belfast was like a plague city. Students from the country wouldn't stay there at the weekend, they'd go home to avoid being shot or blown up.

[103] Unlike similar-sized cities in Great Britian, Belfast doesn't have one daily morning paper, it has two. I know, you're way ahead of me here, but let me spell it out. There's a unionist paper – the Newsletter. And there's a nationalist paper – the Irish News.

"So, the students' union had the staff and the facilities and we were one of the only groups who wanted to use them at weekends.

"When I came out at Queen's I wore a badge at lectures saying 'Yes, I'm homosexual'. I wore it so that my fellow students couldn't ignore the fact that I was gay. A few people had to make themselves known so that society could move on.

"You had to sacrifice yourself for the greater good. There was a little bit of banter that was unkind as a result."

However, while Brian was proudly gay in Belfast, it was several more years before he summoned up the courage to come out in south Armagh:

"I didn't come out to my family until 1976. I was due to appear on a Spotlight[104] about gay people in Belfast. I went down and told my mother and she was very, very nervous about it and about me being on TV.

"I told my brother while he was driving me somewhere and he nearly crashed the car from the shock. It was catastrophic for him.

"And then there was my dad. Every day he'd go to the pub to have a pint of Guinness and then he'd come home, everyone in the pub knew him.

"But after I told him I was gay, he didn't go to the pub for three weeks. But he eventually came round and was supportive.

"I worked at Goodyear at the time and some of my colleagues were evangelical Christians, but they were still friendly to me after Spotlight.

"My boss' boss called me into his office two days after the Spotlight went out. He hadn't seen the programme but he'd heard about one of the scenes where there was a party at my flat and we were all dancing.

---

[104] BBC Northern Ireland's long-running weekly version of Panorama.

"He just asked me 'are you planning on having any gay discos at Goodyear?' And I told him that of course I wasn't, I was here to work.

"And that was that, I went on to get some promotions at Goodyear. I suppose the fact they were an American company helped."

Brian, like Dirk, thinks Paisley's campaign to preserve the criminalisation of homosexuality was central to the rise in hostility towards gay people:

"In the late 70s, when Paisley started with his Save Ulster From Sodomy campaign, I know some people from that period who gave up and moved to London. They haven't been back in 40 years. Paisley was a firebrand who stirred up trouble unnecessarily. He had tried to defeat the civil rights movement in the 60s, even though their demands were very reasonable.

"But he wasn't the only one. The Catholic church was also very opposed to making homosexuality legal but they made that clear through letters to the secretary of state."

Brian sees his life's work as still incomplete after nearly fifty years of struggling for acceptance:

"In the last ten years the DUP have been opposing gay marriage and civil partnerships, using the petition of concern. It was just silly actually.

"Things have changed, there's far more facilities in Belfast for gay people now and in other places like Derry too. And the media has played a big part. When you see gay characters in soaps, for example, it has a mellowing effect on people's attitudes.

"I would say in rural areas and in schools there's still prejudice against gay people. The DUP are still campaigning to stop children learning that homosexual relationships are a normal part of life.

"A lot of people still end up hating themselves because they're gay. You have people who get married and have children before they come to terms with who they are.

"I know someone who was fifty-five when he came out, by which stage he had a wife and four children.

"I'm proud that I've had an effect in terms of changing the law and moving things on. We have equality in the law now in terms of marriage and the age of consent.

"But Northern Ireland is still behind the times."

It's a sentiment which would get a hearty 'too right' from Ryan Cosgrave.[105] He begins by describing his upbringing in rural Northern Ireland in the Nineties:

"The town I grew up in is very depressing. Any type of difference at all was not encouraged. It was a society with quite intense conformity and it probably still is now.

"When I was a teenager, I used to read the Guardian and the New Statesman and I felt like they were windows into a better world, where people weren't marching around in flute bands and reading magazines about tractors.

"There was a lot of homophobia at school, anyone who said they were gay got a hard time. Like a lot of gay people in Northern Ireland, I had a lot of internalised homophobia. I didn't feel positive about being gay.

"There was no way to discuss it so I just sort of bumbled through, self-medicating with alcohol.

"Then one night when I was eighteen, I came out to my parents after I got drunk. They didn't take it well. It was the early 2000s so I think they were worried that I would get AIDS and die, because that was the definition of the male gay experience at the time.

"But they are fine with it now. They've met my partner, they're going to meet his parents soon."

---

[105] Not his real name. At the end of our interview "Ryan" asked me not to use his name. I hope you'll understand that I've had to tweak some of his quotes so as not to give away too much information about him. For instance, in the course of our conversation, Ryan referred to the place he grew up by its name, rather than calling it "my hometown". Suffice to say that Ryan grew up in a conservative small town in Northern Ireland – that's a pretty wide net.

Of all the emigrants I spoke to Ryan seemed to have the most intense feeling of being out of place in Northern Ireland:

"When I went to uni in Britain I was living in halls and it was just a different world.

"I mixed with a group of liberal-minded students and we could have conversations that weren't possible in Northern Ireland – about politics, religion, sexuality.

"I stayed on in GB, started working and I enjoyed it. Even during the pandemic, I felt there was this sense of community where I lived. But my lease was running out, my contract was ending at work so I looked around and I saw this opportunity in Belfast.

"I like my job, I rent a place in a nice suburb of Belfast but I have unresolved issues about the place.

"I went back to the town I grew up in and it's even worse than ever. It's like all other small towns across Britain and Ireland, it's declined in the last 20 years, so many shops have closed, it looks depressing.

"But then there are problems that are uniquely Northern Irish – there's sectarianism everywhere and the extreme boringness of fundamentalist Christianity.

"I have a friend who lives in a small town in central Wales, in a place that is every bit as isolated as my hometown in terms of transport links. But it's got a tourist industry, it's got nice pubs, it's got bookshops.

"There's none of that in my hometown, there's no infrastructure for an interesting life."

Ryan finds life in Northern Ireland's largest city a little more welcoming:

"Belfast has more things going for it, I enjoy the metropolitan areas around the Ormeau Road and the Lisburn Road.[106] They feel like an oasis but they're increasingly expensive to live in. Like a lot of people in their

---

[106] Parts of south Belfast close to Queen's University

thirties, I'm culturally middle class but I'm living a more precarious working-class life.

"The Belfast that I inhabit is tolerant of gay people but I have noticed homophobia here.

"Especially among men over-fifty when they've had a drink. A few days ago, my partner was dropping me off in town, near the Europa Hotel. When we kissed goodbye, this middle-aged fella – he had a crate of beer under his arm – he walked across the street to stare at us through the windscreen.

"So yes, if you're gay in Belfast you'll get weird looks from older men."

At the end of our interview, I remark to Ryan that he's the only emigrant I've spoken to who expresses no fondness for Northern Ireland whatsoever.

Everyone else I talked to for this book seemed to feel, like I do, that the country we left is a sort of wayward relative – maddening, frustrating but fundamentally ours.

A place we love despite everything.

Ryan doesn't feel that way and I was initially disappointed by the thoroughness of his negativity towards Northern Ireland.

But then, pretending to be a millennial for a moment, I checked my privilege. Was it my place – as a straight man – to judge a gay person's attitude towards a society as homophobic as Northern Ireland? I decided that it wasn't.

Kris Gant's life experience is similar to Ryan's – but his attitude towards Northern Ireland is much warmer:

"I'm thirty-four, so I suppose it would be the late Nineties and early Noughties when I start to remember stuff. My mum is from Waringstown where her family still lives. My dad's English but his mum's from Dublin and my mum's mum is from the South as well. My dad was in the British Army and he was stationed in Northern Ireland, that's how my parents met.

"I'm the youngest of four siblings, they're all a lot older than me – twelve to sixteen years. By the time I came along a lot of the big problems in Northern Ireland had calmed down, it was much quieter.

"I grew up in Waringstown, it was a very Protestant, unionist place. But it was quite isolated. I suppose I felt sheltered from the bad things that were happening in other parts of the country."

But, while Kris feels more at ease in Northern Ireland than Ryan does, his experience of the country's education system is strikingly similar:

"I struggled a lot at school with being a shy person. When I went to high school I didn't fit in because I didn't like football like the other boys.

"Being gay in Lurgan...there was a lot of harassment from other students. It was the normal stuff from kids – calling me names. But I'd always had that because I was quiet and because I wasn't from Lurgan.

"When they found out I was gay, maybe at eleven or twelve, the abuse went through the roof. The teachers wouldn't call it out like they would other forms of bullying. After the bullying had gone on for a while, they'd say something like: 'Quiet, that's enough.'

"But they wouldn't address the homophobia, maybe because they agreed with it. Other forms of bullying, they would address, but for me I was just left alone to deal with it.

"I had very little self-esteem so I sort of accepted the bullying."

During his unhappy high school year, Kris came to realise that acceptance was a ferry ticket away:

"I think at the age of fifteen or sixteen I realised that I could move somewhere else where there were more people like me. I wanted to go and live in a big city. I had friends in Belfast and I loved going to see them. I felt way more accepted there but I thought there had to be way more outside of Belfast.

"When it came to applying for unis, I applied for places in Glasgow and London. I ended up in London when I was nineteen and I've lived here ever since. I was pretty determined at that point to live in a big city. I wanted to be around people who thought like me.

"I wanted to live in a more diverse place, not the kind of place where you only interact with people who are the same religion as you and have the same politics as you.

"I think ninety per cent of people at school were like that. But I wanted to be around other gay people, people who had broader minds."

Kris has found leaving Northern Irish society liberating:

"I've become a lot more confident in myself since I left Northern Ireland. I've been seeing a therapist and it's helped me realise that growing up in that prejudiced environment made me very insecure.

"I was always super-aware about what people might think of me. But now I don't care. I feel more at peace with myself. I'm trying to unlearn behaviours I learnt from my family about how to talk to people.

"The way of always being careful of what you say. I remember when I was a kid, I saw an ad on the TV for tampons and I asked my mum what periods were. Instead of explaining it, she just told me that she didn't know, she'd never heard of them either.

"We only ever talk about feelings at a surface level, I find it quite hard to talk to my family about how I feel. I've only just started to do that now with the help of my husband.

"One thing I have noticed though is that English people seem to have more of a gap between family members, between parents and children. I know that I can rely on my parents and they'd do anything for me and I know my sisters are the same with their kids.

"They are almost over-protective, which is nice. My sisters live in each other's pockets and they are there for each other. But they do fight and fall out sometimes."

Kris explains that he and his partner's plan to get married came too soon for the Stormont legislative process:

"When we got engaged in 2018, we weren't allowed to get married in Northern Ireland. So that solved the problem of where we would get married. But I don't think we would've got married in Northern Ireland even if it had been legal at the time.

"The DUP's resistance to same-sex marriage didn't surprise me. I went to school with the children of DUP MLAs, so it was hammered home to me that I wasn't welcome."

Like Brian Gilmore, Kris believes Northern Irish society is slowly shuffling towards the door marked 'tolerance':

"I've got nephews who are at the same school now. From what they tell me, it's a more tolerant place now. So, maybe if I'd been born a bit later, I wouldn't have felt that drive to leave Northern Ireland.

"But it wasn't just the homophobia that drove me away, it was the insularity. There's so much more to the world than the town you grew up in and not everyone is going to be the same as you.

"I knew I was gay from maybe when I was five or six. But people back home they don't like talking about anything awkward.

"There was lots of homophobia in the Noughties but there were also lots of gay celebrities so I would look at them and think: 'Oh, there are other gay people in the world.'

"But my family would make fun of them. When I told my family I was gay they'd say things like 'oh, you're too young to know that'.

"But once they accepted that I was gay, my family have been very supportive.

"Some people in the wider family haven't accepted it because of how they are. And that isn't challenged because they're religious.

"My husband's from England and we go over he notices that my family won't talk about things that upset them. When we visit my family and we're walking round the streets, we definitely don't hold hands."

Despite his understandable reluctance, Kris does seem to have come to terms with his Northern Irish identity:

"When I came to London, I used to avoid other people from Northern Ireland, I wouldn't go up to them when I heard their accent.

"But that's changed now, one of my best friends over here is from Derry. We grew up on opposite sides in Northern Ireland so we can talk about the things that are different and the things that are the same.

"I thought of Northern Ireland as home until a couple of years ago. I got married and we bought a property so that changed my attitude.

"I would never move back to Northern Ireland. I don't even like to visit because I find people's mindsets so restrictive. My husband finds the atmosphere very depressive.

"He says it's a really beautiful country but he doesn't like people's mindsets. I like the scenery, it's a very beautiful place but...no I can't think of anything else.

"Sorry, that makes me sound super-negative. I do get some nostalgic memories sometimes."

After speaking to several gay people who left Northern Ireland, I stop to consider if the homophobia that propelled them to the airport is an all-island problem rather than a specifically Northern one.

The Republic of Ireland has all the same history of religious intolerance. Homosexuality was illegal there for 10 years longer than it was in the North.

Am I blaming Northern Ireland for a wider Irish problem of intolerance?

One person who's in the perfect position to tell me is Vanessa Monaghan, the chair of the London Irish LGBT Network. She moved to London from Meath ten years ago and now seems perfectly at home living with her partner in Lewisham.

When Vanessa began attending events organised by the group, she was struck by the depth of bitterness from many Northerners:

"When I first started connecting with the London Irish LGBT Network at events, I got talking to Northerners over here.

"I couldn't get over the chips that many of them had on their shoulders. The first do I went to, there were people there who'd left in the Seventies and the Eighties and had never gone back.

"There was one person there from Derry who'd left in the early Eighties and told me he'd never been back. There was a younger person from Tyrone who said she would never go home.

"They hated the attitudes they'd encountered in Ireland, the fact that there were no clubs they could go to, that they couldn't be themselves.

"They had this disdain for Ireland, they wouldn't give it a chance, they wouldn't accept that modern Ireland is different.

"They couldn't accept that Ireland had changed and it was like this disdain for the country had been festering all this time. I just couldn't understand that."

Vanessa considered moving to Northern Ireland before the pandemic, but the homophobic atmosphere dissuaded her:

"My mum's from Cavan and my parents live in Meath now, so I thought if I moved to Belfast, they'd only be a bit down the road.

"I have queer friends from Dublin who've moved to Belfast because the rents and house prices are so much cheaper.

"We looked at some places in Belfast. I remember a place we quite liked but there were a load of Union Jacks up on the lampposts round the corner. So, I wondered what would happen when my parents came to visit me with their Southern-registered car? Would that be alright?

"And I thought that probably a lot of people in that area would vote for the DUP. When you go to Northern Ireland and you hear the DUP on the news, their attitudes concern you.

"I don't care about people's politics, but if the politics that someone believes in has the ability to make your life a nightmare, then I'm not going to live there."[107]

After talking to Vanessa, I come away with the impression that, while homophobia still exists across Ireland, there is a distinctly Ulster flavour to the intolerance doled out North of the border.

But this is Northern Ireland we're talking about, so there has to be two of everything.

Ryan, Glen and Khris told me about Protestant homophobia, but what about Catholic homophobia?

Tom O'Reilly is the man who can tell me.

---

[107] Vanessa's story reminded me of my own time looking for student housing to rent in Belfast. My friends and I looked at a place on the Donegall Road, an area which was more loyalisty than studenty. We liked the house but were put off taking it when the letting agent – in uncharacteristic honesty – pointed to the end of the side street and said: "You'll be absolutely fine on this street, just as long as you don't go beyond that corner."

He grew up in north Belfast before moving to Manhattan at the age of eighteen and never coming back.

Tom runs Banc Bar Café in the Murray Hill area of the city. It's not quite an Irish bar but also not-quite-not an Irish bar – sort of Irish-bar-adjacent.

Of all the emigrants I speak to, Tom seems the most comfortable in his own skin. Comfortable running a bar – at one point he breaks off to talk to a colleague 'aye, no bother, you go on your break now' – comfortable living in New York and comfortable being a gay man.

While Ryan, Kris and Gareth all struggled for acceptance from their Protestant families, Tom's Catholic relatives came to terms with his sexuality very quickly:

"When I was eighteen, it would've been 1997, I came out of the closet. My brothers and sister, they already knew. But my mother is very Catholic so I didn't tell her.

"You know, I'd have told her I was going out to Thompson's Garage when I was actually going to the Parliament.[108]

"I didn't come out to her until I was living over here in New York. I would've been 26. It was the last thing she'd been expecting.

"She was annoyed with me for the first twenty-four hours but then she literally did a 360. She still goes to church, but she's also the proud parent of a gay son.

"My partner Donald and I have been together for twenty years. When we go back to Belfast to visit, she loves him more than I do!"

Tom's memories of Belfast seem mainly positive, but the city wasn't exciting enough for him to want to build his life there:

"We're from the Antrim Road at Cavehill, there was myself, and I've two brothers and a sister. Then we moved

[108] One of Belfast's two gay bars in the Nineties. The other being the Kremlin, rather than the aforementioned Thompson's Garage.

down the road to Grasmere after my dad passed away when I was seven. My mum wanted to be closer to her brothers and sisters, who lived round Willowbank.

"There were three sets of families and we were extremely close, my aunt lived next door and my uncle lived across the street.

"We're still the best friends now and I'd be on the phone twice a week to all my friends back home. It was a great wee neighbourhood. Those streets we grew up in there wasn't so much trouble. There was republican flags in some areas and then Union flags in other areas but you definitely felt safe.

"But yeah, leaving Belfast, it was just because I knew there had to be more to life. There was one gay bar – the Parliament – and you'd see the same people there every week.

"I was working at a Mexican restaurant on the Lisburn Road called La Salsa and one of the girls I worked with, she moved to New York and she called me and said I should come over.

"For the first few months I felt out of place in New York because I only knew the one person. But then I started to meet other Irish people. I moved to an Irish area of Manhattan called Sunnyside. It was great because, any time you were out of work, someone would help you out.

"I started out working in the kitchen in the Dog and Whistle but after three months the boss and I agreed the work wasn't for me.

"But I had a friend from Drogheda who got me a job at a gay restaurant on 58th Street – back in the days when there was such a thing as a gay restaurant! I was eight years there, it was just the best job, I made so many friends. And then I moved here to the Banc Bar Café.

"Ten years ago, the manager asked me to start running the place. The hospitality business was something I got into at home at La Salsa.

"I didn't go to college, I went to the tech to try to repeat my GCSEs but that wasn't going anywhere. I don't know anything else but this work.

"I've been doing it 25 years and I'm not jaded at all – the craic's always great."

Tom's strong affection for Northern Ireland coexists with an even more powerful desire never to live there again:

"I've never thought of going back to Belfast. Donald's from the Dominican Republic and, to be honest, I'd much rather retire there when the time comes.

"When I go home now, I get bored. People at home, they've nothing to do on a Monday or a Tuesday, so I just get bored.

"I've been away a long time and Belfast doesn't feel safe anymore. There's a lot of drugs and the shops are never open. I used to like waking down into town but you go there now and there's nowhere to go.

"I just came back from Manchester and the people were lovely, the restaurants were lovely. I just wish Belfast was more like that, more vibrant.

"But I love Belfast people, I just find it easy to connect with other people from Belfast, you know, the craic, the jokes.

"There'd be maybe fifteen people from Belfast who'd be regulars at the bar here, there's people from Poleglass, New Lodge, the Antrim Road. They're working in IT, living the Manhattan dream in the high rises.

"They are doing something I would never do. I just think that's class.

"I love seeing people from Belfast doing well. I'm straight over when I hear a Northern accent 'where are you from? Who do you know?' When I meet someone from Belfast, I'm quizzing them right away so I can tell what religion they are.

"My husband knows what I'm doing now and he teases me about it. But there's something in me that wants to know, that wants to find out if they're a Catholic or a Protestant.

"I mean I don't care either way, I just want to know."

It's impossible to come out of forty minutes with Tom without feeling enthused. He's so confident, so optimistic, so at ease in his own company.

I hope that Kris, Ryan and Gareth – all of whom seem to be struggling for acceptance – can find a place as contented as Tom has located in Manhattan.

But, despite thoroughly enjoying my conversation with Tom, I get a little nervous before I ask him my final question: How would you vote in a border poll?

It's the question I asked at the end of every interview and it always made me feel uneasy.

Asking a stranger about their position on the constitutional question goes against everything you learn about navigating life in Northern Ireland.

Voluntarily bringing up *the* most divisive issue with someone you don't know? Madness.

But it turns out I needn't have worried. Tom gives a very engaged answer...

A LINE ON A MAP

"I talk about a border poll all the time, even my Southern friends, my Protestant friends would know what I think, says Tom.

"My brothers and my sister and I we were never brought up in politics, I don't know how I got so involved.

"You get this thing sometime, where Americans would ask where I'm from and I'd tell them that I'm Irish and I'm from Belfast.

"And then you'd get a wee tilt of the head and they'd say: 'My family's from the real Ireland.' Years ago, I'd have barked at ye for that, but these days my husband just says: 'Jesus, Tom, don't answer that.'

"So yes, I love Michelle O'Neill. I would prefer a united Ireland, but not if it meant going back to the Troubles.

"And if people vote against unity that's fine by me. I always say to my Protestant friends that we would have equal rights for everybody."

After we had talked about the past Northern Ireland they left and the present Northern Ireland they didn't wish to return to, I asked all the emigrants to tell me how they felt about the future Northern Ireland – or indeed if they thought Northern Ireland had a future.

I wanted to know whether the potential for a radical change in Northern Ireland – in effect the end of Northern Ireland – might persuade them to return.

But more than that, I wanted to know how much – after decades away in some cases – they remained engaged in Northern Ireland's fate.

Nearly every emigrant I spoke to perked up when I asked them the border poll question, sitting up, as if to signal: 'Funny you should mention that, Barry, because I've wanted to speak to someone about this...'

Opinions were divided on both the wisdom and likelihood of Irish unity.

But one thing all the emigrants seemed to share was the benefit of being an outsider looking in, using their experience of living in another country to highlight the problems of staying in the union – and the problems of leaving it.

But before hearing from them it's important to explain how Irish unity might come about.

On May 22, 1998, voters in both parts of Ireland backed the Good Friday Agreement – the first time people in every part of Ireland had voted on the same day since the UK general election on December 14, 1918.

The UK parliament then passed the Northern Ireland Act 1998 to implement the wish of the majority of voters in Ireland.

One of the key elements of the agreement – and absolutely central to winning support from nationalists – was the British government spelling out how its rule in Northern Ireland might come to an end.

The act says that a border poll will be called by the Secretary of State for Northern Ireland:

If at any time it appears likely to him that a majority of those voting would express a wish that Northern Ireland should cease to be part of the United Kingdom and form part of a united Ireland.[109]

"If...it appears likely to him" is an ambiguous – and sexist – turn of phrase.

How exactly will the Secretary of State for Northern Ireland – whether he, she or otherwise – decide that it "appears likely" that the pro-unification side might win?

At the time of the act, the secretary of state was Labour's Mo Mowlam, who played a crucial role in brokering the agreement and was so popular in Northern

[109] https://www.legislation.gov.uk/ukpga/1998/47/schedule/1/enacted

Ireland that a playground at Stormont was named after her following her death.[110]

A year after the agreement, Tony Blair carried out a reshuffle and moved Mowlam to Chancellor of the Duchy of Lancaster, possibly the only cabinet role that constitutes a demotion from Secretary of State for Northern Ireland.[111]

Since that day in 1999 when Mowlam got down to the important business of administering the estates and rents of the Duchy of Lancaster, there have been 14 British MPs who have served as Secretary of State for Northern Ireland.

They range from the stubbornly effective John Reid, to the wildly popular Julian Smith, to the utterly forgettable Karen Bradley.

But one thing that united all these disparate politicians – beyond a certain sense of doom every time their plane landed in Belfast – has been a desire to provide no clue whatsoever as to what constitutes their threshold for calling a border poll.

And this is not a criticism.

Both governments have long wanted Northern Ireland's politicians to reduce their obsession with the constitutional question and focus instead on the bread and butter – to take heed of John Hume's frequent requoting of his father's observation that 'you can't eat a flag.'

Providing a benchmark, a target, a running commentary on when there might be a border poll is not in the interests of any secretary of state for Northern Ireland.

But Northern Irish politicians rush into this vacuum to provide their own analysis of when the day of Irish unification might be on the ballot paper.

---

[110] Jenny and I took the kids there when they were younger. It's a great playground.

[111] It's been widely rumoured that Blair demoted Mowlam as revenge after *she* received a standing ovation when he mentioned her work securing peace during his speech at the Labour Party Conference of 1998.

This is particularly true for Sinn Fein who need – psychologically more than anything else – to insist that Irish unity is not only inevitable, but reasonably close.

Otherwise, what did all those IRA members kill and die for?

Unionist politicians, who know a thing about placating the base themselves, are relatively unruffled by the constant predicted demise of Northern Ireland.

It would seem fair to assume that the secretary of state would use assembly elections as their border barometer.

These are held using the wonderfully Irish Single Transferable Vote system of PR, a delight for political geeks and maths nerds alike. When all the quotas have been reached, when the surpluses distributed and when the tallymen have retired to the bar, what you're left with is a legislature that fairly closely reflects the votes of the public.

Not as accurately as the puritan Israeli version, which lets all and sundry into the Knesset, but a lot more closely than the wildly unrepresentative voting system used at Westminster.

In other words, if the voters want a united Ireland, then you'd expect the make-up of the Northern Ireland Assembly to reflect it. Those parties which support reunification – Sinn Fein and the SDLP – should form close to a majority.

But sadly, for those who dream of a nation once again, this is not the case.

In fact, in the twenty-five years during which the assembly has (sometimes) operated, the level of votes and seats for nationalist parties has remained relatively stable, usually a little over forty per cent, sometimes a little under.

And this while the proportion of the voting-age population who are Catholic has increased at each poll.

In 1998, the SDLP were still the dominant party within nationalism, though clearly under pressure. They topped the poll in votes cast on twenty-two per cent - the first time a nationalist party finished above all unionist parties in a Northern Ireland-wide poll.

But they still came second to the Ulster Unionists in terms of seats.

Still, the SDLP's twenty-four seats and Sinn Fein's eighteen took nationalism to forty-two out of 108 – thirty-nine per cent of the seats, matching the two parties' combined share of the vote. Not a mandate for a border poll yet, but a good place to start.

The following assembly election in 2003 was historic. After years of delays in the operation of the Good Friday Agreement because of disagreement over how and when parties whose supporters had guns should get rid of them, the old voting patterns of the Troubles were overturned.

Sinn Fein overtook the SDLP, while the DUP eclipsed the Ulster Unionists. Both of Northern Ireland's new elite have had their struggles in the following decades, but neither of them has seemed in danger of being overtaken by those they consigned to also-ran status in 2003.

But, while the face of Northern Ireland Assembly changed radically in 2003, nationalism remained stuck in its forty per cent cul-de-sac, rather than motoring towards a united Ireland.

In 2003, Sinn Fein and the SDLP swapped seat totals, with the former rising to twenty-four and the latter dropping to eighteen – a fairly obvious indicator that Sinn Fein's growth wasn't being fuelled by former unionist voters.

The nationalist vote did go up in 2003 though, limping over the two-fifths mark to forty point five per cent.

The next poll in 2007 was more encouraging for those who support Irish unity, with the two nationalist parties winning forty-one point four per cent of the vote and picking up two extra seats to go to forty-four – just over forty per cent of the total.

But that election nearly two decades ago has been the high point for nationalists so far.

In 2011 Sinn Fein's slow progress in votes and its extra seat didn't cancel out the SDLP's continuing decline, and the loss of two of its representatives.

At the next vote in 2016, the pattern changed, and this time both nationalist parties went into decline at the same time, winning jut thirty-six per cent of the vote between them and shedding three seats.

Perhaps the best indication of Northern Ireland's dysfunction is that the assembly lasted just a year before another poll was needed.

This time the assembly was reduced from six seats in each of the eighteen Westminster constituencies to five, bringing the total number of seats down from 108 to ninety.

The SDLP managed to lose a few votes, but no seats while Sinn Fein managed to win more votes but lose a seat.

In typical Good Friday Agreement-style, for most of the following five years until the next poll in 2022, Northern Ireland had no government.

But when the vote did come about, we were told how historic it was because Sinn Fein topped the poll meaning in theory – and two years later in practice – they were entitled to appoint the First Minister.

But look beyond the symbolism of a republican leader of the executive and the picture looks much less rosy for a border poll.

Yes, for a party that had jointly run Northern Ireland for twenty years, Sinn Fein did remarkably well in the 2022 election, increasing its vote share by one per centage point to twenty-nine and holding all of its 27 seats.

But the SDLP had a terrible election, losing four of its twelve seats and falling from twelve per cent of the vote to just nine per cent. Crucially, all four of these seats were lost to the centrist party Alliance, who surged overall from eight to seventeen.

If a party as moderate as Alliance can have an article of faith in anything, it's that a border poll is not a priority in any shape or form.

So, to surmise: In 1998 nationalists won thirty-nine per cent of the 108 seats in the Northern Ireland Assembly.

A generation later they won thirty-nine per cent of the ninety seats in the Northern Ireland Assembly.

But, while nationalist parties have struggled to make the case for unity, either to persuadable unionists or to the Stay At Home party, the case for unity is certainly there to be made.

Because, at the same time as the nationalist vote has stagnated at around forty per cent, the unionist vote has fallen significantly.

Unionist parties won fifty per cent of the vote in the first assembly elections after the Good Friday Agreement in 1998. By 2022 this had fallen to forty per cent.

As mentioned, the primary beneficiary of the decline in the unionist vote has been Alliance who, like many of the emigrants I spoke to, are in theory persuadable on the merits of a united Ireland.

But, as things stand, they're utterly unconvinced that the constitutional debate should be prioritised over Northern Ireland's many problems.

The assembly results show that unity is far from a done deal – but they also indicate that the union is dwindling in popularity.

It's all to play for.

Of all the emigrants I spoke to Eamon Eastwood was the most clearly pro-unity. He told me from his home in Melbourne that he thinks a united Ireland is not only welcome, but inevitable:

"I would like to see a border poll, I'd like the country to be united, I do feel strongly about it. You would think it's going to happen at some stage.

"There's some fantastic community building and reaching out going on and we already have some cross-border bodies. It's evident that Britian has no interest in continuing to send over ten billion quid to keep the lights on.

"If we had a united Ireland, there's something deep inside me would think: 'Fuck it, let's go back and live there for a few years.'"

On the other side of the argument, Mark Aiken – who's planning to return to Northern Ireland from Canada – is strongly unionist. He asks me with a little nervousness whether I think there is going to be a border poll before giving me his views on it:

"No-one has given more to be part of the UK than Ulster, so when you hear all this talk of unification, it is concerning.

"I wouldn't pretend to know all the minutiae of the arguments but I obviously have my preference.

"If there's something to do – knocking on doors or whatever – to promote the cause of staying on the UK, then I'll do it."

Most of the other emigrants I spoke to take a less certain position than those of Eamon and Mark.

They raised issues which will be key in any future unity referendum:

How would unionists be accommodated in a united?

What would happen to the Northern health service after unity?

How would a united Ireland pay its bills?

Perhaps because the issue of passports is inevitably high on an emigrant's mind, many of the people I interviewed also brough up Brexit.

When I ask Pete Devenney how he feels about a possible border poll, I'm expecting a response along the lines of 'let them do what they want.'

But instead, he explains how Brexit re-engaged him with the politics of Northern Ireland, even from his home thousands of miles away in New Zealand:

"I completely disengaged in the debate coming up to the Brexit referendum. Two days before the vote, my dad called me and told me to vote because he knew Remain was in trouble.

"I ignored him so I've learnt my lesson. If there was a unity referendum, I would vote, very much so.

"I would vote for a united Ireland, in my heart I would vote for it. What's the best way to explain this? If Ireland was off the coast of South America, the British would have left by now.

"It's only coz we're close that they're still there."

Across the Tasman Sea in Melbourne, Louise McCloskey also references the Brexit referendum when I ask her about a possible vote on unity:

"I haven't really thought about a border poll but I did get my parents to set up a proxy vote for me and the catalyst for that was the Brexit referendum. I didn't realise until the vote happened that I could have taken part in it.

"Votes like that, and a unity referendum, have a big impact so I'd want to take part. Plus, I'm not saying we'd move back but maybe we would.

"I hated the way the Leave campaign tapped into this false narrative that the EU drains money out of the UK that could've been used on the NHS.

"The EU gave a lot of peace funding to Northern Ireland over the years.

"And people in Northern Ireland voted to stay in but they had to leave because of England and Wales.

"Anytime I've been in London I've found that English people know very little about Northern Ireland, they just think 'oh, that's part of Ireland.'"

Over in Manchester, Brexit has also been the key revelation for Ciaran Tracey, guiding him from a position of agnosticism on Irish unity towards a place of some belief:

"I would vote for unity because I think Britain has revealed itself through Brexit. If you still had statesmen like Blair, you might find a convincing argument that they could bring Northern Ireland to a better place.

"But the UK government doesn't give a fuck about northern England, let alone Northern Ireland.

"But I'm not the blood and soil type."

In Rome, Brexit is also top of Niki Sweetnam's mind when I ask her about the possibility of a border poll:

"I couldn't vote in the Brexit referendum, but I certainly would have voted to remain if I could have. I think Brexit was a big boost to the idea that there should be a united Ireland because, economically speaking, it would be the most seamless solution.

"Or at least it would be if the politics could be removed from it. We need to think what's best for economic stability for both the islands.

"Thinking with our hearts never really gets us anywhere."

Talking to me from her flat in Paris, Julie McDonald says she's ready to consider unity following Brexit:

"If there ever was a border poll, I would feel strongly emotionally invested in it.

"But I would want to know about the practicalities of unity, about what it would mean for the health service. And there's a lot of religion in the schools down in the South too.

"But I think Brexit has changed things, it feels like the Republic is a more progressive country than the UK now."

Speaking to me from her home in Sheffield, Nadine McGarry also references Brexit, but in a different way to other emigrants.

For her, the lesson of 2016 is that if you believe in major constitutional change, you need to do your homework:

"If there were a border poll I'd want to understand the options of what a united Ireland would look like.

"You wouldn't want the situation that you had over here with Brexit. The country voted to leave and the next day everyone's googling 'what is Europe?' 'what is the EU?'"

The frequent referencing of Brexit by emigrants, nearly a decade after the vote, shows it is a wound that hasn't healed. Northern Irish people love a grudge. In our culture, eight years is barely any time to nurse a grievance.

The sense of injustice comes from the fact that Northern Ireland voted to remain in the European Union by 56% to 44%. But, as a tiny part of the UK, these votes meant little in the final toll.

The Brexit vote exposed the fundamental mathematics of Britain and Ireland in a way which strengthens the argument for Irish unity.

Northern Ireland is a region of just under two million people. In a country the size of the UK, whose population is closing in on seventy million, it barely matters at all.

But in a united Ireland – a country of seven million people – Northern Ireland would matter ten times as much.

Since 2016, nationalist parties on both sides of the border have been energised, feeling the wind is at their backs as they make the case for constitutional change.

In June 2024, two thousand people gathered at the SSE Arena in Belfast to hear representatives of eleven political parties make the case for Irish unity.

But appeals to unionists to join the debate have largely fallen on deaf ears.

As Malachi O'Doherty explains in his excellent book Can Ireland Be One? the nationalist political class has singularly failed to come up with a plan to accommodate nearly a million unionists into a united Ireland.

Would they be expected to learn Irish?

How would the new state respond if some unionists resisted Irish unity through force?

What happens if a unionist party emerges from an election with the balance of power in the Dail?

Would a united Ireland have a new flag?

Would it join the Commonwealth?

Would it need a new anthem?

Some emigrants brought up these questions as soon as I asked for their thoughts on a border poll.

Liam Devlin, who grew up in west Belfast during the Troubles, seems as ever to think of his Protestant friends when considering how he will feel about a referendum:

"On an emotional level I feel Irish. I would like to think that, in a united Ireland, Protestants who see themselves as culturally British would have more say over the lives they live than they do now. But that's just a hope.

"I think unity will happen but it will take a long time."

Michael Campbell lived in west Belfast during some of the worst years of the Troubles. The constant threat of violence was a key reason for him leaving.

So, it's perhaps not surprising that he raises the prospect of loyalist violence in the event of a yes vote for unity:

"Economically, unity would be really good for Northern Ireland but it would turn things on its head.

"There would be some kind of unionist movement that would spark up and there would be attacks all over Ireland.

"I think we had a de facto united Ireland before Brexit but the unionists wanted to stop that. I think if Britain re-joined Europe, that would be easier than having a border poll.

"The Republic is a powerhouse and their economy is working for them. They have roughly the same population as New Zealand – they have 8,000 homeless people, we have 80,000."

Looking at events from Paris, Charlotte Forbes is also concerned about the prospect of violence around a border poll:

"It could be a watershed moment but I'd be concerned that it could bring all the extremists out of the woodwork.

"But it wouldn't make me want to move back. I'll always be Irish and I'll always be European."

On the other side of the Atlantic, Glenn Chestnutt also fears that the birth of a united Ireland would be bloody:

"In terms of a border poll, I would want to vote and I would take it seriously – I'm one of those people who actually reads manifestos!

"I suppose I would say that, whether we're in Northern Ireland or a united Ireland, I want Protestants to have proper, healthy representation, to feel that our voices are heard.

"Young Protestants have issues around health and education, there are young lads with no memory of the Troubles who are joining loyalist paramilitary groups.

"I saw something saying there are 10,000 loyalist paramilitaries – why do these groups exist? What about these young guys who are fourteen or fifteen, are they going to engage in the process of a border poll?

"Or are they going to pick up a brick or a bottle and go to some guy and say they want to join up?

"There's a lack of leadership in the unionist community. I'm worried that my community will be left behind.

"I worry about how those 10,000 loyalist paramilitaries would react if there's a vote to get rid of the border."

Glenn is one of a number of Protestants I spoke to who have come round to a position of considering the merits of a united Ireland.

Freed from the stultifying conformity of Northern Irish life they have the freedom to consider their identity anew.

Added to this is the universal experience of any Northern Irish person anywhere in the world, of being considered Irish at first meeting, regardless of your religious background.

Ruth Sanderson is a soft yes to Irish unity:

"I think it would be good to have a border poll. I would be open to a united Ireland – or a new Ireland is probably a better way of putting it. Some of my family have a sense that it's going to happen, and that it's OK.

"We all support the same rugby team...in some ways it would be a relief – this has to be resolved somehow.

"But I think that people under-twenty-five are Generation Neither – they don't care that much about national identity."

Tim Wilson, who like Ruth, grew up in a religious Protestant family, has also tempered his unionism with a stiff dash of indifference:

"I know there's people saying we're going to have a united Ireland. Your man, the Taoiseach, was saying that people in the Republic need to decide as well. It would be strange if Northern Ireland decides to leave the UK but the Republic doesn't want us.

"We're going cap in the hand to the mainland UK every day now, I think we'd just turn around cap in hand to Dublin.

"I think I'd follow the debate closely but with an outsider's perspective.

"I'd've been a reasonably strong unionist in the past but I don't feel like a unionist now. The two unionist parties are spending too much time trying to keep the hardcore happy."

Jen Carswell, who swapped Belfast for New Zealand, has warmed to unity given political developments thirteen time zones away from her new home:

"I just say I'm Irish now. I got an Irish passport right after Brexit, I want my kids to be able to live in Europe if they want to.

"I don't think I would be against unity, I'm not massively opposed to it."

Spealing from her solicitor's office in Bristol, Natalie Cooke explains that she has moved to a position of agnosticism on Irish unity – a far cry from her conservative Protestant family back home:

"My parents would be very much against Irish unity but I suppose form a geographic point of view, it would make sense.

"But it would have to be done carefully and delicately."

Perhaps because of her mixed background Tracey Taggart was keen to stress how much of a challenge it would be for the South to take on such a large number of Northern Protestants:

"I think unionist people would have to feel welcome into whatever new Ireland would come. That's one of the things that concerns me – I don't think people in the Republic have got their heads round that.

"If there's a united Ireland then the unionist people are coming. They are as much a part of Ireland as anyone else, they've lived there since the Plantation.

"Unionists would have quite a say in the Dail, people in the Republic need to think about that. I think there's a bit of work to do on Northern Ireland before there could be a united Ireland.

"Maybe we need to wait for a generation to die off."

Eimear Willett, who like Tracey, is the child of a mixed marriage, also thinks first of what unity would mean for Protestants:

"I would definitely want a united Ireland but I'm also aware of the fact that there's so much work needs to be done to accommodate unionists.

"They are fifty per cent of the population and that's not going to change, people who want a united Ireland don't seem to realise that.

"How will you integrate them into schools where you have to speak Irish?

"People just think you'll win a border poll and that'll be that but there's so much work to be done."

Given his experience of growing up as a gay man within the unionist community, it is perhaps little surprise that Gareth Patterson has turned his back on the Union Jack:

"I'm always on the Northern Ireland section of the BBC website. I went through a period of listening to Radio Ulster all the time but my partner got fed up listening to it!

"It's Groundhog Day with the politics but I think having Michelle O'Neill as First Minister shows that things are changing.

"I was brought up as a unionist but I would say I'm a nationalist now, I'd be well up for a united Ireland. I think we need to get rid of the links with Great Britain.

"I think being a gay man has given me the chance to look at other parts of who I am. I've found I have a real passion for being Irish, for the mystery of Celtic Ireland.

"That's something that's grown inside me organically."

Ryan Cosgrave agrees, though his attitude seems more informed by hostility to the UK, rather than enthusiasm for a united Ireland:

"I'm really not sure if I have any Northern Irish traits at all. I've never thought about it. I suppose I'd say that when I'm in Britain I do gravitate to other Irish people but I'm not sure why.

"I always say that I'm Irish but, if it came to a border poll, I'm not sure how engaged I would be in it. There are things I don't like about the UK – it's right-wing, it's militaristic and it's Anglo-centric.

"I don't think the Republic is a wonderful country but I do think it's better than the UK. Northern Ireland has such social and economic problems. It has the constant psychodrama at Stormont.

"I think Northern Ireland is a doomed political project."

Kris Gant has taken a similar journey to Gareth and Ryan. But his thoughts on the relative importance of his politics and his sexuality is revealing:

"I follow Northern Irish politics a bit but if there were a border poll, I'd feel more engaged.

"I would take more interest in that than I did in the same-sex marriage debate because the border issue is a more integral part of my childhood, part of our identity.

"I'm definitely more inclined to the nationalist perspective which is the opposite of my family. It's the one thing we don't talk about – they're fine with me being gay but not with me supporting a united Ireland.

"I wouldn't say unionist homophobia drove me to support a united Ireland. Because, for a long time after I left Northern Ireland, I wasn't engaged in its politics at all because I was so fed up with it.

"It was only later when I became more interested in our history. Ireland was a country long before England arrived."

As a senior Fine Gael politician – not to mention the daughter of one of the founders of the SDLP – Emer Currie's opposition to the Sinn Fein view of a border poll is no surprise:

"If Sinn Fein get into government there will be a clamour for a border poll but I don't think that's the right approach.

"I'm a proud nationalist and I want there to be a united Ireland but I'm open-minded about what it might look like.

"It can't just be hard green against hard orange. I'm trying to create the space in which that can happen but you can't do that with a deadline.

"Their electoral promise will be to demand a border poll but the stats aren't there for it at the minute.

"Young people are more open to constitutional change. I think things have changed since Brexit and young people are now more interested in a different future. And then there are people of our age who are optimistic about the possibility of change but don't want a Sinn Fein version of a united Ireland.

"In some ways our biggest differences aren't the border. The Shared Island Project[112] isn't about constitutional change it's about dealing with the huge disconnect between North and South.

"Some people come at the unity debate from a totally romantic perspective but they don't realise how different the North and the South have become.

"The Shared Island Project is about recognising those differences and trying to overcome them."

Jim McAuley is similarly sceptical about the chances of a Sinn Fein-led government in the South leading the whole island to reunification:

"I don't think unionists need to be particularly concerned that Sinn Fein want to get a border poll on the agenda. All the polls indicate that people will vote to stay in the UK.

"One third of people will always vote for a united Ireland and one third will always vote for the United Kingdom.

"It's the third in between. A lot of them are middle-class Catholics and they will vote for what's best for them economically.

"I think it will be heart versus wallet. And we all know how that ends."

---

[112] In February 2024, the Irish government announced 800 million euros to improve the all-island economy. The funding will pay for, among other things, improved road and rail links and increased training of female entrepreneurs.

Emer and Jim both bring expertise from their lives in politics and academia to explain that those who support Irish unity, perhaps more than anything else, must make the economic argument for it.

Preaching to the converted at big rallies in Belfast and Dublin will butter no parsnips.

Other emigrants who've pursued careers in business also bring up the economic challenge of unity.

Mark Heaney, like Jim, grew up in a very Protestant area. Like Jim, his scepticism about a united Ireland is rooted in economics, rather than culture:

"I have a British and an Irish passport. I got the Irish one for purely practical reasons – it's much easier having two passports for international travel. My daughter got an Irish passport because of Brexit.

"I wouldn't be banging the drum for Northern Ireland being part of Britain but at the same time, I'm not sure Ireland would want us.

"You could have the bizarre situation where Northern Ireland votes for unity and Dublin says to Westminster 'hold on a second – how much money are you going to give us?'

"There's so many people in Northern Ireland who work for the government – the civil service, the NHS, the security services.

"There isn't the industry in Northern Ireland that there is in the South. They've got the big tech companies and the big pharma companies because of all the tax breaks. That's allowed them to keep more of their young people and bring more of them back.

"The education system in Northern Ireland is far superior to anything on the mainland. There's a lot of clever kids who could make it in business if the opportunities were there, but they're not."

Over in Sweden Owen McMeel may be of a different generation and the other religion to Mark, but they are both numbers guys.

And the mathematician in him knows that making the sums work for a united Ireland is quite the complicated equation:

"The South can't afford us. I don't think people in Northern Ireland understand just how much money Westminster puts in – it's a huge amount.[113]

"I think I'd probably get a vote if there were a border poll and my parents would be very much in favour but I would probably vote to keep Northern Ireland separate.

"People in the South don't want us. Even if Sinn Fein end up in government on both sides of the border, I don't think they can persuade enough people to support unity.

"I don't see a nationalist party bringing unionists over to them. I think the nationalist attitude is just to let the births and deaths turn things their way – with a little help from the British government doing things like Brexit."

Emily Shanks' feeling on unity appears to have strengthened since she swapped her career in Belfast as a solicitor for a new life as a consultant in London.

But, just like Owen and Mark, her work head is telling her heart to houl on a wee sec:

"I would feel very strongly about a border poll. I have an Irish passport, I go to Croke Park, confirmations, the whole thing.

"So yes, I'd feel it with my heart.

"But I think it's the people in the South who'll decide, not us. We cost too much money and Westminster has to prop us up. I just don't think the majority of people in the South feel strongly about unity.

---

[113] The gap between the amount of tax the government collects in Northern Ireland and the amount it spends is around £10 billion a year

"There would have to be some sort of economic plan with Westminster for the first 20 years."

Of all the people I speak to, Ciaran Ferrin is the most confident that a border poll is in the post – and he's keen for the knock at the door:

"I believe there will be a referendum in 2030 and I will vote in it if I can. When I was at Féile an Phobail[114] Sinn Fein were saying that there will be a vote in 2030 if they get into power in the South. Mary Lou McDonald, Gerry Adams, Michelle O'Neill, they have all said that."

Ciaran is also confident that the pro-unity side will win:

"I think if people's lives don't get better, with the housing market and inflation, then they will look for dramatic change to change their circumstances. People are toying with the idea that a united Ireland will make it better, so we need to know exactly what it will look like."

Over in Vancouver, Catherine Craig is also thinking in terms of money, but for her the numbers point towards staying in the United Kingdom:

"I feel very strongly about a border poll – I think it would be a waste of time and resources.

"The South don't want us and the British don't want us. The majority of people on the Republic of Ireland have never even visited Northern Ireland.

"They don't understand or care about our politics. On the mainland, they also don't care, no-one cared about us during Brexit.

"There's no easy, seamless way to integrate Northern Ireland into a united Ireland."

In New Zealand, Fidelma McCorry is coming round to the view that unity would work economically:

"Brexit did something that I thought might never be and that was to make a united Ireland seem possible. I

[114] The West Belfast Festival, which takes place at dozens of locations across the city every summer.

remember sitting up watching the referendum, I couldn't believe it.

"I'm a nationalist, a republican with a small 'r'. But having said that, for a long time, Northern Ireland was far better off economically in the UK.

"But things have changed since then. Ideologically I'm in favour of a united Ireland but logically we need to get there too – how would it improve health and education?"

Yvonne O'Hagan, who grew up in a similarly nationalist background as Fidelma, doubts whether an economic case for a united Ireland can be sold to Northern voters:

"I...would...love to see a united Ireland but not through bloodshed.

"We've been occupied by the British like so many other places in the world. We're one island. But will I see it in my lifetime? I'm not sure.

"When I go home, they're still using sterling, still getting benefits, still got the health service. Would they give that all up?"

Perhaps only second to the issue of how a new Ireland will operate economically, is the critical question of how an all-island health service would work.

Northern Irish people have grown very attached to the NHS, not just as a care service but as one of the region's major employers.

Enthusiasm to fully adopt the Southern model – where most adults have to pay to see their GP – is not high in the North.

But at the same time, the Northern NHS has been wheezing alarmingly in recent years, with by far the worst waiting lists in the UK.

As a doctor, health is uppermost in Jenny Ryan's mind when she comes to consider unity. She's concerned about the future of the NHS in Northern Ireland, despite having no illusions about its present:

"I was very frustrated during Brexit that there was no consultation with people in Northern Ireland. People over here didn't care.

"I think there will be a border poll and it worries me what might happen. I think the vote will go for a united Ireland. I think it's difficult to know what they would do about the NHS.

"But the NHS at the minute, it's not even on its knees, it's on its face.

"The waiting lists in Northern Ireland are horrific. Some people are waiting seven years for a knee replacement. And the autism rate in Northern Ireland is much higher than in Great Britain.

"I'm not sure how long it's going to be there."

Katherine Parke also brings up the NHS as key to her scepticism about a united Ireland:

"A lot of people I know would be nationalist or republican and, especially after Brexit, they look to the South more and more.

"But if you listen to the radio, it's cost of living, it's hospital witing lists that are really bothering people.

"I'm much more interested in dealing with that than symbolic concerns about whether to remain in the UK or join the Republic.

"I don't know who would afford us, we're a black hole for public financing.

"I do think we have more in common with the rest of the island of Ireland but I wouldn't want to remove the links with the rest of the UK.

"The cynic in me thinks that of people in the North thought they'd have to pay to see their GP and have their bins emptied – like they do in the south – then there wouldn't be as much republican feeling.

"I do think a united Ireland will come. I think things are moving that way but I don't know when or how.

"I don't see anyone coming forward with a plan for how it would work. I do support a united Ireland but I don't support Sinn Fein's version because that seems like just a united Ireland for one community, not for all communities."

The key factor in any referendum debate will be the undecideds – the 20% of the population who tend to vote Alliance, or not at all.

People who could be persuaded of the merits of a united Ireland, but whose hearts don't lift when they see the green, white and orange fluttering in the wind.

And this key group present both the DUP and Sinn Fein with a cruel irony.

They redesigned the Good Friday Agreement to give each of them a minority veto over the formation of any government.

But, if a border poll ever comes, the veto will pass to a smaller group – Alliance-inclined voters who could go either way.

Just as they will have the last word in a referendum, they will have the last word in this chapter.

Speaking from the world of Dublin public policy, Emma Rooney is one of those who are convincible – but yet to be convinced:

"I would be really, really engaged in a border poll. But I'd be worried if there was a narrow vote in favour. We shouldn't repeat the mistakes of Brexit, where people voted for something without really knowing what they were getting.

"I don't think people down here want to inherit the problems of the North. And what's going to happen with the health service?

"Will we still have the NHS or will we have the Southern system where you have to pay?"

Speaking to me from New Zealand, Annmarie McPolin is similarly sceptical of the prospects of unity:

"If there ever was a border poll, I would definitely disappear down some rabbit holes. I know a bit what it's like because my partner is Scottish and he was engaged in their independence debate.

"But I think the way that politics is structured back home, things won't change.

"What if the new generation coming through wants something different from the two big parties?

Jo Gamage, longing to leave Northern Ireland for New Zealand, is not convinced that unity is the answer:

"I definitely would pay attention to a border poll. I probably would be able to vote but I'd feel bad about voting for something that won't impact me.

"It would be like all those old people who voted Leave knowing they wouldn't live to see the effect of Brexit.

"When I was younger, I wanted a united Ireland because I thought it was wrong that the English and Scottish settlers had taken our land but I've moved on now.

"It would be a massive change. And a massive change for the South too. They have their own problems, the cost of living down there is crazy and they've not got enough houses.

"But my life will be in New Zealand."

Already in New Zealand, Rory Hughes also appeared indifferent to the result of a border poll:

"I would follow a border poll very closely...I don't know it's a very difficult question. I suppose whoever promises me my medication can have my nationality.

"Part of me thinks that a border is just a line on a map and a flag is just a piece of cloth, but that's too simple. What people call themselves is their identity and it's very important to me.

"The Union flag makes me very uncomfortable because it's a flag of great intolerance and I don't quite like the Northern Ireland flag either."

Grace Farrell also feels that Irish unity is not a priority – though she's very much in the minority within her family:

"All my aunties are obsessed with a united Ireland. My family WhatsApp group is full of people posting links about polls showing how it's going to happen.

"I'd love it, but at the same time, I don't really care. I want people in Northern Ireland to have a better quality of life. I would much prefer to keep free healthcare.

"Other things are much more important. Things like the fact that the majority – the majority – of LGBT kids in Northern Ireland have considered suicide.

"It's more authentic to care about the Irish people rather than the border."

Perhaps the day will come when the issues which concern Grace will matter more than flags.

But that day still seems a long way off...

CONCLUSION

Northern Ireland is a maddening place, its insanity apparent to every foreign visitor who sees its peace walls and painted kerbstones for the first time.

But the madness of the place jars even more for those of us who return and look at our homeland with the eyes of the outsider.

In January 2003, at the comparatively ripe old age of twenty-three, I had my first opportunity to look on the place that reared me as an outsider might.

I had come home from Taiwan for a week's break while my English language school was closed for Chinese New Year. As my dad drove me back home through east Belfast I looked at my city as an outsider for the first time.

Some of the strangeness would have struck any resident of East Asia visiting northern Europe in January.

In Taiwan, like many parts of the Pacific, the rain either comes down very, very hard or not at all. But in Belfast that afternoon, there was the damp background hum of drizzle, the backing track for anyone who lives in Britain or Ireland.

Taipei is a festival of neon, with bright shop signs blazing round the clock, even giant illuminated crucifixes outside churches. But in Belfast that Sunday most of the shops we drove past were shuttered in Sabbatarian grey.

However, some of the oddness I observed out of the car window was a uniquely Belfast weirdness, even five years into peace.

On our way home we passed the Short Strand, the only solidly Catholic district in overwhelmingly Protestant east

Belfast. The peace wall diving the two communities was not as high as it had been when I left a year earlier.

It was twice as high.

There had been rioting during the previous summer's marching season and this was the solution – more concrete dividing two equally poor communities whose problems were the same.

And no-one seemed to mind or think that this was strange.

Twenty years on from that afternoon, the peace wall at the Short Strand still stands. And so do all the others in Belfast. Taking down these ugly symbols of sectarianism is – like many other things – not an Executive priority.

Tim Wilson noticed the same on his return to Northern Ireland from years in England.

He imagined he was going back to the place he enjoyed visiting for a week here and there, only to find that full-time residency soon removed the rose-tinted glasses.

The NW200, potato bread and some lovely hills can only do so much before you realise, in Tim's words that "the whole place is stuck in a rut."

Then came the request from someone who he respected to pretend he spoke Ulster-Scots, to help win funding that would otherwise go to the other side.

Jim McAuley is in a sense the opposite of Tim – someone who has almost made the decision to return to Norther Ireland.

But he shares Tim's sense that Northern Ireland enjoys its division far too much:

"I think the high emigration rate is a reflection of a failed society that's largely based on sectarianism. I don't necessarily mean violence, it's the benign apartheid where we have to have two of everything.

"This whole idea that British and Irish are polar opposites. This is still a very conflicted society."

It is this that needs to change if Northern Ireland is to attract more of its emigrants to return.

These are the people who Northern Ireland raised, who the country educated, often to an excellent standard. But they are making their lives – and paying their taxes – somewhere else.

As Matthew O'Toole noted to me, one of his party's previous leaders, Mark Durkan, spoke of the need, fifteen years ago, to dismantle the "ugly scaffolding" of the Good Friday Agreement.

Designations of unionist and nationalist, parallel consent, vetoes to each side etc, etc, etc.

These protections, which could have been temporary, have taken on the air of permanence while bringing nothing but instability.

There was nothing wrong, back in 1998, with mandatory coalition, building as broad a support as possible for a new Northern Ireland emerging from conflict.

The South African parties agreed a similar arrangement to manage the transition from apartheid, with the ANC sharing power with FW de Klerk's National Party, even though Mandela's party won more than sixty per cent of the vote in the first fair elections.

It was a wise measure – but a temporary one.

After five years of artificial coalition, South Africa transitioned fully to a functioning democracy where the party (or parties) who have a majority of seats in parliament form the government.

No South African party has a God-given right to be in power. It's long since time that Northern Ireland followed suit.

The scaffolding that Durkan himself helped construct was needed to build a secure new home, but it looks rustier with each year it remains in place.

In any emerging democracy the peaceful transition of power from one party to another is an absolutely crucial moment.

This has never happened in Northern Ireland. The ugly scaffolding of the Good Friday Agreement makes it impossible.

The building beneath may not be beautiful, but it's time to have a look at it.

The agreement has secured a generation of peace so, of course, it should not be cast aside.

But it's time for thorough reform to reflect a post-conflict Northern Ireland.

Unionist rights can be protected in law even if some or all unionist parties happen to be in opposition. And likewise for nationalists.

Until this happens, Northern Ireland will continue to repel thousands of young people each year through its politically instability and economic under-performance.

On this, the younger emigrants were clear.

Grace Farrell is obviously a bright young woman. But it looks like she will make her mark in life outside of Northern Ireland:

"It is beautiful there. But it's the same patterns on repeat at Stormont. When there is progress it's superficial, Stormont was designed so that nothing really progressive can happen."

Over in Stockholm, Owen McMeel is another great advert for the Northern Irish education system, but it's clear that his potential children will not have the benefit of it:

"Any progress is very slow. There are only 1.8 million people in Northern Ireland – why does it take so long to get anything done?

"In the private sector, I don't think any of those politicians would be keeping their jobs. They'd have to sharpen their pencils.

"In Northern Ireland it's green and orange. A unionist voter isn't going to switch to a nationalist party and vice versa.

"There has to be power sharing of some kind but how long do we continue with it when it's not delivering for the people of Northern Ireland?"

But ironically, it's in the area of education where reform is most urgently needed. Many of the emigrants I spoke to – not least Owen – heaped praise on the schooling they received.

Irish culture generally respects teaching and education more than is the case in Britain.

Many of the emigrants I spoke to had used the good local schools they were able to attend to make sure that the poverty of their birth was not a life sentence.

But many of them also cited the enduring sectarianism of Northern Ireland's schools as a reason not to return.

Niki Sweetnam dreaded a kicking as she travelled to her Protestant school in a Catholic part of Belfast.

Rory Hughes' father hid his tie and blazer in his bag every day to avoid a beating for going through a Protestant area on the way to his Catholic school.

Once in school, many of those I spoke to chafed at their religious education.

Tracey Taggart argued with the nuns about their uncompromising view of Presbyterians. Natalie Cooke became disillusioned with her school's adamant opposition to abortion.

Natalie also brought up the fact that she didn't know any Catholics her own age because they went to separate schools.

The same was true in reverse for Emma Rooney, whose friends were impressed when she finally met some Protestants.

Again the eyes of an outsider helps to illuminate the absurdity here.

Imagine being a visitor to Belfast and you happen to walk past Stranmillis College in south Belfast where (mostly) Protestant student teachers learn how to educate the next generation of (mostly) Protestant children.

You would only need to walk a couple of miles to west Belfast to find another teacher training college – St Mary's – where (mostly) Catholic student teachers learn how to educate the next generation of (mostly) Catholic children.

A society with the population less than that of West Yorkshire may need one teacher training college. But it certainly doesn't need two.

However, like the peace walls that never come down, no-one in power seems concerned about the benign apartheid of separate teacher training colleges, feeding the next generation of teachers into segregated schools.

For many emigrants who have become parents since leaving Northern Ireland, any thoughts of returning ended the moment that tiny hand grabbed their finger for the first time.

When your child is happily learning among her peers in Hobart, Helsinki or Huddersfield why would you want to take her back to your home, where the uniform she wears will mark her out as a Protestant or a Catholic?

Matt Thompson was just one of the many parents who raised the issue of sectarian education. In his case as a factor guiding him towards relocating from London to Edinburgh rather than Belfast.

The route to reversing emigration runs through the classroom. Since integrated education began in 1970, fifty mixed schools have opened.

In many parts of Northern Ireland there is still no choice for parents who don't want their child to have a sectarian education.

The Catholic Church has shown no interest in disbanding any of its schools.

At the very least, the Executive could commit that all new schools should be integrated.

And all politicians who continue to support sectarian education should at least be asked to justify this position.

The economic paralysis that those politicians have allowed to fester is also undermining Northern Ireland's ability to create the jobs that could attract emigrants to return.

In my more recent visits, it's the signs of economic malaise and neglect that have rankled as I pootled round Northern Ireland at a time when it had no government.

In 2022 myself and my extended family spent a pleasant summer week by the side of one of Fermanagh's many loughs.

We visited the nearest town, Lisnaskea, a place I'd never been to before but which has a reputation within Northern Ireland as being a tourist destination. And, as you look at the beautiful Fermanagh countryside you can see why.

But walk down the main street and you'll soon find a hotel right in the heart of the town which is closed down and dilapidated.

Next to the village's Church of Ireland are the ruins of Castle Balfour, which was built during the Plantation. A sign on the castle's walls notes that the site is owned by the Department for Regional Development, a barely functioning part of the then-defunct Stormont administration.

But these owners had made no effort to encourage the curious visitor to open their mind or their wallet.

At such a site in England there would be a tour, maybe a shop, certainly a narrative board. But at Castle Balfour there was nothing, no reason to linger and learn.

And even when Northern Ireland's tourism industry does succeed, it could do more.

The year before I stood befuddled at Castle Balfour, Jenny and I took the kids to Crumlin Road Goal Museum in north Belfast. It's well worth a morning of anyone's time, a fascinating and beautifully maintained tour through Belfast's criminal history.

I particularly enjoyed the fact that, while the Troubles of course featured, they were only a part of the museum's story.

The imprisonment of ordinary decent criminals is equally interesting, as is the depiction of the enforcement of Victorian morality in the prison's earlier years. A walk round the execution wing is powerfully memorable.

At one point you can walk into the tunnel under the Crumlin Road which once connected the jail with the court across the street.

Prisoners would be escorted under the road on their way to and from court, sometimes fighting with each other, or the guards, as drivers passed unknowingly overhead.

But halfway along the tunnel, as the cars roar above you, your way is blocked. The rest of the tunnel belongs to the owners of the courthouse.

Wouldn't it be great to continue through the tunnel to another museum in the listed courthouse?

To wander through its Victorian courtrooms and turn a great morning in north Belfast into a great day.

But the court is a pale imitation of the prison. The court heard its last case in 1998 and since its closure has had several owners, several fires and several grand plans for hotels.

But still it stands vacant, weeds now overgrowing a historic site on one of Belfast's main roads.

It was only many months later that I realised that this little section of the Crumlin Road is a symbol of post-agreement Northern Ireland – it could've been so much more than it is.

If Northern Ireland is to attract more of its emigrants home, it must improve its economy, as Owen McMeel memorably put it, politicians and officials have to "sharpen their pencils."

Landmark buildings should be brought back into use, historic relics properly exploited. As Mark Aiken pointed out after travelling round the Shankill, you can remember the past and still fill in the holes that it left.

Above all, the Northern Ireland Executive needs to focus – as governments of various stripes in the Republic have over the last few decades – on making the most of what they've got.

And in Northern Ireland, its best resource is its people – hard-working, well educated, with resilience beaten into them by history.

As Matthew O'Toole outlined, Belfast can be the affordable Dublin. And Derry – were it ever to get its university – could be so much more than it's been allowed to be so far.

Northern Ireland is the only place in the world that is part of the United Kingdom and, in effect, part of the European Union.

There is a great opportunity here to attract the high-skilled jobs that would persuade a 21-year-old to return from their three years in Dundee to make their life back home.

All that's needed is some political leadership.

Frequently when talking to other emigrants for this book, my mind drifted back to one of the first interviews I did with the academic Dirk Schubotz.

He's the opposite of nearly everyone else in this book, he moved to Northern Ireland rather than from it.

Dirk grew up in communist East Berlin. He left a city which tore down its wall to make his life in one which seems determined to keep all of its walls up. There might not be another person in the world who understands as much as he does about why so many people leave Northern Ireland and why so few go back.

As I sat talking to him on a road parallel to the M62, one thing he said rang out to me over the traffic:

"I found that the young people who were most likely to say they would leave were those who felt estranged from the Protestant and Catholic communities. It was the people who felt they didn't fit in..."

Dirk and I were talking at the time about people who are gay, but he went on to explain that those who went to integrated schools, or who feel Northern Irish, rather than Irish or British, are also more likely to leave.

Northern Ireland is a fiercely conformist, rigidly divided society.

Pete Devenney put this best, when he told me about returning to post-agreement Belfast after a few years in Glasgow:

"The place was small-minded, people were always reminding you about things you did years ago...Northern Ireland is all about schools and systems and jobs where you have to wait for the person above you to die before you get their job."

Most of the emigrants I spoke to mentioned a childhood feeling that they were an outsider.

Gareth Patterson, Kirs Gant and Ryan Cosgrave felt they didn't fit in because they were gay.

Eamon Eastwood felt out of place because he liked soccer as well as Gaelic football.

When Yvonne O'Hagan was told off by her brother for talking to a police officer: "that was when I had my lightbulb moment. I didn't fit in."

Tracey Taggart, as the child of a mixed marriage, never felt at home in the "itchy garment" of Catholicism that didn't fit her right.

Eimear Willett, who like Tracey had a Catholic mother and a Protestant father, felt out of place in Derry. Emma

Rooney never felt comfortable in highly conservative north Antrim.

Liam Devlin seems to have battled with a sense of not belonging since he was a young child:

"The moment you're born, you're given this huge baggage of history and you're not allowed to say: 'I don't want it' you're just not allowed."

Of all the people I spoke to, Jo Gamage seemed to feel the most out of place.

She'd moved back to Northern Ireland from New Zealand after the death of her husband.

I think Jo felt she could talk to me, because it would be too awkward, too cruel, to share her true feelings with her family and friends.

Our lives and our families are not the same.

But, looking back now at the last thing she said to me, I realised I could have said it back to her word for word and it would have been every bit as true for me as it was for her:

"I love Ireland, I had a great childhood but...yeah...it's not where I choose to be anymore.

"I feel like an imposter in Northern Ireland, I don't fit in, I don't really belong here.

"It's complicated, isn't it?"

The End

FURTHER READING

Thanks for reading this far.

I presume the fact that you've completed the book means that you have – or have now developed – an interest in Northern Ireland. I think you'd enjoy the following books, but these are just a few suggestions.

This list is neither exhaustive nor (I hope) exhausting:

The Dirty War, Martin Dillon

Shankill Butchers, Martin Dillon

Can Ireland Be One? Malachi O'Doherty

How to Fix Northern Ireland, Malachi O'Doherty

Lost Lives: The Stories of the Men, Women and Children Who Died as a Result of the Norther Ireland Troubles, Brian Feeney, Seamus Kelters, David McKittrick and Chris Thornton

A Shared Home Place, Seamus Mallon and Andy Pollack

Killing Rage, Eamon Collins

Northern Protestants: An Unsettled People, Susan McKay

Bear In Mind These Dead, Susan McKay

Borstal Boy, Brendan Behan

Agents of Influence: Britain's Secret Intelligence War Against the IRA, Aaron Edwards

The Irish Story: Telling Tales and Making it Up in Ireland, R F Foster

Burned: The Inside Story of the 'Cash-for-Ash' Scandal and Northern Ireland's Secretive New Elite, Sam McBride

Fifty Dead Men Walking: The Heroic True Story of a British Secret Agent Inside the IRA, Martin McGartland

John Hume: The Persuader, Stephen Walker

The Singing Flame, Ernie O'Malley

On Another Man's Wound, Ernie O'Malley

Living With Ghosts: The Inside Story From a 'Troubles' Mind, Brian Rowan

The Bloody Red Hand, Derek Lundy

Reporting the Troubles: Journalists tell their stories of the Northern Ireland conflict, Deric Henderson and Ivan Little

The Long Game: Inside Sinn Fein, Aoife Moore

ACKNOWLEDGEMENTS

My thanks to everyone who helped me with this book.
Sorry to anyone that I forgot to include below.
Any errors below – or above – are mine alone.

Thanks first and foremost to Jenny, Ciara and Fergal who endured living with a distracted husband / father who was frequently on Zoom calls to random strangers with similarly weird accents.

One Sunday afternoon they were good enough to humour me by coming along to an exhibition about the Troubles at the Imperial War Museum in Salford.

And thanks to my wider family – my mum and dad, my sisters Catriona and Anna, my brother Conor and my uncle Bill – for their words of encouragement and for their help in finding interviewees.

Thanks to James Essinger and the staff at Conrad Press for supporting this first-time author through the publication process and to Zoe Verner for her help promoting the book.

My old friend and New Zealand émigré Pete Devenney provided the morale-boosting first interview as well as support and encouragement throughout. It was halfway through our chat, scribbling down his story in shorthand while exhausted after yet another 3am start to the day, that it dawned on me that this might just work.

Caoimhe Ní Mhaolagáin from the Washington Ireland Program provided absolutely invaluable assistance by connecting me to younger people who have left Northern Ireland. Without her help, this book might never have made it past the ninety per cent finished mark.

Thanks to all of the people who talked to me about their experience of leaving Northern Ireland: Alana Cahoon, Liam Devlin, Ruth Sanderson, Jo Gamage, Tim Wilson, Michael Campbell, Jen Carswell, Annmarie McPollin, Yvonne O'Hagan, Fidelma McCorry, Tracey Taggart, Jenny Ryan, Eamon Eastwood, Rory Hughes, Gareth Patterson, Jim McAuley, Glenn Chestnutt, Mark Aiken, Ryan Cosgrave, Kris Gant, Mark Heaney, Tom O'Reilly, Julie McDonald, Charlotte Forbes, Niki Sweetnam, Emily Shanks, Louise McCloskey, Matthew Thompson, Grace Farrell, Eimear Willett, Katherine Parke, Ciaran Ferrin, Emma Rooney, Owen McMeel, Catherine Craig, Natalie Cooke and Nadine McGarry.

I was touched by the way that they were all generous with their time and willing to talk about painful periods of their lives.

Ciaran Tracey spoke to me about his own experience of leaving Northern Ireland, as well as providing the excellent advice to "write without fear and edit without mercy."

Another old friend, Emer Currie, provided a valuable insight into her remarkable life on both sides of the border.

Sara Farmer from Christchurch Irish Society provided a very productive link to Northern Irish people in New Zealand.

Ronan McDonald from the University of Melbourne helped me find emigrants in Australia.

On the other side of the Pacific, a similarly helpful role was played by Cathy Murphy from the Eamonn O'Loghlin Irish Canadian Immigration Centre.

Elsewhere in Canada, Rev Dennis Glazier of Vimy Loyal Orange Lodge connected me with Mark Aiken.

Shauna Kelly-Lefevre from Mna na hEireann ensured that this book isn't entirely Anglophone by connecting me to Northern Irish women living in continental Europe.

Back in the English-speaking world, Nuala Ginty from the Women's Irish Network played a similarly helpful role.

Matthew O'Toole was very generous with his time, given that he leads Northern Ireland's Opposition.

Marc Strathie from the Institute of Directors helped outline the economic damage of high emigration.

Adam Murray from Cara Friend was hugely helpful in connecting me with gay people from Northern Ireland.

Brian Gilmore and Vanessa Monaghan both provided insight into the challenges of being gay in Northern Ireland.

The academics and researchers who helped me pick through the issues related to the topic: Ann Watt of Pivotal, Dirk Schubotz and Tom Hulme from Queen's University, Belfast.

Damien McNally was very generous with his time when talking about trans-generational trauma, taking the time to talk to me about the murder of his father.

My day-job editor Catherine Norman was always encouraging and helped me to navigate our employer's declaration of interest bureaucracy.

My colleague Scott Duffield connected me with his old friend Rory Hughes.

Thanks to all my 5 Live Breakfast colleagues who offered encouragement, particularly Sarah Rock and Vuyelo Ndlovu.

Thanks to the two authors whose (vastly superior) works indirectly inspired this book.

Halfway through the writing of this book, I realised it was a very pale imitation of Svetlana Alexievich's epic *Second Hand Time: The Last of the Soviets,* in which she gives the fallen empire's citizens the room to talk about living through the collapse.

Closer to home, I also took inspiration from Derek Lundy, whose book *The Bloody Red Hand* explains Northern Ireland with an engaging blend of the personal and the historical.

Finally, thanks to the musicians who provided the inspiration and the title of this book, as well as the soundtrack to much of its composition.

Thanks first to the aforementioned Noah Kahan, whose song Homesick came on my Spotify one day in early 2024 as I struggled home along a bunged M62.

In the track, he sings about his native New England – a place he clearly loves but finds endlessly infuriating: "This place is such motivation, for anyone tryna move the fuck away from hibernation."

As I listened to those words I realised I wanted to write about my equally frustrating homeland.

I would never have had Noah Kahan's music on in the first place had I not stumbled across it a few months earlier while listening to Olivia Rodrigo's Live Lounge on BBC Radio 1, in which she performs a spellbinding cover of his track Stick Season.

Her music provided much of the backdrop to the writing of this book. I'm listening to Logical as I type this sentence.

Finally, thanks to The Pogues, whose music has been a part of my life since my Uncle Bill sent me a copied cassette of If I Should Fall From Grace With God more than 30 years ago.

In a very strong field, the finest of all songs on the album is Thousands Are Sailing.

It's a lament to the many millions of us who've left Ireland and includes a line that's always stuck with me.

Towards the end of the song Shane MacGowan notes the infuriating tendency of we exiles to romanticise the country we've abandoned:

Where e'er we go, we celebrate
The land that makes us refugees.